Charles Coppens

The art of oratorical composition

Charles Coppens

The art of oratorical composition

ISBN/EAN: 9783337305253

Hergestellt in Europa, USA, Kanada, Australien, Japan

Cover: Foto ©Thomas Meinert / pixelio.de

Weitere Bücher finden Sie auf **www.hansebooks.com**

A. M. D. G.

THE ART

OF

ORATORICAL COMPOSITION,

BASED UPON THE

PRECEPTS AND MODELS OF THE OLD MASTERS.

BY

REV. CHARLES COPPENS, S.J.,

Author of "A Practical Introduction to English Rhetoric."

NEW YORK:
SCHWARTZ, KIRWIN & FAUSS,
42 BARCLAY STREET.

CONTENTS.

BOOK III.—ORDER OR ARRANGEMENT OF THOUGHTS.

BOOK IV.—DEVELOPMENT OF THOUGHT.

BOOK V.—MEMORY AND ELOCUTION.

BOOK VI.—THE DIFFERENT SPECIES OF ORATORY.

PREFACE.

In this treatise on oratorical composition it has been the author's aim to present the student with the wisest precepts of the most authoritative writers. Among the ancients Aristotle, Cicero, and Quintilian are his principal guides; among modern works he has freely consulted the *Ars Dicendi* of Rev. Jos. Kleutgen, S.J.; the *Guide du Jeune Littérateur* of Rev. Jos. Broeckaert, S.J.; the *Grammar of Eloquence* of Rev. M. Barry, and the *Sacred Eloquence* of Rev. Thomas J. Potter, both of All-Hallows', Dublin; the *Lectures on Eloquence and Oratory* delivered by our great American statesman, John Quincy Adams, when Boylston professor in Harvard University; the *Lectures on Rhetoric and Belles-Lettres* of Rev. Hugh Blair, D.D., of Edinburgh University; besides a multitude of treatises, reviews, etc., which have furnished abundant matter. In general the author has preferred to let others speak in his stead whenever it could well be done. He has endeavored to illustrate the precepts by numerous extracts from the best productions of ancient and modern orators. The entire treatise is the growth of many years of teaching.

In preparing it for the press one of the principal difficulties has been to combine thoroughness with brevity: to strike a proper medium between the superficial treatment so common in modern text-books and that multiplicity of terms and distinctions which made the satirist exclaim :

> "All a rhetorician's rules
> Teach nothing but to name his tools."

The author does not expect to please every taste—this is impossible ; but he hopes to have written a useful work for the earnest student. If any be disposed to find fault with him for having given so little that is professedly his own, he would answer them in these words of J. Q. Adams' Inaugural Oration at Harvard (vol. i. p. 28): "In the theory of the art and the principles of exposition novelty will not be expected ; nor is it, perhaps, to be desired. A subject which has exhausted the genius of Aristotle, Cicero, and Quintilian can neither require nor admit much additional illustration. To select, combine, and apply their precepts is the only duty left for their followers of all succeeding times ; and to obtain a perfect familiarity with their instructions is to arrive at the mastery of the art."

THE AUTHOR.

St. Louis University,
St. Louis, Mo., March 1, 1885

INTRODUCTORY.

1. In a didactic treatise like the present it is both useful and conformable to general practice to begin with a clear definition of the subject treated. **Oratory is defined** in Webster's Dictionary: *The exercise of rhetorical skill in oral discourse.* It is not, then, co-extensive with rhetoric, but only a branch of it—that branch, namely, which treats of *oral* as distinguished from *written* discourse. As oratorical compositions are thus a species of "rhetorical compositions," it is necessary next to explain the precise meaning of the term *rhetoric.*

2. **Rhetoric,** from ῥέω, to flow, originally designated the power or art of using language *fluently.* Like most other words, it has been employed with some variety of meaning. Aristotle defines rhetoric: *The art of inventing whatever is persuasive in discourse.* Thus, as it regards persuasion, it is distinguished from grammar, which deals with mere correctness of language. Aristotle's definition appears preferable to Webster's, which is, "the art of composition"; for this would include grammar as a branch. Adopting, then, the definition of Aristotle, we may develop it more fully by considering the meaning of its terms. Rhetoric invents *whatever is persuasive in discourse.* Now, to *persuade* signifies to influence or control the minds and wills of others; and for this purpose not only thoughts, but also the arrangement and proper expression

of thoughts, are to be conceived and invented. Hence the same definition may be thus more fully expressed : Rhetoric is *the art of inventing, arranging, and expressing thought in a manner adapted to influence or control the minds and wills of others.* Oratory is *that branch of rhetoric which expresses thought orally.* As it has so many elements in common with the other species of rhetorical composition, the thorough study of oratory will throw much light upon the entire field of literary productions.

3. **Eloquence** is a term whose meaning is often confounded with oratory and rhetoric. Blair, in his *Lectures on Rhetoric and Belles-Lettres,* defines it as "the art of persuasion," and, in a wider sense, as "the art of speaking in such a manner as to obtain the end for which we speak." We prefer, with Webster's Dictionary, to define eloquence as *the expression or utterance of strong ·emotion in a manner adapted to excite correspondent emotions in others.* Thus eloquence, inasmuch as it deals with *strong emotions* only, is less extensive in meaning than oratory ; but as it is not confined to oral discourse, it is, in this respect, more extensive, and applies also to written language ; so that we may say an "eloquent essay," and even, with Webster, an "eloquent history."

4. Oratory, as here explained, is **a noble art,** worthy of the study of the noblest and the most earnest minds. **Cicero** thought it worth his while to write seven distinct treatises on this subject ; and the praise which he bestows on it in his first book *De Oratore* shows how enthusiastically he admired the power of the orator. "Nothing appears to me more excellent," he writes, "than the power of holding enchained the minds of an assembly by the charm of speech, of fascinating their hearts, impelling their wills whithersoever you desire, and diverting them from whatsoever you please. This one accomplishment has ever

exerted the chief attraction and influence among every free people, especially in times of tranquillity and repose. For what is so admirable as that, among an infinite multitude of men, there should rise up one who alone, or almost alone, can do what nature intended to be done by all? Or what is so pleasing to hear and understand as an oration adorned with wise maxims and noble expressions? Or what is so powerful and so grand as that the speech of one man should control the movements of the people, the consciences of the judges, and the dignity of the senate? What besides is so noble, so honorable, and so glorious as to succor the suppliant, to cheer the afflicted, to free from evil, to save from danger, to retain men in the bonds of society? . . . Not to name any further advantages—for they are almost innumerable—I shall briefly say I feel convinced that on the influence and the wisdom of a perfect orator depends not only his own dignity, but also, to a very great extent, the safety of multitudes and the welfare of the whole republic. Wherefore continue as you are doing, young men, and apply earnestly to that study in which you are engaged, that you may be an honor to yourselves, a help to your friends, and a treasure to your country" (*De Or.* i. 8).

5. **Lord Brougham** evidently had this passage in his mind when, in his inaugural discourse pronounced before the University of Glasgow, he bestowed the following encomium on oratory: "It is but reciting the ordinary praises of the art of persuasion to remind you how sacred truths may be most ardently promulgated at the altar, the cause of oppressed innocence be most powerfully defended, the march of wicked rulers be most triumphantly resisted, defiance most terrible be hurled at the oppressor's head. In great convulsions of public affairs, or in bringing about salutary changes, every one confesses how important an

ally eloquence must be. But in peaceful times, when the progress of events is slow and even as the silent and un- heeded pace of time, and the jars of a mighty tumult in foreign and domestic concerns can no longer be heard, then, too, she flourishes, protectress of liberty, patroness of improvement, guardian of all blessings that can be showered on the mass of humankind ; nor is her form ever seen but on ground consecrated to free institutions. ‘Pa- cis comes, otiique socia, et jam bene institutæ reipublicæ alumna eloquentia ’—Eloquence is the companion of peace and the associate of leisure, trained up under the auspices of a well-established republic. To me, calmly revolving these things, such pursuits seem far more noble objects of ambition than any upon which the vulgar herd of busy men lavish prodigal their restless exertions. To diffuse useful information ; to further intellectual refinement, sure fore- runner of moral improvement ; to hasten the coming of the bright day when the dawn of general knowledge shall chase away the lazy, lingering mists even from the base of the great social pyramid—this indeed is a high calling, in which the most splendid talents and consummate virtue may well press onward, eager to bear a part."

6. **National Variations.** In comparing these two ex- tracts it will, we think, be apparent that Cicero is more taken up with the beauty of eloquence, without, however, ignoring its usefulness ; and Lord Brougham attends more to its utility, without ignoring its beauty. In fact, the great orators of England formed themselves upon the vigorous model of Demosthenes. Now, Demosthenes aimed more at "power and efficiency"; while Cicero, in most of his orations, appears to aim rather at "oratorical effect." Hence the **English conception of eloquence** is plainer but not less noble, and is even better suited to ordinary use ; on the other hand, the **Latin** affords finer models of the

epideictic or demonstrative kind, which has also its proper place. It appears to us that the **French**, whether led to it by their national character or by special circumstances, have viewed oratory more after the manner of the Latins, and owe in part to this characteristic of their taste the magnificence of many of their orations. "In general," says Blair (Lect. xxvi.), "the characteristical difference between the state of eloquence in France and in Great Britain is, that the French have adopted higher ideas both of pleasing and persuading by means of oratory, though sometimes in the execution they fail. In Great Britain we have taken up eloquence on a lower key; but in our execution, as was naturally to be expected, have been more correct. In France the style of their orators is ornamented with bolder figures, and their discourses carried on with more amplification, more warmth and elevation. The composition is often very beautiful; but sometimes also too diffuse, and deficient in that strength and cogency which renders eloquence powerful."

It is, of course, not meant that the English possess no magnificent orations, nor even that magnificent oratory is exceptional with them; but only that the great British orators have not made splendor so much an object as the Latins and the French, but have rather studied the vigor of the highest model of orators—Demosthenes. We shall see in the chapter on demonstrative oratory that **American** eloquence aims at the perfection of the Latin.

7. In the study of oratory on which we are about to enter we shall follow the order which appears the most natural. The orator must have acquired certain qualities, which will be the sources of his success. He must then set to work systematically to prepare his speeches. He will first collect materials or thoughts for his oration; next he will arrange these in suitable order, then proceed to de-

velop or express them to advantage, afterwards memorize and deliver his discourse.

Hence we have the following **division**: The first book will treat of the Sources of Success in Oratory; the second, of the Invention; the third, of the Arrangement; the fourth, of the Development or Expression of Thoughts; the fifth, of Memory and Delivery. A sixth book is added on the various Species of Oratory.

This division agrees with Quintilian's in his *Institutes*, or "Education of an Orator," the most thorough and systematic work ever written on this subject. He devotes the first portion of his treatise to the early training of the coming orator; then (b. iii. c. iii. 1) he lays down this formal division: "The whole art of oratory, as most of the greatest writers have taught, consists of five parts · invention, arrangement, expression, memory, and delivery" The various species of oratory are explained in the course of his work.

BOOK I.

8. To attain such eminence in oratory as to deserve the praises above quoted, the **highest talents** are required. In fact, real eloquence, which we have defined . *the expression of strong emotion in a manner adapted to excite correspondent emotions in others,* is to a great extent a gift of nature. Our own great orator, **Daniel Webster,** justly considered it to be such. He said : "When public bodies are to be addressed on momentous occasions, when great interests are at stake and strong passions excited, nothing is valuable in speech, farther than it is connected with high intellectual and moral endowments. Clearness, force, and earnestness are the qualities which produce conviction. True eloquence, indeed, does not consist in speech. It cannot be brought from afar. Labor and learning may toil for it, but they will toil in vain. Words and phrases may be marshalled in every way, but they cannot compass it. *It must exist in the man, in the subject, and in the occasion.* Affected passion, intense expression, the pomp of declamation, all may aspire after it—they cannot reach it. It comes, if it comes at all, like the out-breaking of a fountain from the earth, or the bursting forth of volcanic fires, with spontaneous, original, native force. The graces taught in the schools, the costly ornaments and studied contrivances of speech, shock and disgust men when their own lives and the fate of their

wives, their children, and their country hang on the decision of the hour. Then words have lost their power, rhetoric is vain, and all elaborate oratory is contemptible. Even genius itself then feels rebuked and subdued as in the presence of higher qualities. Then patriotism is eloquent, then self-devotion is eloquent. The clear conception, outrunning the deductions of logic; the high purpose, the firm resolve; the dauntless spirit speaking on the tongue, beaming from the eye, informing every feature, and urging the whole man onward, right onward to his object—this, this is eloquence, or rather it is something greater and higher than all eloquence : it is action, noble, sublime, godlike action."

9. But it is not altogether a gift of nature. For even when the occasion is most favorable and the subject most inspiring it is not the uneducated man that can stand forth and control a nation. "Even genius itself then feels rebuked and subdued as in the presence of higher qualities." *It must exist in the man*, says Webster, but in the educated man. The great orator is a *genius*, but a **cultivated genius,** whose every power is developed to its fullest proportion. Such a genius was Daniel Webster himself; such were Calhoun and Clay among us ; such were Chatham, Pitt, Burke, and Fox in England ; Sheridan, Curran, Grattan, and O'Connell in Ireland ; Bossuet, Bourdaloue, Massillon, Fléchier, and Fénelon in France ; such were Cicero himself at Rome, and Demosthenes and Pericles at Athens. In these and all great orators of every land, without a single exception perhaps, assiduous labor perfected the man ; careful study and training contributed, as well as native power, to raise the orator above his fellows.

10. Even without extraordinary talent a **careful training** can achieve much towards the formation of an effi-

cient and elegant speaker. For it is not with oratory as
it is with poetry and other ornamental arts. In public
speaking, even mediocrity has its value. Besides, "between mediocrity and perfection," says Blair (Lect. xxxiv.),
"there is a wide interval. There are many intermediate
spaces, which may be filled up with honor ; and the more
rare and difficult may be complete perfection, the greater
is the honor of approaching to it, though we do not fully
attain it. The number of orators who stand in the highest class is, perhaps, smaller than the number of poets
who are foremost in poetic fame ; but the study of oratory has this advantage over that of poetry : in poetry one
must be eminently good or he is insupportable :

> " ' Mediocribus esse poetis
> Non homines, non Di, non concessere columnæ.'
> —*Horace.*

> " ' For God and man and lettered post denies
> That poets ever are of middling size.'
> —*Francis.*

In eloquence this does not hold. There one may hold
a moderate station with dignity. Eloquence admits of a
great many different forms, plain and simple as well as
high and pathetic ; and a genius that cannot reach the
latter may shine with much reputation and usefulness in
the former."

11. Still it remains true that a **considerable amount of
natural talent** is requisite. "It is my opinion," says
Cicero in his first book *De Oratore*, "that nature and
genius contribute most to the powers of eloquence ; for
the mind and genius ought to be endowed with certain
quick faculties which, rendering invention acute, make expression and its embellishments copious, and memory
strong and retentive. It is very well if these faculties
be animated or excited by art, but it is not in the power

of art to supply all these qualities—they are the gifts of
nature. . . . There are some men so stammering in
their expression, so harsh in their tone of voice, so forbidding in their look, so unwieldy and rustic in person,
that neither genius nor art could ever make them orators ;
while there are others so happily formed, so endowed by
nature with fitness for the same attainments, that they
seem not only to be born but moulded by the hand of
God for oratory. . . . Natural abilities have been deem-
ed so necessary that Apollonius of Alabanda, a master of
rhetoric, would not allow those whom he thought could
never become orators to lose their time in attending his
lectures. He dismissed them to embrace that art or profession for which he judged them to be most fitted by
nature."

12. In his second book *De Oratore* Cicero lays down
this practical rule : "Therefore, in forming an orator, I
first ascertain the extent of his abilities. He must have
acquired a certain amount of learning ; he must have
heard some speaking and done some reading ; he must
have received special precepts. I would then try what
suits him best ; what he can do with his voice, his lungs,
his breath, and his tongue. If I think that he can reach
the level of eminent speakers I will not only advise him
to persevere in labor, but, if I think him a man of principle and honor, I will urge him to go on—such lustre,
in my judgment, does a man who combines integrity with
eloquence shed over an entire nation. But if I think,
after he has done his best, that he can only rise to mediocrity in eloquence, I shall then leave him to himself to
follow his own inclination, without giving him any great
trouble. But if he have anything distinctly unfavorable
and shocking in his manner I shall then advise him to
discontinue, or direct his views to some other profession

CHAPTER I.

SPECIAL TALENTS.

13. We shall now consider what natural powers are most necessary for an orator, and what training will aid to develop each of them. Among the gifts of nature we may mention first **a strong mind,** quick to conceive ideas, clear in judging of their agreement or disagreement, unerring in drawing the right conclusions from a train of reasoning. This is the *vis mentis* spoken of in the familiar maxim of the ancients: *Pectus est quod disertos facit, et vis mentis*—"It is the heart and mental power that make men eloquent." The mind may be much developed and strengthened by a thorough course of classical and mathematical studies, by reading polemical works remarkable for cogent reasoning, but especially by the study of logic and philosophy. Much meditation will be of the utmost advantage; and it is, perhaps, one of the greatest drawbacks to the intellectual power of the present generation that, engrossed by a variety of pursuits and whirled along by the excitement of the hour, few men have that leisure for meditation which the great minds of former times enjoyed. "The wisdom of a scribe cometh by his time of leisure," says Ecclesiasticus (xxxviii. 25), "and he that is less in action shall receive wisdom. With what wisdom shall he be furnished that holdeth the plough?" etc.

14. A second gift is a great **sensibility of the passions** or the heart, called *pectus* in the maxim just quoted. "By passion," says Blair (Lect. xxv.), "I mean that state of

the mind in which it is agitated and fired by some object it has in view. A man may convince, and even persuade, others to act, by mere reason and argument. But that degree of eloquence which gains the admiration of mankind, and properly denominates one an orator, is never found without warmth or passion. Passion, when in such a degree as to rouse and kindle the mind without throwing it out of the possession of itself, is universally found to exalt all the human powers. It renders the mind infinitely more enlightened, more penetrating, more vigorous and masterly than it is in its calm moments. A man actuated by a strong passion becomes much greater than he is at other times. He is conscious of more strength and force; he utters greater sentiments, conceives higher designs, and executes them with a boldness and a felicity of which, on other occasions, he could not think himself capable." "But chiefly with respect to persuasion is the power of passion felt. Almost every man in passion is eloquent. Then he is at no loss for words and arguments. He transmits to others, by a sort of contagious sympathy, the warm sentiments which he feels; his looks and gestures are all persuasive; and nature here shows herself infinitely more powerful than art. This is the foundation of that just and noted rule: *Si vis me flere, dolendum est primum ipsi tibi*—'If you wish me to weep you must first grieve yourself.'"

15. **Sensibility** of the passions **may be cultivated** by reading the best poets and hearing the greatest orators, but especially by the acquisition of the social and the civil virtues, which will readily enkindle the proper passions when the occasion requires; thus a man who sincerely loves his country or his fellow-man will feel his passions aroused at the sight of oppression or misfortune.

16. A third gift necessary for an orator is a **lively imagi-**

nation. Quintilian, speaking of one of its effects, remarks: " What the Greeks call *Phantasies* we call *Visions*, by which the images of absent things are so represented to the mind that we seem to behold them with our eyes as present before us; whoever shall be able vividly to conceive those visions with his imagination will have great power to excite the passions." "These remarks," as the *Grammar of Eloquence* justly observes (p. 194), " regard the operations of the imagination generally, and not the mere figure called vision. The imagination creates admiration by its beauties of description, astonishes by its brilliant imagery, delights by the happy resemblance which its painting bears to nature, and by its magic spell hurries the hearers into love, pity, grief, terror, desire, aversion, fury, or hatred. It arouses in others the ardent feelings which gave itself birth in the speaker's mind, and opens up at pleasure all the deep fountains of rage, of laughter, and of tears."

17. **Power of will** is a fourth requisite. This faculty, which selects good and rejects evil, though free in its choice, is nevertheless very differently disposed in different persons, partly by nature and partly as a result of habits gradually acquired. " The orator," says Barry (p. 201), " must have a strong, firm, unconquerable will to maintain his personal character by probity of life and fidelity to his cause and duty; to acquire additional knowledge and greater perfection in his profession by unceasing application ; and to deport himself with respectability, with advantage to himself, his clients, and his country. To succeed in this nothing is more useful than to have regular and fixed habits, to husband time by distributing it into separate hours for study, business, and relaxation." Some one has defined genius to be the power of devoting one's self to an object ; if so, then a strong will is often the source and always the condition of genius.

18. **Memory** is another gift. "What," says Cicero, "shall I say of that treasury of all knowledge—memory? For unless this faculty be the faithful repository of all the thoughts and inventions, we know that all the other qualifications of an orator, even though they be perfect, must be fruitless." "Eloquence displays the power of memory in its full light; for in eloquence the memory retains the greatest quantity of matter, and not only the order of things but of words, and in such an abundance that patience fails the hearer sooner than memory fails the speaker" (Barry). A faithful memory is a gift of nature, but it can be wonderfully improved by constant exercise and by habits of regularity.

19. That the speaker's **outward appearance** may add much to the effect of his words is at once apparent, and a favorable appearance is evidently a gift of nature; so likewise is a **strong and melodious voice.** The latter can be greatly improved by judicious cultivation, as was that of Demosthenes. It may not be improper to recall in this place the energetic and **persevering efforts** which this greatest of orators made to improve his natural gifts and to remove his natural defects. "He bade adieu," says Plutarch in his life of Demosthenes, "to the other studies and exercises in which boys are engaged, and applied himself with great assiduity to declaiming, in hopes of being one day numbered among the orators. . . . He built himself a subterraneous study, which has remained to our times. Thither he repaired every day to form his action and exercise his voice; and he would often stay there for two or three months together, shaving one side of his head, that if he should happen to be ever so desirous of going abroad the shame of appearing in that condition might keep him in. . . . As for his personal defects, Demetrius the Phalerean gives us an account of the remedies he applied

to them, and he says he had it from Demosthenes himself in his old age. The hesitation and stammering of his tongue he corrected by speaking with pebbles in his mouth ; and he strengthened his voice by running or walking up-hill and pronouncing some passage in an oration or poem during the difficulty of breathing which that exercise caused. He had, moreover, a looking-glass in his house, before which he used to declaim and adjust all his motions."

CHAPTER II.

MORAL VIRTUES.

20. But far more important than any physical power in the orator are the **moral virtues** with which nature and his own efforts, with the help of God's grace, have adorned his soul. "In order to be a truly eloquent or persuasive speaker," says Blair (Lect. xxxiv.), "nothing is more necessary than to be a virtuous man. This was a favorable position among the ancient rhetoricians : *Non posse oratorem esse nisi virum bonum*—'That no one could be an orator except a good man.'" It is the chief duty of education to make men virtuous ; any system of training which does not put virtue in the first place is a false system. Now, the virtues most necessary for an orator are :

21. **1. Probity**. "The greater this power of eloquence is," says Cicero (*De Or.* iii. 14), "the more strongly does it need to be supported by probity and the greatest prudence ; if you give fluency of speech to a man destitute of these virtues you will not so much have made an orator as have put a sword in the hands of a madman." "If the power of creation," remarks J. Q. Adams, "could be delegated to mortal hands, and we could make an orator as a sculptor moulds a statue, the first material we should employ for the composition would be integrity of heart. The reason why this quality becomes so essential is that it forms the basis of the hearer's confidence, without which no eloquence can operate upon his belief." This is a reason, but not the chief reason.

22. **2. Temperance**—*i.e.*, habitual moderation with regard to the natural appetites. To this Blair refers when he says : "Nothing is so favorable as virtue to the prosecution of honorable studies. It prompts a generous emulation to excel ; it leaves the mind vacant and free, master of itself, disencumbered of those bad passions and disengaged from those mean pursuits which have ever been found the greatest enemies to true proficiency." And he quotes these words of Quintilian : "If the management of an estate, if anxious attention to domestic economy, a passion for hunting, or whole days given up to public places of amusements, consume so much time that is due to study, how much greater waste must be occasioned by licentious desires, avarice, or envy ! Nothing is so much hurried and agitated, so contradictory to itself, or so violently torn and shattered by conflicting passions as a bad heart. Amidst the distractions which it produces what room is left for the cultivation of letters or the pursuit of any honorable art ? No more, assuredly, than there is for the growth of corn in a field that is overrun with thorns and brambles."

23. **3. Public spirit**, or love of country and the highest interests of society. "On all great subjects and occasions there is a dignity, there is an energy in noble sentiments which is overcoming and irresistible. They give an ardor and a flame to one's discourse which seldom fails to kindle a like flame in those who hear, and which, more than any other cause, bestows on eloquence that power, for which it is famed, of seizing and transporting an audience. Here art and imitation will not avail. An assumed character conveys none of this powerful warmth. It is only a native and unaffected glow of feeling which can transmit the emotion to others. Hence the most renowned orators, such as Cicero and Demosthenes, were no less distinguished for some of the high virtues, as public spirit

and zeal for their country, than for eloquence.   Beyond
doubt to these virtues their eloquence owed much of its
effect ; and those orations of theirs in which there breathes
most of the virtuous and magnanimous spirit are those
which have most attracted the admiration of ages " (Blair,
Lect. xxxiv.)

24. When we mention love of country among the virtues
of an orator we do not mean that *utilitarianism* which
looks only to the advantages of the present hour.   The ancient orators often maintained that virtue practised for its
own sake is the highest interest of society, as Plutarch
teaches when he says (Life of Demosthenes) : " Panatius,
the philosopher, asserts that most of Demosthenes' orations
are written upon this principle, that virtue is to be chosen
for her own sake only ; *e.g.*, the oration on the Crown,
that against Aristocrates, that for the Immunities, and the
Philippics.   In all these orations Demosthenes does not
exhort his countrymen to that which is most agreeable or
easy or advantageous, but he points out honor and propriety
as the first objects, and leaves the safety of the state as a
matter of inferior consideration."   This conduct of Demosthenes placed his popularity above the reach of fickle fortune, so that when the battle of Chæronea was lost " the
people," says Plutarch, " not only acquitted him, but treated
him with the same respect as before, and called him to the
helm again as a person whom they knew to be a well-wisher
of his country."

25. **4. Compassion for the unfortunate.**   " Joined with
the manly virtues he should at the same time possess
strong and tender sensibility to all the injuries, distresses,
and sorrows of his fellow-creatures ; a heart that can easily
relent, that can readily enter into the circumstances of
others, and can make their case his own " (Blair, xxxiv.)
The influence and power which every appearance of public

spirit and compassion for the unfortunate imparts to a man who is thought by his hearers to possess these virtues are strikingly exhibited in the case even of unprincipled demagogues, such as a Garibaldi, a Mazzini, and the orators of the Reign of Terror in France.   Men like these exert a powerful influence over their followers.   Still it is well to remark that they cannot be called orators in the true sense of the word, for we must estimate an orator's greatness by the admirable effects which he produces.   Now, such speakers produce nothing admirable ; their work is destruction, and their path is strewn with the ruins of all that is most noble and precious.   Instead of raising the people above self-interest, as Demosthenes did, they debase their hearers by strengthening their selfish inclinations.

26. **5. Benevolence.**   "It is the most captivating of all human qualities, for it recommends itself to the selfish passions of every individual.   Benevolence is a disposition of the heart universal in its nature, and every single hearer imagines that temper to be kindly affected towards himself which is known to be actuated by good-will to all.   It is the general impulse of human nature to return kindness with kindness, and the speaker whose auditory, at the instant of his first address, believes him inspired with a warm benevolence for them has already more than half obtained his end " (Adams, Lect. xv.)

27. **6.** "**Modesty** is a kindred virtue to benevolence, and possesses a similar charm over the hearts of men.   Modesty always obtains the more, precisely because it asks nothing. Modesty lulls all the irritable passions to sleep.   It often disarms, and scarcely ever provokes, opposition.   These qualities are so congenial to the best feelings of mankind that they can never be too assiduously cultivated.   In them there is no contradiction.   If they do not always succeed, they never totally fail.   They neutralize malice, they baffle

envy ; they relax the very brow of hatred and soften the features of scorn into a smile. But the purest of virtues border upon pernicious failings. Let your benevolence never degenerate into weakness, nor your modesty into bashfulness " (ib.)

28. **7.** " A decent **Confidence** is among the most indispensable qualifications of an accomplished orator. Arrogance stimulates resentment ; vanity opens to derision ; but a mild and determined intrepidity, unabashed by fear, unintimidated by the noise and turbulence of a popular assembly, unawed by the rank or dignity of an auditory, must be acquired by every, public speaker aspiring to high distinction. It is as necessary to command the respect as to conciliate the kindness of your hearers " (ib.)

29. **8.** " This decent and respectful confidence is but a natural result of the perfect and unalterable **self-command** which, though last, is far, very far, from being the least ingredient in the composition of an accomplished orator. If it be true of mankind in general that he who ruleth his spirit is greater than he that taketh a city, to no description of human beings can this pre-eminence of self-dominion be so emphatically ascribed as to the public speaker. . . When the ebullitions of passion burst in peevish crimination of the audience themselves, when a speaker sallies forth armed with insult and outrage for his instruments of persuasion, you may be assured that this quixotism of rhetoric must eventually terminate like all other modern knight-errantry, and that the fury must always be succeeded by the impotence of the passions " (ib.)

30. **9.** To these virtues we may add, with Blair, **a habit of application and industry** : " It is not by starts of application, or by a few years' preparation of study afterwards discontinued, that eminence can be attained. No ; it can be attained only by means of regular industry, grown into

a habit, and ready to be exerted on every occasion that calls for industry. This is a fixed law of our nature, and he must have a high opinion of his own genius indeed that can believe himself an exception to it. . . . Nothing is so great an enemy both to honorable attainments and to the real, to the brisk and spirited enjoyment of life, as that relaxed state of mind which arises from indolence and dissipation. One that is destined to excel in any art, especially in the art of speaking and writing, will be known by this more than by any other mark whatever : an enthusiasm for that art—an enthusiasm which, firing his mind with the object he has in view, will dispose him to relish every labor which the means require."

CHAPTER III.

KNOWLEDGE.

31. Having spoken of the natural powers of an orator and of his moral virtues, we shall add a few remarks about the knowledge which he should possess.

And, first, he will need a clear and full **knowledge of the particular profession** in which his oratorical efforts are to be exerted. If he be a lawyer, let him have a thorough knowledge of the law ; if a divine, let him be a deep theologian ; if a statesman, let him be well acquainted with all that concerns the prosperity of nations, particularly of his own country, with its wants, its resources, etc.

32. In addition to this special knowledge every orator needs a considerable amount of **general knowledge.** In fact, Cicero insists that *omnibus disciplinis et artibus debet esse instructus orator*—" An orator should be versed in all the branches of learning." By this he means that he should at least have received a liberal education, embracing the thorough study of language, history, philosophy, and a certain familiarity with the finest productions of poetry and with the general circle of polite literature.

33. Almost all the great speakers who have reflected so much honor on the English language were **classical scholars,** who from boyhood had developed all their powers of mind by a liberal education, and, of course, had studied the masterpieces of ancient oratory in their original tongues. " Burke, Chatham, Fox, and Pitt," says Chauncey A. Goodrich in his Introduction to *British Eloquence,* " stand, by

universal consent, at the head of our eloquence." Now, all these were eminent for classical attainments. Our own Daniel Webster and Calhoun had richly profited by the advantages of a classical education; and they are undoubtedly our greatest orators. For of Webster the judgment passed on him by Lowndes has been generally accepted, that "the North had not his equal, nor the South his superior," and Calhoun was his rival in the South.

34. Of the knowledge of **history** Cicero says: "Do you not perceive how far history is the business of an orator? I doubt if it be not his principal business." "The orator," observes Quintilian, "ought to furnish himself with a great number of examples, as well ancient as modern, and therefore ought not only to be acquainted with the records of history, with traditions, and with the events of the day, but he should not neglect even the fictions of the more celebrated poets" (xii. 4). "History," says Dionysius of Hali carnassus, "is philosophy teaching by example." Now, example is universally acknowledged to be more efficacious than precept. The great orator and statesman Edmund Burke owed much of his success to his historical knowledge.

35. As to **philosophy**, two of its departments—viz., logic and ethics—are indispensable to an orator; the former "to forge the weapons which oratory is to wield," the latter to guide the statesman and the lawyer, and even the divine, in the studies of their respective professions. For, as J. Q Adams notices (Lect. xv.), "a truly virtuous orator must have an accurate knowledge of the duties incident to man in a state of civil society. He must have formed a correct estimate of good and evil; a moral sense which in demonstrative discourse will direct him with the instantaneous impulse of intuition to the true sources of honor and shame; in judicial controversy, to those of justice; in de-

liberation, to the path of real utility ; in the pulpit, to all the wisdom of man and all that the revelation of heaven have imparted of light for the pursuit of temporal or eternal felicity."

36. **Familiarity with the finest productions** of poetry and with the general circle of polite literature, and especially with the most perfect specimens of ancient and modern oratory, is indispensable to a perfect orator. Hume has somewhere remarked that " he who would teach eloquence must do it chiefly by examples." Without these, precepts would be almost powerless ; and universal practice has sanctioned the reading of Demosthenes' and Cicero's orations in colleges as one of the most direct preparations for an oratorical career. Likewise the most excellent orations of modern orators should be carefully studied, and even their more familiar business speeches will be read with much profit.

37. **In a word,** " The orator," says Cicero, " must have a forest of materials and thoughts. . . . Indeed, it is my opinion that within the province of an orator everything falls that belongs to the advantage of his countrymen and the manners of various nations, whatever regards the habits of life and the conduct of governments, civil society and the public feeling, the laws of nature and the morals of mankind. Though he is not obliged to answer distinctly, like a philosopher, on those subjects, he should at least be competent to interweave them dexterously into his oration on the cause at issue ; he ought to be able to speak on such topics in the same manner as the men who founded laws, statutes, and states, in a plain, straightforward manner, with luminous perspicuity, without metaphysical disputation, and without dry or profitless cavilling."

38. To induce young men to strive after the highest per-

fection of the ideal orator, such as Cicero conceived him, J. Q. Adams, at the end of his fourth lecture, thus addresses the Sophomores in Harvard University: " To whatever occupation your future inclinations or destinies may direct you, that **pursuit of ideal excellence** which constituted the plan of Cicero's orator and the principle of Cicero's life, if profoundly meditated and sincerely adopted, will prove a never-failing source of virtue and of happiness. . . . It must be the steady purpose of a life, maturely considered, deliberately undertaken, and inflexibly pursued through all the struggles of human opposition and all the vicissitudes of fortune. It must mark the measure of your duties in the relations of domestic, of social, and of public life ; must guard from presumption your rapid moments of prosperity, and nerve with fortitude your lingering hours of misfortune. It must mingle with you in the busy murmurs of the city, and retire in silence with you to the shades of solitude. Like hope, it must ' travel through, nor quit you when you die '—your guide amid the dissipations of youth, your counsellor in the toils of manhood, your companion in the leisure of declining age. It must, it will, irradiate the darkness of dissolution, will identify the consciousness of the past with the hope of futurity, will smooth the passage from this to a better world, and link the last pangs of expiring nature with the first rapture of never-ending joy."

BOOK II.

ON THE INVENTION OF THOUGHT.

39. "The power of eloquence can never appear," says Cicero (*De Or.* i. 11), "but when the orator is a complete master of his subject." Now, it is the aim of the following precepts on Invention to aid the orator in "mastering his subject." Hence their importance. "Invention," says Blair (Lect. xxxi.), "is without doubt the most material and the groundwork of the rest." "But with respect to this," he adds, "I am afraid it is beyond the power of art to give any real assistance." It would, indeed, be a great pity if art were so powerless with regard to what is acknowledged to be the most important task of an orator. Happily, however, such minds as Aristotle, Cicero, and Quintilian among the ancients, and many of the greatest rhetoricians among the moderns, judge differently from Dr. Blair. We shall attempt to follow their teachings, both on account of the authority which their writings carry with them, and because the experience of many years devoted to the teaching of rhetoric has convinced us that the study of invention is most efficacious in developing the minds of the young and making them prefer solid thought to idle declamation. The absence of such precepts from the *Lectures* of Dr. Blair greatly impairs the value of a work so admirable in many other respects, and we are not surprised to hear Macaulay designate Blair as a superficial

critic, which epithet applies to him chiefly on account of this very omission.

40. We shall divide this book on Invention into the following chapters : 1. A General View of the Intended Speech ; 2. Sources of Thought ; 3. Intrinsic Topics ; 4. Extrinsic Topics ; 5. Topics of Persons and Moral Topics ; 6. Use of the Topics ; 7. An Example for Practice.

CHAPTER I.

A GENERAL VIEW OF THE INTENDED SPEECH.

41. Before we proceed to search for thoughts on any subject or matter it is necessary to fix the following points clearly in our minds.

1. What is the **subject** on which we are preparing to speak? Thus, when William Pitt spoke on the abolition of the slave-trade, his subject was the *Slave-Trade*, not *Slavery;* this latter would be a very different matter.

42. **2.** What **question** is to be answered about the subject? In the example just mentioned the question was, *Whether the slave-trade should be immediately abolished?* For such abolition was the motion then before the House of Commons, and in support of it Pitt delivered his famous speech, "one of the ablest pieces of mingled argument and eloquence which he ever produced," as Chauncey A. Goodrich remarks in his *British Eloquence* (p. 579). To mistake the subject or the question is a disgraceful fault called *ignoratio elenchi—i.e.*, missing the point. For instance, such a mistake was the cause of much misrepresentation and useless ill-feeling at the time of the late Vatican Council, when many leading journalists inveighed so vehemently against the *infallibility* of the. Pope. They mistook it for the *impeccability* of the Pope, and thus confounded a solemn teaching of the Catholic Church with an error which no Catholic believes.

43. **3.** What is the **end intended** in the speech, or what does the speaker hope to accomplish? For instance, does

he aim chiefly at convincing the minds of his hearers? or does he rather aim at controlling their wills? or does he wish mainly to please? Thus Webster in his two speeches at the Bunker Hill Monument aimed at *pleasing*, in his speech in Knapp's trial at *convincing*, in that on the Presidential Protest at *convincing and persuading*. To aim chiefly at display or pleasure, when there is a more serious task before us, would incur only the contempt of sensible men. Besides, we must not forget what Cicero remarks (*De Orat.* ii. 77): "While we bring others to our opinion by three means, by explaining, by conciliating, and by moving, we must ever pretend to do but one thing—*i.e.*, we must appear to aim at nothing but explanation; the other two must permeate the parts of an oration as the blood permeates the body." Certainly it would be improper to tell our hearers that we are going to please or to move them; but no sensible man can object to have the matter explained to him and proofs presented to convince his mind.

44. **4.** What is the exact **state of the question**—*i.e.*, what is the precise point on which the parties differ, or on the decision of which the success of the speech will chiefly depend? This is also called **placing the question on its proper footing,** and it is of especial importance in argumentative speeches. In doing this properly the ability of a lawyer or the skill of a debater will often appear to the greatest advantage. Thus in Daniel Webster's speech in the Dartmouth College case the general question was, whether certain acts of the Legislature of New Hampshire "were valid and binding on the plaintiffs, without their acceptance or assent"? The decision of this question Webster causes to turn on this particular point: *Whether or not the former trustees had obtained vested rights as sacred as the rights of private pro-*

perty? If they had, no Legislature could violate them; and he maintained that they had. His opponents had to maintain either that such was not the fact or that the decision did not depend on this precise point.

45. **5.** What are the **presumptions** in the case—*i.e.*, what may be taken for granted until it is disproved? The following are some of the principal presumptions, common to many subjects :

(*a*) In a **criminal** case the accused party is presumed innocent until his guilt is proved. This throws the burden of proof on the accuser; it is enough for the defence to show that the proofs adduced by the prosecution are not conclusive, no matter how plausible.

(*b*) In **civil claims** the presumption is in favor of the actual possessor—*i.e.*, the one who holds actual possession need not produce his title till he who wishes to eject him has proved a legal claim ; if a doubt remains as to the validity of this claim the present occupant remains in possession.

(*c*) **Legal documents** must be supposed to be genuine till they are proved to be counterfeit.

(*d*) In **legislation** no new law should be made till it is shown to be an improvement.

(*e*) **Uncertain laws** do not bind—*i.e.*, our liberty is not to be hampered by a law whose existence is doubtful.

(*f*) **What is known to have been done** must be presumed to have been validly done ; *e.g.*, title-deeds, writs issued by officials, are supposed to be valid, unless there is positive proof to the contrary.

(*g*) The presumption is **in favor of morality** and the common good ; thus the presumption is against infidel speculations, since these debase man and loosen the bonds of society by removing the highest sanction of the natural law.

(*h*) The presumption is **in favor of what exists** and against a change ; thus even the Redeemer, when he came to put an end to Judaism, proved his divine mission by manifest miracles.

46. The various distinctions of subject, end, question, and state of the question are treated by J. Q. Adams under the one name of **state of the controversy**. His treatment of this matter appears to us so excellent that we shall be excused if we quote him here at some length.

"The first and most important of these (essential particulars)," he says (Lect. viii.), "is what the ancient rhetoricians term the state of the controversy. . . . A full and clear understanding of it, applied to the usages and manners of our own times, is one of the most important points in the whole science. . . . It is the *quod erat demonstrandum* of the mathematicians. It is the mark at which all the speaker's discourse aims; the focus towards which all the rays of his eloquence should converge ; and, of course, varies according to the nature and subject of the speech. In every public· oration the speaker ought to have some specific point, to which, as to the goal of his career, all his discourse should be directed. In legislative or deliberative assemblies this is now usually called the *question*. In the courts of common law it is known as the *issue*. In polemical writings it is sometimes called the *point*. In demonstrative discourses it is dilated into the general name of the *subject ;* and in the pulpit the proper state is always contained in the preacher's text. It therefore belongs to every class of public speaking, and is not confined to judicial or deliberative oratory, where alone you would, at first blush, suppose the term controversy could properly be applied. It is, indeed, probable that it first originated in judicial contests, where it always remained of most frequent use. To the other classes it was transferred by analogy. Whoever speaks in public must have something to prove or to illustrate. Whatever the occasion or the subject may be, the purpose of the orator must be to convince or to move. Every speech is thus supposed to be founded upon some controversy, actual or implied. Conviction is the great purpose of eloquence, and this necessarily presupposes some resistance of feeling or of intellect upon which conviction is to operate."

47. "I told you that the state of the controversy was one of the most important points of consideration in the whole science of rhetoric. As I have explained it to you in its broadest acceptation, it is to the orator what the polar star is to the mariner. It is the end to which every word he utters ought directly or indirectly to be aimed; and the whole art of speech consists in the perfect understanding of this end, and the just adaptation of means to effect its accomplishment. This may, perhaps, appear to you to be so obvious and so trivial a truth as to require no illustration. And yet you will find throughout your lives, in the courts of law, in the legislature, in the pulpit, nothing is so common as to see it forgotten. Our laws have found it necessary to provide that in town-meetings nothing shall be done by the inhabitants unless the subject or state of the controversy has been inserted in the warrant that calls them together. In all our legislative bodies rules of order are established for the purpose of confining the speakers to the subjects before them; and certain forms even of phraseology are adopted, into which every question must be reduced. Yet even this is not sufficient to restrain the wandering propensities of debate. . . ."

"The difficulties of ascertaining the true state are, indeed, in all practical oratory, much greater than a slight consideration would imagine. They arise principally from three sources, which, in the language of the science, are called co-ordinate, subordinate, and contingent states.

48. " 1. **Co-ordinate states** occur when there are more questions than one, which, separately taken and independent of all the rest, involve all the merits of the case. Such are the several charges of Cicero against Verres. Such are the impeachments of modern times, both in England and in our own country. Every article contains a co-ordinate state with all the rest ; and they may be met with distinct and separate answers to each charge or by one general answer to all.

49. " 2. **Subordinate states** are questions distinct from the principal point, controvertible in themselves and more or less important to its decision. . . . In deliberative eloquence you will find a remarkable instance of subordinate states, skilfully adapted to the main state, in Burke's speech on his proposal for conciliation between Great Britain and her then American colonies. His main state was the necessity of the conciliation. Why? Because America could not be subdued by force. This is a subordinate state. But the proof of his main position depended entirely upon its demonstration ; and it was a truth so unwelcome to his audience that it was incumbent upon him to place every part of his argument beyond the power of cavil. The depth and extent of research, the adamantine logic, and the splendor of oratory with which he performs this task has, in my own opinion, no parallel in the records of modern deliberative eloquence. It was for wise and beneficent purposes that Providence suffered this admirable speech to fail of conviction upon the sordid and venal souls to whom it was delivered. As a piece of eloquence it has never been appreciated at half its value." (See the analysis of the oration below, Number 147.)

50. "**3. Incidental states** are questions arising occasionally, and more or less connected with the main question without being essential to it. They are common to every species of oratory, though of rarer use in the desk, where they generally partake of the nature of digressions. But in legislative assemblies every proposition for an amendment offered on a bill upon its passage, and at the bar every occasional motion for the postponement of a trial, the admission of a witness, the disqualification of a juror, or the like, introduces an incidental question having some relation to the main state of the controversy. . . ."

51. We shall conclude these extracts with this judicious remark of the same lecturer. Speaking of the state of the question, he says : " But it is also **of high importance to the hearer** of every public speaker. For although some of you may never intend to follow the practice of public speaking, yet you will all occasionally be hearers ; and, with your advantages of education, all will be expected to be judges of the public orators. You have been justly told that there is an art of silent reading : the art of collecting the kernel from the shell, of selecting the wheat from the tares. Let me add—for it is only another modification of the same truth—that there is an art of hearing. And one of the most elaborate exercises is to ascertain the state of the public speaker's discourse."

52. **Examples.** We think it useful to exemplify such exercises by applying the explanations of this chapter to some of the most renowned orations of the greatest orators. We shall begin with the **Philippics of Demosthenes.** Philip, King of Macedon, whom the Athenians at first despised as a barbarian upstart, had acquired considerable power. Partly by skilful intrigue, partly by energetic war-measures, he was constantly extending his dominions and baffling all the efforts of the Athenians to stop his progress through

Thessaly into Greece, which was weakened by intestine dissensions. In Athens itself there was a party of politicians who favored his ambition. Demosthenes had made it the constant aim of his public life to defeat the crafty foe and his secret partisans. In several of his speeches, but especially in his three Philippics, the relations of Athens with Philip were the *subject* under consideration ; the *question*, which Adams would call *the state of the controversy*, was, whether they should adopt certain vigorous war measures to oppose him ; but the *state of the question*, or what Adams would call the "subordinate state," was not always the same. In the first speech it is whether there is any use in adopting vigorous measures, or, in other words, whether there is any hope of success remaining. In the second and third Philippics the state of the question is, *whether Philip is truly an enemy*, as the orator maintains he is. "The subject of this speech is simple," says Libanius, referring to the third oration ; "for while Philip spoke words of peace, but did many deeds of war, the orator advises the Athenians to arise and punish the king, since a great danger threatened themselves as well as all the Greeks in common." The *end intended* in each of the Philippics was to arouse his countrymen to adopt energetic measures. Demosthenes did not, with the mass of Athenian orators, study to gratify the ear of a refined and fastidious audience by beautiful sentiments clothed in magnificent language ; but to convince and persuade was his great object, to which all other things were made subservient.

53. We shall next examine the speech of **Cicero for Milo.** Milo, a candidate for the consulship in Rome, and a leader of the conservative party, while on an official journey, accompanied by his wife and a numerous suite of retainers, had been met by his enemy, Clodius, a violent leader of the radical party, who was attended by a numerous body of

armed slaves. A quarrel arose and Clodius was slain. How far Milo contributed to this result we do not exactly know; Asconius gives us one account of it and Cicero another. Cicero, who had formerly been driven from Rome by this same Clodius, undertook the defence. His speech on that occasion, as retouched afterwards and published by himself, is one of the most skilful specimens of pleading in existence. The matter, or *subject*, was the murder of Clodius. The *question* was not whether Milo killed Clodius, but whether he—or rather his slaves acting without his orders—killed the aggressor justly, *i.e.*, in self-defence. *The state of the question*, on which Cicero artfully makes the whole question turn, is this : *Which of the two waylaid the other ?* He presents the accusers as having argued that the murder had evidently been preconcerted, and that Milo had planned it. Cicero fights them on their own ground : supposing the murder had been preconcerted, he clearly shows that Milo could not have planned it ; therefore that Clodius must have waylaid his enemy, and Milo's party have acted in self-defence.

54. Lastly, we shall review one of the best speeches of **Daniel Webster**. As we shall often have occasion to speak of this great orator, it may not be amiss to quote Orestes A. Brownson's opinion of Webster's *Works :*

"We shall look in vain," says he (*Review*, July, 1852, p. 366), "in the whole range of American literature for works that can rival these six volumes before us. In general the end is just and noble, and, with few exceptions that we could reasonably expect, the doctrines set forth are sound and important. No man has written among us who has given utterance to sounder maxims on politics and law, and no one has done more to elevate political and legal topics to the dignity of science, to embellish them with the charms of a rich and chaste imagination. and to enrich them with the wealth accumulated from the successful cultivation of the classics of ancient and modern times. The author has received from nature a mind of the highest order, and he has cultivated it with care and success. We see in every page, every sentence of his writings vast intellectual power, quick sensibility, deep and tender affection, and a rich and fervid imagination ; but we see also the hard student, the traces of long and painful discipline under the tutelage of the most eminent ancient and modern masters. Nature has been bountiful, but art has added its full share in making the author what he is ; and the combination of the two has enabled him to produce works which in their line are certainly unrivalled in this country, and we know not where to look for anything in our language of the kind really superior to him. As an orator Mr. Webster has all the terseness of Demosthenes, the grace and fulness of Cicero, the fire and energy of Chatham, and a dignity and repose peculiarly his own."

55. The circumstances which led to **Webster's Speech in the Trial of J. F. Knapp** were as follows : A peaceful old man, Mr. White, had been brutally murdered in his bed at night. Four men were suspected of complicity in this foul deed and were arrested. One, probably the actual murderer, committed suicide ; another, by name J. F. Knapp, was accused as a principal in the murder. Mr. Webster was employed as attorney for the prosecution. He proves, in the first part of his masterly oration, that the murder was the result of a conspiracy, to which the culprit was a party. Next he shows that the same culprit rendered actual aid to the murderer, or at least was on hand with the purpose of doing so ; this would make him a principal, in the language of the law. The *subject* is the murder of Mr. White ; the *question*, whether Knapp was a principal to it. Webster makes the question hinge on this precise

point, *Whether Knapp was in Brown Street by appointment with the murderer for the purpose of aiding in the murder.* The defence had argued that Brown Street was not a good place whence to render aid. Webster argues that it need not be ; it is enough that Knapp was there by appointment with the perpetrator, which supposed fact he endeavors to prove by a most skilful sifting of the circumstantial evidence. And the argument is all the more remarkable for its cogency if, as Mr. E. C. Whipple asserts in his late edition of Webster's great speeches, " Knapp was not in Brown Street for that precise purpose which the orator ascribes to him."

CHAPTER II.

SOURCES OF THOUGHTS.

56. When a clear and distinct conception has been formed of the subject on which we are to discourse, and of the precise question to be answered about it ; and when we have determined what point we should select for the state of the question, we can next proceed to find an abundant supply of thoughts on the subject. This will enable us to deal with it so thoroughly, lucidly, and even elegantly as to attain the end for which we speak.

Now, a thought which is intended to convince the hearers is called an **argument**—a word which Webster's Dictionary correctly defines as " a proof or means of proving ; a reason offered in proof to induce belief or convince the mind." However, the word argument has been used by many rhetoricians in a wider sense, and some call an **oratorical argument** *any thought that suits the orator's purpose*, whether it be intended to convince, to please, or to persuade. We are now to consider the sources whence arguments can be derived.

57. These sources are called **Topics** by the Greeks, **Common-Places** (*Loci Communes*), or **Seats of Arguments** (*Sedes Argumentorum*) by the Latins—all figurative expressions, as if the arguments were to be found in certain localities by any one who would know how to look for them. This is exactly the way in which Cicero views this matter when he endeavors to show us the importance of such Topics, reminding us at the same time that it requires a careful

search to discover the arguments which they contain. " If I wished to point out a mass of gold," he says, " that is buried in several places, it would be enough if I should describe the signs and marks of the places where it lies, for then the person to whom I described it might find and dig it up with ease and certainty ; thus, after I have made myself master of these marks which indicate where arguments are to be found, I say that all the rest is to be accomplished by careful searching. For when these sources are impressed upon the mind and upon the reasoning faculties, and arranged so as to serve upon all occasions, nothing then can escape the orator, not only in his contests at the bar, but in every kind of public speaking " (*De Or.* ii. 41).

58. **The invention of these Topics** is ascribed to Gorgias, the sophist, which fact is perhaps no great commendation ; but no logical mind will thence conclude that they are mere sophistry. " If it be true," remarks J. Q. Adams, " as by the concurrent testimony of all the ancient rhetoricians we are assured, that Gorgias was the inventor of what are called topics, or common-places, of oratorical numbers, and of a general plan for extemporaneous declamation upon every subject, he must be considered as one of the principal improvers of eloquence. These things are peculiarly liable to be abused ; but they have been of important use to all the celebrated ancient orators, and to none more than to Plato himself " (Lect. iii.)

59. The Topics may be thus **defined**: *Certain leading considerations which can be applied to any subject for the purpose of studying it in itself and in all its relations to other things, so as to acquire a clear and full knowledge of the matter under consideration.*

60. They may be variously **distinguished**: some regard things, others persons, and some the motives of persons.

The last are called *Moral Topics.* Those regarding things are usually divided into two classes, now commonly called *Intrinsic* and *Extrinsic.* The Intrinsic Topics are found in the matter itself which is treated of ; the Extrinsic exist outside of it and independent of it. Aristotle called the former *Artificial,* because it requires art to find the arguments by means of them and bring them out of the nature of the subject ; the latter he called *Inartificial,* because the arguments furnished by them are not to be skilfully made up by the orator, but exist already—such are deeds, written documents, witnesses, authorities, oaths, etc. (*De Orat.* ii. 27).

CHAPTER III.

INTRINSIC TOPICS.

61. If any one be inclined to find fault with us for introducing here a number of classifications, distinctions, and technical terms, we can only plead in our own defence that the same is done and must be done wherever accurate knowledge is aimed at, in rhetoric as well as in philosophy, in physics, and chemistry, or in the study of law and medicine.

We are studying how to dissect a subject and examine all its parts. In this portion of our task we shall mostly follow in the footsteps of the distinguished modern philosopher and rhetorician, Rev. Joseph Kleutgen, S.J., who has treated this matter with equal brevity and clearness.

62. Examining with him, 1st, the **Nature** of the subject, we find in it these four topics, *Definition*, *Enumeration*, *Genus*, and *Species;* 2d, the **Name** of the subject, we find *Notation* and *Conjugates;* 3d, its **Relations** to other things, we have *Cause and Effect*, *Antecedents and Consequences*, and *Circumstances;* 4th, its **Comparison** with other things, we meet with *Contrariety*, *Likeness*, and *Likelihood.* More topics might be mentioned, but these are the principal of the intrinsic kind. On each of these we shall speak with some detail.

Article I. Definition.

63. The **definition** states in clear and exact language what is meant by the subject under consideration. This is

one of the most important topics. Many speeches are vague and ineffectual because the speaker has taken no pains to define his subject clearly to his own mind and to the minds of his audience. Often a debate or a case before a court of justice is gained by a clear definition.

64. As an example of this we may adduce the masterly plea of **Erskine in behalf of Lord Gordon.** "Lord George Gordon," says C. A. Goodrich (*British Eloquence*), "a member of the House of Commons, was a young Scottish nobleman of weak intellect and enthusiastic feelings. He had been chosen president of the Protestant Association, whose object was to procure the repeal of Sir George Saville's bill in favor of the Catholics. In this capacity he directed the association to meet him in St. George's Fields, and to proceed thence to the Parliament House with a petition for the repeal of the bill. Accordingly about forty thousand persons of the middle classes assembled on Friday, the 2d of June, 1780, and, after forming a procession, moved forward till they blocked up all the avenues to the House of Commons.

"Lord Gordon presented the petition, but the House refused to consider it at that time by a vote of 192 to 6. The multitude now became disorderly, and, after the House adjourned, bodies of men proceeded to demolish the Catholic chapels at the residences of the foreign ministers. From this moment the whole affair changed its character. Desperate men, many of them thieves and robbers, took the lead. Not only were Catholic chapels set on fire, but the London prisons were broken open and destroyed; the town was for some days completely in the power of the multitude.

"When order was at last restored the magistrates, as is common with those who have neglected their duty, endeavored to throw the blame on others—they resolved to make

Lord George Gordon the scape-goat. He was accordingly arraigned for high treason ; and such was the excitement of the public mind, such the eagerness to have some one punished, that he was in imminent danger of being made the victim of public resentment." Kenyon, his senior counsel, had failed in his defence.

65. Erskine, then a young man, saved him by laying down a clear and correct *definition of High Treason*, which was the indictment against him. He proved that the crime of high treason, in the only meaning in which it could apply to the case, supposed *premeditated open acts of violence, hostility, and force;* and he was able to show from copious testimonies that such *premeditated open acts* were totally foreign to the mind of his client. The whole speech is worthy of careful study. Lord Campbell is enthusiastic in its praise. "Here I find," he says, "not only great acuteness, powerful reasoning, enthusiastic zeal, and burning eloquence, but the most masterly view ever given of the English law of high treason, the foundation of all our liberties."

66. A speaker should strive to find or make up such definitions as even his adversaries cannot refuse to accept. A lawyer will properly draw his definitions from Blackstone, Kent, etc. For ordinary purposes our great lexicographers, Webster and Worcester, are usually good authorities. It may not be amiss, however, to remark that abstract philosophical terms, and in general all words relating to matters about which the English mind is less solicitous, are often very imperfectly defined in these works. There is, perhaps, no class of terms with regard to which this defect is more striking than such as are connected with the Catholic religion, its rites and ceremonies. (See an article on this subject in the *American Catholic Review* for April, 1880.) For such matters the *Catholic Dictionary* of Addis and

Arnold may be relied on as furnishing correct definitions.

67. When the orator prepares his own definition he may do so philosophically or oratorically. A **philosophical definition** gives the *genus*, or class, to which the subject belongs, and, along with the genus, it states the *specific difference—i.e.*, the peculiar property or properties by which this subject is distinguished from the other species of the same genus. For instance, "Painting is the fine art which expresses the beautiful by means of colors ; music is the fine art which expresses the beautiful by means of sound." The genus is *"fine art"—i.e.*, an art intended to express the beautiful. One fine art differs from another in the method of expressing the beautiful : painting expresses it by means of color, music by means of sound ; *color* and *sound*, then, are the specific difference.

68. The **oratorical definition** aims more at effect than at strictness of meaning or exactness of expression. The *Grammar of Eloquence* presents the teachings of rhetoricians on this subject as follows: An oratorical definition or description is made in **six ways:**

1. By **enumerating** the parts of which it is composed, as, "Oratory is an art which consists of invention, arrangement, style, and delivery."

2. By **effects**; as when sin is defined "the pest of the soul, the stain of conscience, the destroyer of spiritual life, the dishonor of human nature, the ruin of the world."

3. By **affirmation.** St. John Chrysostom thus defined the Cross of Christ : "The Cross of Christ is the way to the wandering, the guide to heaven, the hope of those who suffer injury, the bridle of the rich, the army which opposes the proud, the death of a voluptuous life, a rudder to the seafaring, a haven to the shipwrecked, an asylum to all the world."

4. By negation. Such a definition declares what a thing is not, that we may the better know what it is. Affirmation and negation are sometimes united. Thus Cicero describes Verres : "We have brought before your tribunal, not a thief, but a robber ; not a sacrilegious wretch, but an open enemy to all that is sacred and religious ; not an assassin, but the most cruel butcher of our citizens and our allies."

5. By adjuncts or circumstances. Of this we can adduce no finer example than that quoted by J. Q. Adams (Lect. ix.) He says: "Thus, in the funeral oration of Turenne by Fléchier, the orator, to display with greater force the combination of talents required for commanding an army, resorts to an oratorical definition. 'What,' says he—'what is an army? An army is a body agitated by an infinite variety of passions, directed by an able man to the defence of his country. It is a multitude of armed men blindly obedient to the orders of a commander and totally ignorant of his designs ; an assembly of base and mercenary souls for the most part, toiling for the fame of kings and conquerors, regardless of their own ; a motley mass of libertines to keep in order, of cowards to lead into battle, of profligates to restrain, of mutineers to control.'"

6. By comparisons and metaphors. Plutarch defines beauty thus : "A bland enemy, a pleasant ravisher, a deceitful torturer, a snare to our feet, a veil to our eyes."

ARTICLE II. ENUMERATION.

69. This topic furnishes an abundance of striking, and often most appropriate, arguments. **Enumeration** examines separately and in detail, or passes rapidly in review, the various parts of a subject. "The letters of Junius," says J. Q. Adams, "ranking in the very first line of elo-

quence, but far lower in moral and political wisdom, make frequent use of enumeration. His first letter, for instance, contains an enumeration of the high offices of state which composed the administration, with a commentary to prove that they were all held by weak and worthless men. In his address to the king he asks him on what part of his subjects he could rely for support if the people of England should revolt ; and then answers by enumerating all the other classes of people then composing the British Empire, and proving that he could depend upon none of them " (Lect. ix.) A similar example is found in the peroration of Edmund Burke's opening speech at the trial of Warren Hastings.

70. Enumeration is well suited to open up vast fields of thought on many subjects. Thus Rev. Thomas N. Burke, O.P., enters on his lecture entitled " The Catholic Church the Salvation of Society " with a happy enumeration, saying : " We may analyze society, as I intend to view it, from an intellectual standpoint. Then we shall see the society of learning, the society of art and literature. Or we may view it from a moral standpoint. . . . What has this society produced intellectually, morally, and politically ? "

71. As the parts of a whole subject may be separately considered, so may lesser divisions be more rapidly enumerated with happy, and often with brilliant, effect. We find mental greatness thus presented : " These sights are grand, whether we behold them in the philosopher, fathoming the depths of mind ; in the geologist, quarrying out science from the rock and the fossil ; or in the chemist, deducing the laws of life and death from the crucible and laboratory—whether we see them in the artist, busied in the magnificent creations of the chisel and the pencil ; or in the poet, entering into the treasure-house of imagination and stringing those rosaries of thought, the jewelled

epic and the sparkling song; or in the astronomer, soaring to the planets, measuring their paths, weighing their mass, and calling them by their names. But, after all, what is it? A few systems, a few poems, a few discoveries, the writing of a few names in rubies—and that is all of mental greatness " (Dr. Stephens). In a similarly glowing style Cicero, on the Manilian Law, advocating the appointment of Pompey to direct the war against Mithridates, enumerates the countries over which Pompey had already passed in his rapid conquests.

ARTICLE III. GENUS AND SPECIES.

72. In rhetoric a general proposition is called a **thesis**, as, " Poets deserve praise "; a particular proposition is called a **hypothesis**, as, " Virgil is an excellent poet." Now, it often happens that a speaker, while treating a thesis, will find it useful to dwell for a while on some special hypothesis, usually in illustration of his thesis. He is then said to draw an argument from the topic of **Species**. For instance, in Thomson's " Seasons " the poet, describing the effects of heat in the torrid zone, refers thus to the particular pestilence which destroyed the English fleet at Carthagena under Admiral Vernon :

> " You, gallant Vernon, saw
> The miserable scene ; you pitying saw
> To infant weakness sunk the warrior's arm
> Saw the deep-racking pang, the ghastly form,
> The lip pale quivering, and the beamless eye
> No more with ardor bright.   You heard the groans
> Of agonizing ships from shore to shore ;
> Heard nightly plunged, amid the sullen waves,
> The frequent corse," etc.

Thus, too, Lord Brougham, in his inaugural discourse

turns from his general theme, which is the praise of eloquence, to extol the merit of Demosthenes, Cicero, etc.

73. On the other hand, when dealing with a hypothesis
the orator may speak of the whole class or genus to which
his subject belongs. He then draws an argument from the
topic of **Genus.** " These topics are often employed," says
J. Q. Adams, " in argumentative oratory, and the speaker's
talent is discerned in the art with which he descends from
a general to a special proposition, or ascends from the special to the general."

74. The most familiar **example of the topic of genus** is
that passage of Cicero's oration for the poet Archias in
which he ascends from the praise of his client to the praise
of poets and poetry in general, rightly judging that whatever honors poets in general honors Archias in particular.
For, even in the strictest reasoning, whatever can be predicated of a whole class can be predicated of each species
and individual of that class.

75. But the reverse of this does not hold : it is a fallacy
to reason from a portion or an individual to a whole class.
Scientists are guilty of this **sophistry** when upon some particular observations they build up a general theory and
call it a scientific conclusion. For instance, Sir Charles
Lyell, calculating the annual increase of the alluvium at
the Delta of the Nile, allows thirty thousand years for the
formation of the deposit. But Lyell, to justify his calcu-
lation, should prove that in former times the deposit was
not more rapidly formed than at present. His fallacy consists in deducing from the rate of deposit at one time the
same rate of deposit at all times. This is fallacious reasoning.

In further illustration of this fallacy we may, with J. Q.
Adams, quote an epigram of Prior :

> " Yes, every poet is a fool—
>   By demonstration Ned can show it ;
>   Happy could Ned's inverted rule
>   Prove every fool to be a poet."

76. In his oration in Knapp's trial Webster has two beautiful passages drawn from the topic of Genus: one when he develops the general thesis, "*Murder will out*" (*Webster's Works*, vol. vi. pp. 53, 54), and immediately after it when he observes, "*Such is human nature that some persons lose their abhorrence of crime in their admiration of its magnificent exhibition*" (ib. 54, 55)—a passage on which they would do well to meditate who are so fond of adorning the narrative of crime with the richest charms of language in sensational novels and periodical literature.

77. When the topic of Genus is well managed it always produces a **happy effect** ; it makes us *rise above our subject*, as when Webster at Bunker Hill rises from the laying of a corner-stone to a consideration of the mighty changes that had come over the world within the last fifty years (*Amer. Oratory*, ii. p. 444).   So likewise Edward Everett, speaking at Cambridge on the fiftieth anniversary of the Declaration of our Independence, rises above his subject to consider the nature of all good government (ib. p. 467).

78. Still this topic is to be used with much **caution,** for it departs from the exact subject to dwell on something more general ; and a speaker who has frequent recourse to it would deal with generalities and fail to produce any definite effect on his audience.

Such generalities as speakers frequently drift into, for want of an intimate acquaintance with their subject, are also called **Common-places.**   They are very objectionable ; and the odium of this particular meaning of the term has often been attached in English literature to the general common-places or topics which we are now explaining.

79. That abuses may be avoided, observe these **cautions**: 1st. Never insist long on a genus, unless it be a matter rarely treated.

2d. Never refer a trifle to an important genus; this fault the poet ridicules, saying :

> " Non de vi, neque cæde, nec veneno ;
> Sed lis est mihi de tribus capellis."
>
> —*Martial.*

> " Talk not of arson, rape, nor murder dire ;
> Give me my kids—'tis all that I desire."

80. The ancient rhetorician Apthonius mentions this topic of genus as one of the school exercises, or **Progymnasmata**, usually given to boys for composition—*e.g.*, the praise of patriots, of orators, of soldiers, etc. It is an easy exercise, and readily lends itself to a declamatory style giving more sound than sense. But when this defect occurs, it is not owing to the topic itself, but to the mismanagement of the writer.

81. Lastly, it must be remarked that the meaning of the word **hypothesis**, explained in this article, is not to be confounded with another meaning of the same term, equivalent to **supposition**—*i.e.*, something not proved, nor even asserted, but merely assumed for the sake of argument. Adams takes the word in this latter meaning when he says (Lect. ix.) : " The hypothesis of an orator bears the same proportion to his thesis that traverse bears to plain sailing in navigation. It is not included under the topics, but includes them all under a different modification. Hypothesis is the potential or subjunctive mood of rhetoric, frequently used in every kind of public discourse. It is peculiarly calculated to excite attention and rivet the impression of the topics employed under it. Read, for instance, Junius' address which I have already quoted, and

commonly called his Letter to the King. It is, however, in form a hypothetical speech to the king, introduced in a letter to the printer; and a considerable part of its force is owing to the hypothesis upon which it is raised. Hypothesis is a favorite artifice with all orators of a brilliant imagination. It gives a license of excursions of fancy which cannot be allowed to the speaker while chained to the diminutive sphere of relatives. In deliberative and judicial orations it affords an opportunity to say hypothetically what the speaker would not dare to say directly. The artifice is, indeed, so often practised to evade all restraint in speech that there is at least no ingenuity in its employment. The purposes for which it is resorted to from this motive are often so disingenuous that in seeing it used and abused, as you will upon numberless occasions throughout your lives, you will probably go a step beyond the conclusion of the philosophical clown in Shakspere and settle in the opinion that there is much vice as well as much virtue in *If.*"

Article IV. Notation and Conjugates.

82. **Notation** draws an argument from the name of the subject, **Conjugates** from kindred words; both may be called the topic of **Etymology.** This topic is not a very copious source of arguments, but when it is applicable it may yield a clear proof. For there is often much virtue in a name. For instance, in a debate " whether Louis XIV. or Charlemagne was the greater man," the very name of the latter, which means Charles the Great, shows that posterity has recognized his uncommon greatness, whereas the efforts of many French writers to attach the same epithet to the name of Louis XIV. have not been generally approved.

83 The virtue that lies in a name arises either from the

fact that the name expresses the nature of the subject (*e.g.*, Lutheranism, Calvinism, Protestantism, Church of England, etc.), or from the fact that the name has been imposed by Almighty God (as Peter, John, etc.) or by general consent (as Alexander the Great, Washington the Father of his Country, etc.)

There is a specimen of this topic in the speech of Webster "On the Tariff," where he argues thus : " Allow me, sir, in the first place, to state my regret, if, indeed, I ought not to express warmer sentiments, at the names or designations which Mr. Speaker has seen fit to adopt for the purpose of describing the advocates or the opposers of the present bill. It is a question, he says, between the friends of an ' American policy' and those of a ' foreign policy.' This, sir, is an assumption which I take the liberty most directly to deny," etc. The entire passage is well worth studying ; the retorting of the argument is masterly.

For a second example see Bayard's speech on the Judiciary, where the orator comments on the words, " The judge *holds* his office from the President " (*American Eloquence*, ii. p. 71). Another striking example is found in Father Burke's lecture on Catholic Education (vol. i. p. 363) : " Do they know how to *educate ?* " etc.

ARTICLE V. CAUSES AND EFFECTS.

84. There is scarcely a subject on which the topics of *Cause* and *Effect* will not be found suggestive of good arguments. The *Grammar of Eloquence* explains them thus : Cause is that which produces an effect, or that by whose power and influence something exists or happens. A cause may be *efficient*, as fire is the efficient cause of heat ; or *material* as a piece of marble is the material cause of a

statue ; or *instrumental,* as a sword is the instrumental cause of death inflicted with it ; or *formal,* as a soul is the formal cause of man's being what he is, as distinguished from all other animals ; or *final,* as victory, or peace, or territory may be the final cause of war, or the cause of engaging in war.

85. The following **example** will illustrate all these causes combined : a statue of Washington owes its existence to the artist as the efficient cause ; to his tools as the instrumental ; to the marble, say, as the material ; to the figure of the hero as the formal ; and to the decoration of a hall as the final cause.

86. The way of **reasoning from causes** is :

First, to infer effects from them : He is sowing the whirlwind : he will reap the storm.

Cicero uses the *final* cause thus : " If we consider what excellence and dignity belong to human nature, we shall understand how disgraceful is a life of softness and effeminacy, and how honorable is a frugal, continent, austere, and sober deportment."

Secondly, by denying the causes, to deny the effects ; as, Milo could gain no advantage by attacking Clodius ; therefore he cannot be supposed to have done it.

Thirdly, by proving the possibility of effects from the power of causes to produce them ; as, Miracles are not impossible to-day, for God's arm is not shortened.

87. **Effect** is that which results from a cause, and therefore the cause is proved by it ; as, There is much order in the world, therefore much wisdom in its Maker. Effects are as numerous and as various as the causes which produce them. Cicero, in his plea for Archias, eulogizes the *effects of literature* thus : " Other things do not belong to all times, nor to all ages, nor to all places. But *studies* are the nourishment of youth, the delight of old age ; they adorn

prosperity, while in adversity they afford a refuge and a consolation ; they delight us at home, they are no burden abroad ; they remain with us by night, on our travels and in the retirement of our villas." In his book *De Senectute* this eminent writer makes the following admirable observations on the *effects of voluptuousness :* "Listen, my excellent young friends, to an old speech of the distinguished Archytas of Tarentum, which was communicated to me when, in my youth, I was staying at Tarentum with Quintus Maximus. He used to say that nature had inflicted no worse plague on men than the desire of bodily pleasure, because the passions, greedy of this pleasure, were prone to pursue it rashly and with unbridled license. Hence, he said, arose treason, and revolutions, and secret dealings with the enemies of our country ; there was no crime, no great outrage, to the commission of which the love of voluptuous pleasure did not impel. He maintained that adulteries and all such wickedness were brought on by no other enticements than sensuality ; and that while nature or a god had given to men nothing more precious than reason, nothing was more hostile to this divine gift and blessing than the love of pleasure. For where passion reigns there is no room whatever for self-command, nor can virtue exist in the realms of voluptuousness. . . . Therefore nothing was so detestable, so destructive as bodily pleasure."

88. All **oratory is full of examples** of these topics. The more philosophic the mind, the more it is inclined to seek the causes of all things. Ordinary people trouble themselves little about causes, but they can understand effects ; and few things move an audience more than a clear and forcible statement of the effects which a proposed measure is apt to produce. Edmund Burke is always asking, "Why? whence? by what means? for what

end? with what results? etc." We have a fine specimen of these two topics in a speech of J. C. Calhoun (*Works,* vol. iv. p. 450) congratulating France after her Revolution. Why should we congratulate her so soon? he asks; she has only pulled down, but what has she built up?—*i.e.,* he finds no cause for congratulation. Next he examines the effects which such congratulation would produce on other nations. Lord Chatham, in his speech Against Search-Warrants for Seamen, vividly traces the bad effects which such a measure would produce (*Brit. Eloq.,* p. 79). The entire speech is drawn from the topics explained in the present article.

ARTICLE VI. CIRCUMSTANCES.

89. The topic of Circumstances is another copious source of arguments. **Circumstances** are such things as do not necessarily belong to a subject, but happen to attend it on the present occasion ; they may be summed up in the following verse :

> *Quis? quid? ubi? per quos? quoties? cur? quomodo? quando?*
> " Who? where? by whom? how? when? how oft? and why?"

If these be applied—to take an example from sacred oratory—to the scene of the Redeemer dying on Calvary, it will appear at once how many appropriate thoughts may be suggested by the topic of circumstances.

90. **Four kinds** of circumstances are most suggestive of arguments—viz., those of persons, things, places, and times.

1. **The persons** may be chief agents, accomplices, witnesses : we may consider their race, nation, country, sex, age, etc., as will be explained more fully when we come to consider the Topics of Persons (chapter v.)

2. **The things** may precede, accompany, or follow the event.

3 and 4. Of the topics of **place** and **time** Cicero gives us a good example in his speech for Milo: "Let us now consider which of the two nobles was more favored by the place where they met." "Approach to the city by night should have been avoided rather than sought by Clodius."

Lawyers have constantly to deal with *circumstantial evidence :* for them the sifting of all the circumstances is one of the chief means of success in the defence or in the prosecution of the culprit.

91. A masterpiece of this study of circumstances is found in the oration of Cicero for Milo. Cicero is trying to prove that Milo could not have waylaid Clodius. It is interesting to observe how clearly and skilfully he proceeds. He shows us Milo starting out, and makes us accompany him and study all his movements before, during, and after the affray in which Clodius perished. Every circumstance appears to proclaim the innocence of Milo and the guilt of Clodius. The speech of Webster in Knapp's trial displays a similar power in sifting circumstantial evidence.

92. But it is not only at the bar that circumstances should be carefully studied ; the following extract from Grattan's speech on Moving a Declaration of Irish Rights shows us the efficiency of this topic in another field of eloquence: "England now smarts under the lesson of the American war. The doctrine of an imperial legislature she feels to be pernicious ; the revenues and monopolies attached to it she found to be untenable. Her enemies are a host pouring upon her from all quarters of the earth ; her armies are dispersed ; the sea is not hers ; she has no minister, no ally, no admiral, none in whom she long confides, and no general whom she has not disgraced. The balance of her fate is in the hands of Ireland. You are not

only her last connection; you are the only nation in Europe that is not her enemy. Besides, there does of late a certain dampness and supineness overcast her arms and councils, miraculous as that vigor which has lately inspired yours. With you everything is the reverse. Never was there a parliament so possessed of the confidence of the people, etc." (*Brit. Eloq.*, p. 387).

ARTICLE VII. ANTECEDENTS AND CONSEQUENTS.

93. We mean by **Antecedents** such things as ordinarily and naturally precede an event, and by **Consequences**, or **Consequents**, such as are apt to follow. Thus a man's former conduct is called his antecedents, and it furnishes a means to form conjectures regarding his future conduct. For though it does not follow that a person who has once stolen will steal again, still there is a presumption that he may do so. Thus Cicero shows from the violent character of Clodius, on the one side, that he was likely to be the aggressor, and from the usually pacific conduct of Milo, on the other, that the latter did not plan the assault. As to consequents, he proves from the calm behavior of Milo after the affray that he was not conscious of any crime. Thus, too, Demosthenes is ever interpreting the actions of Philip by his antecedents.

94. Politicians bring up the antecedents of rival candidates and of rival parties. Henry Clay, in his "Speech on the New Army Bill," refutes an opponent by an argument drawn from his antecedents in the following words (*Amer. Eloq.*, ii. p. 266): "But I beg the gentleman's pardon; he has indeed secured to himself a more imperishable fame than I had supposed. I think it was about four years ago that he submitted to the House of Representatives an initiative proposition for the impeachment of Mr. Jefferson. The House condescended to consider

it. The gentleman debated it with his usual temper, moderation, and urbanity. The House decided upon it in the most solemn manner; and although the gentleman had somehow obtained a second, the final vote stood one for, and one hundred and seventeen against, the proposition," etc.

95. **Remark** that Antecedents and Consequences considered as proofs lie, as it were, in a middle region between causes and effects on the one hand, and circumstances on the other. For there is a *necessary* connection between causes and effects, and a merely *accidental* connection between an event and its circumstances; but there is a *natural* connection between a man's present conduct and his antecedents, and between a fact and its consequences.

96. In English, *Consequents* and *Consequences* are two words often used as mere synonyms of the word *effects;* they are not so used on the present occasion, unless effect be taken in a looser and wider sense than philosophers assign to that term. True, it matters little by what name you call the topic, provided it furnishes good arguments. But it is very important that a thing should not be considered as an effect or a consequence when it follows another only accidentally; and still this fallacy of *Non causa pro causa*, as philosophers call it, is not uncommon. We may mention as an example in point the insinuation of the infidel historian Gibbon, that the decline of the Roman Empire was owing to the spread of Christianity.

ARTICLE VIII. CONTRARIES.

97. The topic of **Contraries** consists in making a thing more clear and striking by presenting it by the side of another thing entirely different or opposite. A scene of horror is made more impressive by contrasting it with

a scene of peace and happiness, as black seems darker by the side of white. Thus Cardinal Manning (*Miscell.,* p. 178) makes the *revival* of Catholicity in England more striking by comparing it with the former *prostration* of the Church there.

Edward Everett, to extol the glory of a *volunteer* army, contrasts it with a *mercenary* army: "It was the people in their first capacity of citizens, and as freemen, starting from their beds at midnight, from their firesides and fields, to take their own cause in their own hands. Such a spectacle is the height of the moral sublime, when the want of everything is fully made up by the spirit of the cause, and the soul within stands in place of discipline, organization, and resources. In the prodigious effort of a veteran army, beneath the dazzling splendor of their array, there is something revolting to the reflecting mind. The ranks are filled with the desperate, the mercenary, the depraved; an iron slavery by the name of subordination merges the free will of one hundred thousand men in the unqualified despotism of one. The humanity, mercy, and remorse which scarce desert the individual bosom are sounds without a meaning to that fearful, ravenous, irrational monster of prey, a mercenary army," etc. ("On the First Battles of the Revolution ").

98. This topic is variously **used in reasoning**. Sometimes by proving one point we disprove its opposite; *e.g.,* " Roscius loved his father; therefore he did not wish to kill him " (Cicero).

Or from opposite causes we argue that opposite effects should be expected; *e.g.,* "If it is characteristic of barbarians to live for the present hour only, wise men should provide for all the future, even for eternity " (Cicero). " Philip would advise you to disband your army; therefore you ought to retain it " (Demosthenes).

ARTICLE IX. LIKENESS OR SIMILITUDE.

99. **Likeness** or **Similitude**, also called **Resemblance**, is the topic which compares like things. Nothing helps more than a well-chosen similitude to make an abstract argument clear to an audience. The following **rules** must be observed :

1. We should draw our similitudes from objects well known to the audience.

2. From objects that are noble. Some one has said that the distinction between an elegant and a common writer lies in the association of noble thoughts used by the one and of common thoughts by the other   Dean Swift's "Art of Sinking in Poetry" is worth consulting on this matter.

3. We should make the points of resemblance strikingly clear.

100. Edward Everett abounds in similitudes ; he thus proves the necessity of *education :* "Contemplate at this season of the year one of the many magnificent oak-trees of the forest covered with thousands and thousands of acorns. There is not one of these acorns that does not carry within itself the germ of a perfect oak, as lofty and as wide-spreading as the parent stock ; which does not enfold the rudiments of a tree that would strike its root in the soil, and lift its branches toward the heavens, and brave the storms of a hundred winters. It needs for this but a handful of soil to receive the acorn as it falls, a little moisture to nourish it, and protection from violence till the root is struck. It needs but these, and these it does need, and these it must have ; and for want of them, trifling as they seem, there is not one out of a thousand of those innumerable acorns which is destined to become a tree. Look abroad through the cities, the towns, the villages of our beloved country, and think of what materials their population, in many parts

already dense and everywhere rapidly growing, is, for the most part, made up. . When an acorn falls upon an unfavorable spot and decays there we know the extent of the loss—it is that of a tree, like the one from which it fell; but when the intellect of a rational being, for want of culture, is lost to the great ends for which it was created, it is a loss which no one can measure either for time or for eternity." If applied to moral or religious education these thoughts are strikingly true. .

101. There is a charming little volume, called *The Happiness of Heaven*, which in numerous passages exemplifies most happily the power and the beauty of the topic similitude. Here is an example : "What is the diamond? It is nothing more than crystallized carbon or charcoal. There is nothing in the whole range of science which can be so easily and so positively proved as this. The famous diamond Koh-i-noor, or mountain of light, which now sparkles in the British crown, and which is worth more than half a million of dollars, could in a few moments be reduced to a thimbleful of worthless coal-dust ! Yet how great a difference in appearance and value between that precious gem and a thimbleful of coal-dust ! Again, what are other gems, such as the ruby, the sapphire, the topaz, the emerald, and others? They are nothing more than crystallized clay or sand, with a trifling quantity of metallic oxide or rust which gives to each one its peculiar color. Yet what a difference between these sparkling and costly jewels and the shapeless clod or sand which we trample under foot ! . . . The most beautiful flowers and their exquisite perfumes, as well as the delicious fruits to which they give birth, are all made of the very same elements of matter as the bark, the wood, and the root of the tree that bears them. . . . Now, if in the natural order God can and does transform coarse and shapeless matter

into forms so beautiful and so glorious, what shall we say, of the beauty and perfection into which he will change our vile bodies?" etc.

102. **Fables** are specimens of this topic, and they have been used by the wisest men with happy effect. Thus Demosthenes prevented the Athenians from surrendering their orators to Philip by relating the fable, "The sheep giving up their dogs to the wolves to obtain peace." By the fable, "The Stomach and the Hands," Menenius Agrippa brought the plebeians back to Rome from Mons Sacer.

103. A far nobler species of similitude is found in those admirable **Parables** which our Blessed Saviour used so copiously to instruct his followers, and in which, even to the present day, the wisdom of Heaven is distilled like gentle dew into the highest and the lowest minds on earth.

ARTICLE X. LIKELIHOOD OR PROBABILITY.

104. The **Comparison of Probability** or **Likelihood** is a topic which proves a conclusion to be probable or improbable by comparing it with other matters more or less or equally probable. There are three kinds:

1st. The **Comparison a majore** argues from a greater probability to a less, thus: *If what was more likely did not happen, then that which is less likely is not apt to happen;* e.g., "Our ancestors did not allow even a Grecian state to grow too powerful: will you allow a barbarian to become master of Greece?" (Demosthenes, Third Phil.) The *conclusion* in this kind is always *negative*.

2d. The **Comparison a minore** argues from a less probability to a greater, thus: *If what appeared less likely has nevertheless happened, then what appears more likely may be expected to happen;* e.g., "Many persons guilty of less offences were condemned to death; therefore Catiline should be condemned, who is guilty of greater " (Cicero, first Catil.) " Our ancestors waged many wars to punish slighter insults ; therefore we should wage this war to avenge more grievous injuries " (id. Manil. Law).   The *conclusion* is always *affirmative.*

3d. The **Comparison a pari** argues equal truth from equal likelihood, thus : *If what had a certain probability did happen, then an event of like probability may be expected to happen ; e.g.,* " If you will restore liberty to the negroes because it was unlawfully taken from them, you must also restore their lands to the Indians " (Pinkney on the Missouri Question).   The *conclusion* may be *affirmative or negative.*

105. It may not be useless to add some further **examples.** Everett argues : " *We tend the body : much more must we tend the mind.*"   He says : " The body is not starved except in cases of cruel necessity. Not starved ! It is nourished and pampered by whatever can provoke or satisfy the appetite ; the healthy child is nursed and nourished up into the healthy man ; the tiny fingers which now weary with the weight of the rattle will be trained up to a grasp of steel ; the little limbs will learn to stretch unfatigued over plain and mountain, while the inward intellectual being will be allowed to remain unnourished, reglected, and stinted. A reason capable of being nurtured into the vigorous apprehension of all truth will remain uninformed and torpid, at the mercy of low prejudice and error. A capacity which might have explored all nature, mastered its secrets, and weighed the orbs of heaven in the golden scales of science, shall pass through life clouded with superstition, ignorant of the most familiar truth, unconscious of its own heavenly nature. There is the body of a man, sound, athletic, well proportioned ; but the mind within is puny, dwarfed, and starved. Could

we perceive it with our bodily sight we should pity it.
Could the natural eye measure the contrast between a
fully-developed and harmoniously-proportioned intellect
on the one hand and a blighted, stunted, distorted, sickly
understanding on the other, even as it compares a diseased
and shrivelled form with the manly expansion and vigorous
development of health, we should be moved with compassion ; but so completely do we allow ourselves to be the
slaves of material sense that many a parent, who would
feel himself incapable of depriving a child of a single
meal, will let him grow up without ever approaching the
banquet of useful, quickening knowledge " (" On Education
the Nurture of the Mind ").

106. " What man is there among you, of whom if his
son shall ask bread, will he reach him a stone? or if he
shall ask him a fish, will he reach him a serpent ? If you
then, being evil, know how to give good gifts to your
children, how much more will your Father who is in heaven give good things to them that ask him ? " (St. Matt.
vii. 9).

" He that spared not his own Son, but delivered him up
for us all, how has he not also with him given us all
things ? " (Rom. viii. 32).

" If in the green wood they do these things, what shall
be done in the dry?" (St. Luke xxiii. 31).

107. To the comparison *a pari* may be referred the narration of single facts. Thus our Blessed Redeemer relates
the fate of Dives and of Lazarus. Thus, too, Rev. T. N.
Burke (*Lectures*, vol. ii. p. 169) relates the despair and
(p. 170) the death of a drunkard as a warning to all the
intemperate. This is a popular and powerful kind of argument.

CHAPTER IV.

EXTRINSIC TOPICS.

108. Of the **extrinsic topics** some are common to all eloquence, others peculiar to certain species of oratory. Common extrinsic topics are *authorities* and *examples*, which we shall now consider. Of those peculiar to certain species of eloquence we shall treat in connection with each species.

ARTICLE I. AUTHORITIES.

109. **Authorities** are the sayings of persons who enjoy great credit for knowledge of a given subject. Thus Cicero quotes Demosthenes, who says that the chief point in eloquence is "elocution" or "delivery." Here Demosthenes is adduced as an authority; and as Cicero quotes this with approbation, he, too, becomes to us an authority. It will be noticed that the word *authority* is used in various senses: sometimes it means a *person*, sometimes the *saying* of a person, and sometimes the *weight* of the saying. It is evident that good authorities must have great weight with every sensible audience, since they give us the opinions of men who command esteem and confidence.

110. The highest possible authority is **God's word,** or the testimony of Holy Writ. This is the chief argument in the pulpit; it may sometimes be appropriately introduced in profane eloquence, but in such cases it should not be frequently used, nor fully developed, nor minutely discussed, for all feel that such treatment belongs by right to men who are commissioned to interpret the word of God. "*How shall they preach, unless they be sent?*" asks St. Paul

111. Another weighty authority is that of **Common Consent**—*i.e.*, the agreement of all sensible men on certain leading truths which reason or experience has taught. Thus reason teaches all men the existence of God, the accountability of men, the immortality of the soul, etc. Cicero uses this topic in Milo's defence when he says: "There is, then, not a written but an inborn law, which we have not drunk in nor learned, . . . that we may repel violence by violence."

112. **Proverbs** are received expressions of general convictions which have been handed down through generations. They possess great authority, as embodying the wisdom and experience of ages, and evidently not invented for the occasion. Thus Edmund Burke, On the Bristol Election, brings a strong argument to a fine point by a received maxim: "Look, gentlemen, to the whole tenor of your member's conduct. Try whether his ambition or his avarice have jostled him out of the straight line of duty, or whether that grand foe of all offices of active life, that master-vice in men of business—a degenerate and inglorious sloth—has made him flag and languish in his course. This is the object of your inquiry. If your member's conduct can bear this touch, mark it for sterling. He may have fallen into errors, he must have faults ; but our error is greater and our fault is radically ruinous to ourselves if we do not bear, if we do not even applaud, the whole compound and mixed mass of such a character. Not to act thus is folly—I had almost said impiety. *He censures God who quarrels with the imperfections of men.*"

ARTICLE II. EXAMPLES.

113. **Examples,** in the widest sense of the word, may be defined *narratives of facts calculated to persuade.* They are *extrinsic* proofs when, besides the resemblance or com-

parison which they contain, they derive additional weight from the person to whom they are attributed ; *e.g.*, " Justus Lipsius, the most learned man of his day, rejoiced on his death-bed that he had belonged to a confraternity or sodality of the Blessed Virgin Mary." If any dying man were spoken of as having thus rejoiced, the fact would afford an argument *a pari* to show that practices of devotion are a source of consolation when life is over ; but the weight of the argument is much increased by the mental superiority of Lipsius. It is often proper to add some commendation of the persons whose words or actions are quoted, as is done here with Justus Lipsius by adding "the most learned man of his day."

114. The **use of this topic** of examples in eloquence is copious and very effective. *Verba docent, exempla trahunt*— "Words convince, examples persuade," says an old proverb. All men can understand examples, but not all can follow a course of reasoning. Both Cicero and Demosthenes constantly quote the examples of the old Romans and Greeks. Thus in his first Catilinian oration Cicero proves that Catiline should be put to death, by quoting examples of similar measures adopted by illustrious Romans against criminals of the same class.

115. Erskine, prosecuting Williams for publishing Tom Paine's *Age of Reason*, among many able arguments exhibits the examples of great minds that were sincerely Christian :   " In running the mind along the numerous list of sincere and devout Christians I cannot help regretting that Newton had not lived to this day to have had his shallowness filled up with this new flood of light. But the subject is too awful for irony. Newton was a Christian—Newton, whose mind burst forth from the fetters cast by nature upon our primitive conceptions; Newton, whose science was truth," etc.   He thus continues

naming and eulogizing his authorities till he concludes his eloquent enumeration with the following words : " Thus you find all that is great, or wise, or splendid, or illustrious among created beings—all the minds gifted beyond or- dinary nature, if not inspired by their universal Author for the advancement and dignity of the world, though divided by distant ages and by the clashing opinions distinguish- ing them from one another, yet joining, as it were, in one sublime chorus to celebrate the truths of Christianity, and laying upon its holy altars the never-fading offerings of their immortal wisdom " (Goodrich, *Brit. Eloq.*, p. 764).

CHAPTER V.

MORAL TOPICS AND TOPICS OF PERSONS.

ARTICLE I. MORAL TOPICS.

116. The **moral topics** are considerations of the justice and glory, the facility and agreeableness, the utility and necessity, of the measure under discussion. These do not supply a new class of arguments, such as could not have been discovered by the intrinsic and extrinsic sources, but they are a different and often an easier means to the same end; *e.g.*, the **glory** and **advantages** are *effects*, **facility** and **agreeableness** are *circumstances*, etc. In fact, the moral topics are only a special application of the other topics. They are more frequently used to supply general heads, under which the arguments may be arranged.

117. We shall present a few **examples**: 1. Grattan, on moving a Declaration of Irish Rights, considers the *justice*, the *facility*, and the *necessity* of this measure. Still, there is not a single argument adduced by him which might not have been found by means of the extrinsic and intrinsic topics. In all cases, however, where a special measure is recommended or opposed, these moral topics should be employed, as it is but right that the speaker should view the measure in connection with its justice, honor, facility, etc.

118. 2. When, in 1788, the first and second sections of the first article of the United States Constitution were under consideration in the convention of Virginia, Edmund Randolph advocated the "Union" as *advantageous*, *necessary*, and *honorable*. In his peroration he sums up his

arguments as follows (*Amer. Eloq.*, i. p. 173): "I have labored for the continuance of the Union. I believe that our safety, our political happiness and existence, depend on the union of the States; and that without this union the people of this and the other States will undergo the unspeakable calamities which discord, faction, turbulence, war, and bloodshed have produced in other countries. The American spirit ought to be mixed with American pride—pride to see the Union magnificently triumphant. Let that glorious pride which once defied the British thunder reanimate you again."

On the same occasion Patrick Henry spoke several times in reply to Randolph, ever insisting that neither *advantage*, nor *necessity*, nor *honor* demanded the acceptance of the Articles of Union, but that all these motives combined to condemn these Articles.

ARTICLE II. TOPICS OF PERSONS.

119. **Topics of Persons** are, as Blair defines them, the "heads from which any one can be decried or praised" (Lect. xxxii.) Hence they are especially useful for what is called Demonstrative Oratory, which is chiefly employed in praising and blaming. But as passages containing praise or blame may, to some extent, find an appropriate place in any other species of oratory, we treat of the Topics of Persons in this place among the *general* topics. Quintilian, in fact, considers them before he treats of any other source of arguments.

120. The following are the principal: 1. **Birth.** It is honorable to be of a good family, and not less honorable to have risen from an humble parentage to high distinction by one's personal qualities and exertions.

2. **Nation or country.** All nations have their peculiar

characters and manners, laws and usages, influencing the life of their citizens.

3. Sex. Some acts are more probable, some are more heroic, in one sex than in another; as when, among the early Christians, a St. Agnes, a St. Cecilia, or a St. Catherine baffled the combined power and cruelty of their persecutors.

4. Age. Wisdom is more surprising in a youth than in an aged man, and faults are less excusable in riper years: we do not expect of young Telemachus the maturity of aged Mentor.

5. Education and discipline. From the perfection or defect of these, certain results may be validly presumed, or at least they are made less improbable.

6. Habit of body. A Thersites in form is not apt to be a Cicero in mind or character.

7. Fortune. The parsimony that might grace a Cincinnatus might disgrace a Crœsus.

8. Condition or station. It makes a great difference to a jury whether a witness be a professional man or a country lad, a relative or a stranger to the accused; as is well exemplified in the comments of Webster on the testimony of Knapp's father in the trial of the son.

9. Passions or inclinations. A man's known character for justice or injustice, for avarice or extravagance, for mercy or cruelty, for good or bad principles, often determines belief or disbelief in acts attributed to him.

10. The way of living. Thus a person without any known means of self-support is more readily suspected of petty larceny than a wealthy banker.

11. Profession or occupation. A soldier, a merchant, and a lawyer will not make the same impression upon a jury.

12. Power, influence, eloquence, or reputation. All of these may create presumptions of probable consequences, or they may suggest titles to general esteem.

Such applications of these topics as are peculiar to panegyrics will be considered in their proper place under Demonstrative Oratory (b. vi. c. iii. 2).

CHAPTER VI.

USE OF THE TOPICS.

121. We have elsewhere quoted J. Q. Adams as remark-ing of the topics that *these things are peculiarly liable to be abused.* It is, therefore, necessary to lay down careful di-rections for the employment of such oratorical resources.

122. And first we must remind the student that *these topics are not supposed to dispense with talent or extensive knowledge.* "But these Common-Places," says Cicero (*De Or.*, ii. 30), "can be of use to that orator only who is skilled in business, either by the practice which riper age supplies or by that diligence in listening and thinking which anticipates maturity of years. For if you bring me a man who is a stranger to the customs of our city, to the examples, the laws, the manners, and the predilections of our citizens, no matter how ready a speaker he may be, these topics will be of little use to him for the inven-tion of arguments."

123. Besides, *no one should imagine that the topics dispense with diligence.* "Art will only show you where to search, and where that lies which you are anxious to find ; the rest depends on care, attention, reflection, watchfulness, assi-duity, labor—in a word, as I have repeatedly said, on dili-gence " (*De Or.*, ii. 35).

124. We shall now give a few **practical rules** for the use of the topics :

Rule 1. A *beginner* should on every subject apply all the topics ; a *practised speaker*, especially if he has been trained to this process, will turn at once to those which are most directly fitted to his present purpose.

Rule 2. Of the arguments thus discovered we should **reject**: (*a*) All *trivial* ones, as they make the cause appear weak ; (*b*) Those *not strictly to the point*, as only fit for declamation ; (*c*) *Incorrect* and *inconclusive* ones, as being unworthy of us ; besides, being readily refuted, they create a prejudice against our cause ; (*d*) Such as are sound, but *too hard to handle* successfully, either because they require reasoning too subtle for the audience, or because they awaken too much prejudice, or ill become our person, age, condition, or talent.

Rule 3. Among the substantial arguments left we should **select** the best, being more solicitous to present weighty proofs than to display a long array of speculations: *Non numeranda, sed ponderanda*—" Arguments are not to be valued by number but by weight," says the proverb. We should also remember that the argument which is best in itself may not be best before the present audience in their present mood and their present circumstances, lest it be said of us, as of Edmund Burke :

" He kept on refining,
Thought of convincing, while they thought of dining."

Rule 4. *Weak arguments*, if used at all, should be accumulated or passed over lightly, as not needed but only indicative of what might be said ; thus they are apt to make a favorable impression, as if the speaker had an abundance of proofs in reserve.

125. Of this judicious selection of thoughts we may add a few **examples**:

1. Demosthenes, while anxious to reanimate the confidence of the Athenians in the First Philippic, confines himself to these topics :

(*A*) *Cause:* " The only cause of your prostration lies in your indolence."

(*B*) *Antecedents:* "You conquered formerly by your activity, and Philip became victorious by his activity."

(*C*) *Effects:* "As soon as you begin earnestly many cities will join you; while if you remain inactive no one will begin."

126. **2.** William Pitt, in his speech On the Abolition of the Slave-Trade, dwells chiefly on these topics: (*A*) The abolition is *expedient ;* (*B*) It is *just ;* (*C*) The continuance of the trade is *unjust.* To prove the first point he examines the probable effects of abolition; in the second he argues that the effects will violate no vested rights; to prove the third he considers the causes and the circumstances of the slave-trade.

127. When the topics are applied according to the precepts and explanations so far given, there is evidently no danger of the abuse which Blair condemns in his thirty-second lecture, saying: "One who had no other aim but to talk copiously and plausibly, by consulting them (the topics) on every subject, and laying hold of all that they suggested, might discourse without end; and that, too, though he had none but the most superficial knowledge of his subject. But such discourses could be no other than trivial." He adds very correctly: "What is truly solid and persuasive must be drawn *ex visceribus causæ*—from a thorough knowledge of the subject and profound meditation on it." This is just the point: what more *thorough knowledge* can be had of any subject than that which embraces a clear and correct definition of it, a study of all its parts, of its causes and effects, its circumstances, its likeness and points of opposition with other things—in a word, of all that the topics direct us to investigate? We can scarcely imagine that so judicious an author as Dr. Blair could have failed to set a high value on the Common-Places, if he had examined them with the diligence which they deserve.

128. There is no discourse of considerable merit which is not a proof of the **applicability of these topics.** Blair's own lectures are illustrations of this. Thus, if we simply consult the brief analysis appended to each lecture, we shall find that the author usually considers the definition of each subject, enumerates its parts or species, traces its causes and its effects, etc. ; *e.g.*, in Lecture iv. he examines : 1. The meaning or *definition* of the sublime ; 2. Its foundation or chief *cause ;* 3. *Examples* of it ; 4. Its *nature* or essential requisites ; 5. Its sources or special *causes ;* 6. The faults opposed or *contrary* to it.

129. Lastly, we must observe that the topics do not dispense us from *reading for information* on the subject : no one pretends that they are all-sufficient of themselves. On the contrary, one who applies them to any subject will, by means of them, soon find out what points are not sufficiently clear to him, and he will thus be directed by the topics in his reading and consultation. For instance, should one undertake to write a discourse on so familiar a theme as *liberty*, he is apt soon to find out, perhaps to his own surprise, that his ideas on the very nature or definition of liberty are rather vague, and that he needs to consult Blackstone or some other author to clear or to inform his mind.

130. There are even occasions when a speaker knows so little about his intended subject that he finds it necessary to begin at once to read on the matter before applying the topics at all. Such reading for information is called by Rev. M. Bautain (*Art of Extempore Speaking*) the **indirect method of studying a subject**—the application of the topics being the *direct* method, superior to the other. When we thus attempt to read on a subject it is not usually from orations that we are to derive our information on the given matter ; but whatever we may read

we shall be benefited by observing the following **directions** taken from the work just quoted (English translation) :

131. "Always read pencil in hand. Mark the parts which most strike you, those in which you perceive the germ of an idea or of anything new to you. Then when you have finished your reading make a note; let it be a substantial note, not a mere transcription or extract—a note embodying the very thought which you have apprehended, and which you have already made your own by digestion and assimilation."

132. "Above all, let these notes be short and lucid ; put them down one under the other, so that you may afterwards be able to run over them at a single glance."

133. "Mistrust long readings from which you carry nothing away. Our mind is naturally so lazy, the labor of thought is so irksome to it, that it gladly yields to the pleasure of reading other people's thoughts in order to avoid the trouble of forming any itself ; and thus time passes in endless reading, the pretext of which is some hunt after materials, and which comes to nothing. The mind ruins its own sap and gets burdened with trash : it is as though overladen with undigested food, which gives it neither force nor light."

134. "Do not drop a book until you have wrested from it whatever relates the most closely to your subject. After that go on to another and get the cream off, if I may so express myself, in the same manner."

135. "Repeat this labor with several until you find that the same things are beginning to return, or nearly so, and that there is nothing to gain in the plunder ; or until you think that your understanding is sufficiently furnished, and that your mind requires rest to digest the nutriment which it has taken. Rest awhile, for this intellectual di gestion " (p. 169, etc.)

136. Of the *selection* and the *assimilation* Bautain uses this neat illustration : " Then will he (the reader) do as the bee does, which rifles the flowers ; for, by an admirable instinct which never misleads it, it extracts from the cup of the flowers only what serves to form the wax and the honey, the aromatic and the oleaginous particles. But, be it well observed, the bee first nourishes itself with these extracts, digests them, transmutes them, and turns them into wax and honey solely by an operation of absorption and assimilation. Just so should the speaker do. Before him lie the fields of science and literature, rich in every description of flower and fruit—every hue, every flavor. In these fields he will seek his booty, but with discernment ; and, choosing only what suits his work, he will extract from it, by thoughtful reading and by the process of mental tasting (his thoughts all absorbed in his topic and darting at once upon whatever relates to it), everything which can minister nutriment to his intelligence, or fill it, or even perfume it—in a word, the substantial and aromatic elements of his honey, or idea—but ever so as to take in or to digest, like the bee, in order that there may be a real transformation and appropriation, and consequently a production possessed of life and destined to live."

CHAPTER VII.

AN EXAMPLE FOR PRACTICE.

137. We shall conclude our comments on the topics by applying these precepts to a particular subject.

Suppose I am to write a speech, or an essay, or an article on **Religious Liberty.** I must first settle with myself whether I am expected to produce an abstract or philosophical discussion, or whether I have a practical end to attain—*e.g.*, to instil into my hearers a greater love of such liberty, or perhaps to disabuse them of a wrong conception of it. This clear idea of my purpose or end will, of course, direct me in the choice of my arguments.

138. 1. Applying the topic of **Definition,** I find it necessary to remove all vagueness and to form to myself a clear and correct conception of true religious liberty, distinguishing it from religious license, as civil liberty is distinguished from civil license ; for liberty is not the absence of all restraint, but *the absence of undue restraint.* On the true conception of liberty I may read passages in *Balmes' Protestantism and Catholicity in their Effects on the Civilization of Europe*, pp. 79, 80, 228, 229.

2. The praise of all true liberty would give us a specimen of the topic **Genus**; a reference to the Magna Charta would be an argument from the **Species.**

3. Upon the **name** Liberty I may remark that there are few words which are more abused. Thus the revolutionists in the Reign of Terror in France deluged Paris with the blood of its noblest and most inoffensive citizens in the name of liberty.

4. The **causes** which have produced religious liberty may next be studied. At one time the maxim generally prevailed, *Cujus regio, ejus religio*—" The religion of the ruler is binding on his subjects "—and religious liberty was almost unknown. Christianity did not force the pagans or the Jews to become Christians, but it taught that conversion must be voluntary and sincere. Christianity, then, is the great source of religious liberty. On the other hand, exaggerated claims in behalf of private judgment would make all due restraint impossible, or at least illogical, thus producing religious license, the absence of all law and order in religion.

5. The **effects** of religious liberty may be considered philosophically or historically, also as affecting the individual or society at large, as bearing fruit for this world or for the next.

6. We may consider the **opposite** condition of society— viz., religious tyranny, giving its history and describing its effects.

7. We may institute a **comparison** with civil liberty, arguing that, if such sacrifices are made by nations to secure the latter, greater sacrifices should be made to secure the former.

8. We may quote the praises of religious liberty as spoken by venerated **authorities,** and call attention to **examples** of its existence ; *e.g.*, in the early colony of Maryland, and in the whole United States subsequently to the first constitutional amendment.

9. The **moral topics** may show us how just, useful, pleasing, and necessary it is to protect religious liberty.

BOOK III.

139. We shall next consider how the thoughts of a speech are to be arranged. All rhetoricians attach great importance to the plan or method of an oration. This **plan**, however, is not subject to any certain fixed and unvarying rules from which no departure is ever allowed. On the contrary, it will **vary** with the ever-varying circumstances of the speaker, his subject, and his audience, and especially with the end intended, which must regulate all the details of every task. It is, therefore, impossible to lay down oratorical plans for every conceivable occasion, as no military academy would presume to lay down plans for future battles. Still, a general should be familiar with all the evolutions through which an army can be put, and he can derive great advantage from the study of the plans adopted in former battles by military geniuses. Similarly, the student of oratory should make himself familiar with all conceivable dispositions of arguments, and study with great care the plans followed by great minds : then, when his own oratorical contests begin, on which, perhaps, as much may depend as on many a battle, he will marshal his forces to the best advantage, being not a little assisted by his familiarity with all manners of combinations.

140. Order may be defined *a disposition of parts suited to obtain a certain effect.* It implies intelligence, and as such it is not only useful but also beautiful.

141. All order supposes some **principle of order**—*i.e.,* some leading thought which directs us in disposing the parts. Thus in a library the contents of the books, their sizes, their manner of bindings may be various principles of order; frequently several principles are combined, some affecting the chief divisions, others the subdivisions.

142. In a speech the principle of order may be *natural* or *oratorical.*

CHAPTER I.

THE NATURAL ORDER.

143. The **natural order** is either *historical, distributive,* or *logical.*

ARTICLE I. THE HISTORICAL ORDER.

144. The **Historical Order** arranges parts with regard to the time of their occurrence. It is the obvious or natural order when a succession of facts makes up the matter of a speech. Thus Cicero, in his oration for Milo, examines successively: 1. All that led to the slaying of Clodius; 2. The circumstances of the affray; 3. The subsequent conduct of Milo—*i.e.*, the *antecedents,* the *circumstances,* and the *consequents.*

145. We have another specimen of the historical order in **Webster's Speech in Knapp's Trial,** which we shall briefly analyze.

Introduction. The orator excuses himself for appearing as the prosecutor.

Preparatory Refutation of certain prejudices.

Division. Two parts: 1. There was a conspiracy to murder White, and the culprit was one of the conspirators. 2. He was a principal in the actual murder.

Part I. The Conspiracy.

Proposition: 1. It existed—proved from its effects.

2. Defendant was a party to it.

Proof 1. Presumption arising from his supposed interest in it.

Proof 2. His intention of stealing White's will—proved by testimony.

Proof 3. His actual connection with the conspiracy.

(*a*) Proved by testimony of what preceded the murder.

(*b*) Shown by signs after the murder.

Part II. He was a Principal in the Murder.

1. *General maxims* explained—definition of a " principal " fully discussed.

2. *Application* of these—state of the question clearly put.

Proposition : Defendant is a principal—*proved* from accumulation of circumstantial evidence.

1. He was a party to the conspiracy, as proved.

2. He cannot prove an *alibi*.

3. Witnesses certify he was there. The orator sums up evidence so far established.

4. Testimony of Rev. Mr. Coleman separately considered.

Peroration : Enumeration of the arguments.

146. The Second Part of **Burke's Speech on American Taxation** is another fine model of the historical order. He considers : 1. The *first period*—*i.e.*, the policy of the Navigation Act ; 2. The *second period*, or the attempts to raise a revenue from America ; 3. The *third period*, or Lord Rockingham's administration, with Repeal of the Stamp Act ; 4. The *fourth period*—*i.e.*, new taxes .aised by Townsend.

147. The French are remarkable for regularity in all their literary productions, particularly in the plans of their orations. " In this respect," says J. Q. Adams, " they must be acknowledged far superior to their British neighbors. The English, indeed, in their literary compositions of all kinds have been generally too inattentive to the principles of method " (Lect. xix.) Here is a sample taken from a lecture of D'Aguesseau, of wh m Dr. Blair speaks as being one of the most eloquent orators that have adorned the bar in any country. He is treating of the **Decay of Judicial Eloquence in France.**

Introduction : Eloquence, like all good things, may decay—has done so in France.

Preparatory Refutation : The cause is not lack of talents, of aids, of proper subjects.

Proposition: The cause lies in us.

I. *In the dispositions with which we come to the bar :*
  1. Inferior talent ; 2. Low views ; 3. Superficial preparation.

II. *Our conduct at the bar :*
  1. In *youth*, eagerness to appear ; hence no study ; examples ;
  2. In *manhood*, multiplicity of business ; hence ignorance of principles, neglect of form ;
  3. Hence, in *old age*, tardy regret.

Peroration : A short exhortation to remedy the evil.

ARTICLE II. THE DISTRIBUTIVE ORDER.

148. The **Distributive Order** arranges things which are existing at the same time into a number of groups, so that all the thoughts of the same group have some obvious connection with one another.

149. Here are a few **examples** :

I. **The Third Philippic of Demosthenes.**

Introduction: We have rendered our situation as distressing as possible ; now listen to me, and you may yet redress all.

1st Part. Proposition: Punish Philip and his agents. (*Distributes* motives :)
  1. *Philip* has long been attacking us ;
  2. *All Greece* is in danger, and you must defend it ;
  3. *His agents* among you are deceiving you.

2d Part. Proposition: Set to work with energy. (*Distributes* motives :)
  1. *Philip* is approaching rapidly ;

2. *His agents* are active ;

3. *The ruined states* ought to be a warning to you ;

4. Till *we* ourselves begin, no one will join us.

Peroration: Whoever has a better advice to give, let him give it.

150. II. **Cicero, on the Manilian Law**, arranges his praise of Pompey under four heads : 1. His skill in war ; 2. His virtue ; 3. His authority ; 4. His success.

151. III. **D'Aguesseau**, to prove that the orator should know human nature, views *man :*

1. **With regard to his various faculties:**

    (*a*) *The mind,* which is to be convinced ;

    (*b*) *The heart,* which is to be moved ;

    (*c*) *The imagination,* which is to be interested.

2. **With regard to his different conditions** he views human nature :

    (*a*) *In the orator*—he must adapt his speech to his age and talent ;

    (*b*) *In the client*—he is to be defended with the ability of a lawyer and the superiority of an orator ;

    (*c*) *In the judge*—he is to be addressed differently in different ages ;

    (*d*) *In the audience*—they wish to have their opinions respected.

152. IV. **Edmund Burke's oration previous to the Bristol election.** The orator refutes the charges :

    1st *charge,* neglect of constituents ;

    2d *charge,* giving free trade to Ireland ;

    3d *charge,* relief of insolvent debtors ;

    4th *charge,* relief of Roman Catholics.

This last is developed in the *historical order :*

    (*A*) Reasons for the persecuting laws ;

    (*B*) Enacting of the laws ;

(*C*) Execution of the laws;

(*D*) Author of the repeal;

(*E*) Reasons for the repeal—enumerated in the *distributive order:*

    (*a*) Generous loyalty of Roman Catholics;

    (*b*) Claims of humanity;

    (*c*) Beneficial effects on British Empire;

    (*d*) Beneficial example found in foreign countries.

Refutation of objections.

A more minute analysis of this able speech is found in Goodrich's *British Eloquence* (p. 292, etc.)

ARTICLE III. LOGICAL ORDER.

153. **The Logical Order** is the order of reasoning—*i.e.*, it presents the thoughts as links of one connected chain of reasoning. This reasoning makes up the whole speech, or a considerable part of it. In his Discourse on the Manilian Law, Cicero unites all his arguments thus: "An important war needs a great commander; but this is an important war, therefore it needs a great commander; but such is Pompey eminently; hence we should choose Pompey."

154 **Edmund Burke, On Conciliation with America,** develops the following enthymeme: "We cannot conquer America; hence we must make certain concessions." It will be noticed that in the development of the plan the three principles of the natural order are combined. (See above, number 49.)

Introduction: The subject is one that requires systematic views; reluctance of the speaker to come forward, though invited to do so.

Proposition : Seek peace through conciliation.

Part I. You cannot conquer America.

I. State and circumstances of America. (*Distributed:*)

 1. Population ; 2. Commerce ; 3. Agriculture ; 4. Fisheries.

II. Inefficiency of force in such a case. (*Distributed :*)
 This force is : 1. Only temporary ; 2. Uncertain ; 3. Injurious ; 4. Unprecedented.

III. Spirit of America and its causes. (*Distributed :*)
 1. Origin of the colonies ; 2. Form of government ; 3. Religion ; 4. Domestic institutions ; 5. Education ; 6. Remoteness. Hence the spirit of Americans, firm and intractable.

IV. Only three ways possible of dealing with this spirit :
 1. To remove causes of offence ; 2. To prosecute as criminal ; 3. To make concessions. (The reasoning here is : *Force cannot conquer a powerful nation animated by the spirit of independence,* I. IV. *But America is such,* II. III. *Therefore, etc.*)

Part II. What should be the nature of the concessions ?
The right of taxation is not now the question ; but, as an act of policy, Americans should be allowed the rights of Englishmen.

 I. Taxation for revenue must be publicly renounced.
  1. Inconsistency of insisting on it ; 2. The contest arose from taxation ; 3. Precedents of rights of Englishmen granted to (*a*) Ireland, (*b*) Wales, (*c*) Chester, (*d*) Durham.

 II. America, not represented in Parliament, can aid the crown by grants of provincial assemblies.—To explain clearly what will be the status of the colonies he lays down a number of connected resolutions, defending each of them, and refuting objections.

 III. Lord North's scheme not satisfactory ; proposed plan preferable.

 IV. No direct revenue ever to be expected from America.

CHAPTER II.

THE ORATORICAL ORDER.

155. The **Oratorical Order** is that which departs design-edly from the natural order to avoid some special difficulty or to gain some special advantage, sacrificing regu·larity to usefulness.

156. **Examples**—I. When **Demosthenes** spoke his **First Philippic** the natural order of time would have been : 1. Set to work energetically ; 2. Adopt such and such measures against Philip ; 3. The result will be great and certain. But, seeing the Athenians so dispirited, he begins with the last.

157. II. When **Hannibal encouraged his troops** on the Alps in sight of Italy, Livy makes him speak : 1. Of the circumstance of place : " Here you must conquer or die "; 2. Of the effects: " A rich booty before you "; 3. Of the circumstances of persons in both armies : " Victory is easy "; 4. Of the ·causes of the war : " Remember the provocation." The natural order would have been : causes, circumstances, effects.

158. III. **Cicero, in behalf of Milo,** uses the natural order : 1. The charge is false ; but, 2. Even if true, Milo should be acquitted as a public benefactor. While **Demos-thenes, on the Chersonesus,** uses similar arguments, but inverts their order : 1. Even if the charge were true you should not disband the army ; but, 2. The charge is false.

159. The natural order would require that we keep together **arguments bearing on the same moral topic** : *e.g.,*

such as prove a measure *just* would occupy one group ; such as prove it *easy* another ; such as prove it *necessary* a third, etc. But it may occasionally suit the purpose of the orator to depart from this in order to secure some special advantage.

160. As to the succession of **arguments of different strength,** it appears more natural to begin with the least strong and to proceed in the form of a climax ; but the oratorical order readily departs from this for a special reason. "It has been also a subject of inquiry," says Quintilian (b. v. c. 12), "whether the strongest proofs should occupy the foreground, to take immediate possession of the minds of the audience; or should be reserved for the end, to leave the strongest impression upon their minds as they go away ; or should be distributed, some in the beginning and some in the end, the weaker being placed in the middle (an arrangement based on the order of battle described in Homer ; for the *Iliad* tells us that Nestor placed strong men in front, the weak in the middle, and the best soldiers in the rear) ; or, lastly, whether the orator should begin with the weakest and rise by gradation to the strongest. In my judgment this will depend on the nature and exigencies of the cause, provided always that the discourse shall never fall away from vigor into debility."

161. *Cicero is* more positive (*De Or.*, ii. 77). He says : "I must find fault with those who place their weakest arguments first ; and I think that they, too, are in fault who, when they employ many advocates—a custom which I have never approved—always desire the least efficient to speak first. For the very nature of things requires that you reach as soon as possible the expectations of the audience. If they are disappointed in the beginning the orator must labor much harder in the succeeding part of the pleading;

and a cause is in danger when you do not from the beginning prepossess the hearers in its favor. Therefore, as in the case of the advocates one of the best should speak first, so in pleading your strongest points should be first urged, provided always, as regards orators and arguments, that the distinguishing excellence of an advocate or an argument be reserved for the final appeal. Middling arguments—for those that are faulty should be rejected—should be thrown into the middle and enforced in a body."

162. The rule *ut augeatur semper et increscat oratio*—" that the speech should ever grow and swell "—regards the effect produced on the minds of the hearers ; *i.e.*, that their conviction and impulse be ever strengthened, and their interest never flag. It does not require that each succeeding argument be stronger in itself than the preceding.

163. If there is **but one strong argument**, let it be stated first, and, after some weaker ones have been treated, let the strong one return in a new shape. " In all grave and difficult cases," says the *Grammar of Eloquence* (p. 399), " the orator should *never fear to repeat*, as often as he deems it useful, his strong arguments, provided he repeats them with variety. . . . Demosthenes on the Crown, Cicero for Milo, and O'Connell in his numberless speeches on the rights and wrongs of his country, have all had recourse to repetitions with great success."

164. In connection with the proper place for each of the arguments Quintilian makes some remarks about the greater or less **distinctness** with which they should be developed : " If the proofs be strong and cogent they should be proposed and insisted on separately ; if weak, it will be best to collect them into one body. For it is right not to obscure the strong ones by jumbling them together, that

each may appear distinct in its native vigor ; but those that are intrinsically weak derive strength by mutual support. . . . For example, an advocate may urge against a person who is accused of killing another in order to inherit his fortune : ' You expected to come in for the property, and the property was considerable ; you were in pecuniary difficulties, and the people to whom you owed money were then pressing you harder than ever ; you had also incurred the displeasure of the man who had appointed you his heir, and you knew that he determined to change his will.' Those arguments taken separately are weak and common ; but collectively their power is felt, not as a·peal of thunder, but as a shower of hail" (b. v. c. 12).

CHAPTER III.

PLAN OF A DISCOURSE.

165. Having so far studied the invention of abundant and appropriate thoughts upon the given subject, and the various principles of order or arrangement, we are now ready to determine upon some suitable plan for our speech —a plan which will, as far as circumstances admit, combine the beauty of regularity with the higher consideration of greatest efficiency. As Rev. M. Bautain, in his *Art of Extempore Speaking*, has devoted uncommon care and labor to the composition of the plan, we can do no better than quote freely from his pages. True, he supposes the speech to be *extempore ;* but he means by this term that the speech has been carefully studied, according to all the precepts so far explained, that the sketch or plan is to be traced on paper, but that the oration will remain *without a preliminary arrangement of phrases.* Whether the speech be written in full or thus partly improvised, the preparation of the plan will be the same.

166. "The plan of a discourse is *the order of the things which have to be unfolded.* You must, therefore, begin by gathering these together, whether facts or ideas, examining each separately in its relation to the subject or purport of the discourse, and all collectively in their mutual bearings on it. Next, after having selected those which suit the subject, and rejected those which do not, you must marshal them around *the main idea* (the state of the question) in such a way as to arrange them according to their rank and importance with respect to the result which you

have in view. But, what is worth still more than even this composition or synthesis, you should try, when possible, to draw forth by analysis or deduction the complete *development of one single idea*, which becomes not merely the centre but the very principle of the rest. This is the best manner of explaining or developing, because living things are thus produced by nature, and a discourse, to have its full value and full efficiency, should imitate her in her vital process, and perfect it by idealizing that process. In fact, reason, when thinking and expressing its thought, performs a natural function, like the plant which germinates, flowers, and bears fruit " (p. 116).

167. "Sometimes the **idea** thus conceived is developed and **formed rapidly,** and then the plan of the discourse arranges itself on a sudden, and you throw it upon paper, warm with the fervor of the conception which has just taken place, as the metal in a state of fusion is formed into the mould and fills at a single turn all its lineaments. It is the case most favorable to eloquence—that is, if the idea has been well conceived and is fraught with life " (p. 178).

168. " But, in general, one must not be in a hurry to form the plan. In nature life always needs a definite time for self-organization, and it is only ephemĕral beings which are quickly formed, for they quickly pass away. Everything destined to be durable is of **slow growth,** and both the solidity and the strength of existing things bear a direct ratio to the length of their increase and the matureness of their production. When, therefore, you have conceived an idea, do not hasten—unless it be perfectly clear to you at the first glance—to throw it into shape. Carry it for a time in your mind," etc.

169. " The moment you feel that your idea is mature, and that you are master of it in its centre and in its radiations, its main or trunk lines, take the pen and **throw upon paper**

what you see, what you conceive in your mind. If you are young or a novice, allow the pen to have its way and the current of thought to flow on. There is always life in its first rush, and care should be taken not to check its impetus or cool its ardor. Let the volcanic lava run; it will become fixed and crystallize of itself" (p. 197). "Nevertheless, **beware of introducing style** into the arrangement of your plan; it ought to be like an artist's draught, the sketch which, by a few lines unintelligible to everybody save him who has traced them, decides what is to enter into the composition of the picture, and what place each object shall occupy. Light and shadow, coloring and expression, will come later" (p. 196).

170. "Make your plan at the first heat, if you be impelled to do so, and follow your inspiration to the end; after which leave things alone for a few days, or at least for several hours. Then reread attentively what you have written, and give a new form to your plan; that is, rewrite it from one end to the other, leaving only what is necessary, what is essential. **Eliminate** inexorably whatever is accessory or superfluous, and trace, engrave with care the leading characteristics which determine the configuration of the discourse and contain within their demarcations the parts which are to compass it. Only take pains to have the principal features well marked, vividly brought out, and strongly connected together, in order that the division of the discourse may be clear and the links firmly welded" (p. 197).

171. What, however, is to be done **if the idea**, no matter how long it is carried and revolved in the mind, **does not seem to take shape?** The same author answers: "You must *take pen in hand*. Writing is a whetstone or flattening engine, which wonderfully stretches ideas and brings out all their malleableness and ductility" (p. 194).

First take note of any thought which may appear suitable to *introduce* yourself or your subject to the audience. Next determine whether it will be proper to *narrate* certain facts or explain your position before beginning to reason.

See what *proposition* you will lay down, whether openly or at least in your own mind.

Study what *division* you can make of your *arguments*, and in what order you can marshal your logical forces.

Consider where *pathos* is apt to find a place naturally.

Reflect whether any *objections* or difficulties may still remain which will have to be refuted or removed before concluding.

Lastly, find some suitable *conclusion* for your speech. Take note of each clear thought which then suggests itself to your mind.

172. Hence it will be seen that these **eight parts** may occur in an oration : The *Introduction* or *Exordium*, the *Narration* or *Explanation*, the *Proposition*, the *Division*, the *Proofs* or *Argumentation*, the *Pathetic*, the *Refutation*, and the *Conclusion* or *Peroration.* We have said that these eight parts may occur, but they need not all occur ; some excellent speeches will contain no more than two or three of them.

173. When these several parts occur they will usually do so in the **order** in which they have just been mentioned. Still, there may be some variations in this ; *e.g.*, a part, or even the whole, of the Refutation may sometimes be placed right after the Introduction when it is important to clear away prejudices or misconceptions. The Pathetic may occur almost anywhere, and even several times in the same speech. We shall treat of it in connection with Argumentation, with which it is usually combined.

CHAPTER IV.

ANALYSIS AND SYNOPSIS.

174. For the thorough study of masterpieces it will be useful to add some further explanation.

To Analyze (ἀνά-λύω) is to take apart; thus a chemist is said to analyze a compound substance when he resolves it into the simple elements contained in it. Applied to literary compositions, it means to examine a piece in all its details, seeing what are its divisions and subdivisions; what it pretends to explain, to prove, or to refute; what arguments it employs to gain its end; how these are arranged, developed, etc., etc.—in a word, it is to bring to light all that the composition contains, whether of matter or of form, of truth or of artifice.

175. To show the **importance** of analyzing, we may remark that it is the most thorough manner of studying a model; in fact, without such a process the reading of masterpieces is comparatively of little use.

176. **A Synopsis** (σύν-όψις) is a brief sketch of the entire composition, presenting at one glance all that the analysis has discovered, the skeleton, as it were, of the masterpiece which has been taken apart, or of a new piece which is in course of composition.

177. Its principal **advantage** is this: that it enables us to see the additional value which each part derives from its combination with the other parts; and thus we realize the skill displayed by a master-mind in the preparation of his materials to produce the desired composition.

178. A good synopsis might contain the following points:
I. A brief statement of the *circumstances* in which the oration was delivered.

II. *The End intended* and *the State of the question.*

III. The *chief obstacles* to be overcome.

179. IV. **The plan of the speech**—*i.e.,*

1. The *Introduction*, stating what special effects are aimed at and how these are attained.

2. The *Proposition and Division*, very exactly stated, often distinguishing between the apparent and the real proposition.

3. A statement of what is *Narrated or Explained.*

4. *The Arguments*, sketching to the eye their divisions and subdivisions, and noting the artifices employed.

5. *Pathos*—what passions? and how excited?

6. *Refutation*, if any, briefly stating the objections and the answers.

7. *Peroration*, stating what is aimed at, and how it is attained.

180. V. **The effects** produced by the speech, with a brief *criticism* of the chief excellences and the defects of the model analyzed.

181. Examples of Synopses.

I. Cicero's Oration on the Manilian Law.

I. Pompey had just finished the war against the pirates; Manilius had moved the appointment of the same general to finish the protracted war against Mithridates, King of Pontus.

II. *End intended:* to make the people vote for the appointment of Pompey.

III. **Plan.**

1. *Introduction:* formal, solemn; gains *benevolence* by modesty, gratitude, devotedness; *attention* by promising a rich theme.

2. *Proposition:* I will speak for Pompey (*i.e.,* I advocate his appointment).

3. *Exposition* of distress in Asia (brief and vivid).

4. *Division,* formal :

   1. The war necessary ;

   2. Vast ;

   3. Needs a great commander.

5. *Arguments :*

Part I. War necessary, on account of—

   1. *Our glory :*

      (*a*) Insult great ;

      (*b*) Unavenged ;

      (*c*) Enemy powerful ;

      (*d*) Glory of ancestors to be maintained.

   2. *Our allies :* tableau of their distress, their hope.

   3. *Our revenues :*

      (*a*) Riches of Asia ;

      (*b*) Useless in time of fear.

   4. *Private fortunes :*

      (*a*) In Asia ;

      (*b*) At home.

Part II. War vast : (transition by way of objection).

   1. *What has so far been done*—cold praise of Lucullus.

   2. *Why ineffectual :*

      (*a*) Mithridates escaped ;

      (*b*) Is reinforced ;

      (*c*) Roman armies restless ;

      (*d*) Sympathy with Mithridates ;

      (*e*) Our defeat ;

      (*f*) Lucullus recalled.

Part III. The commander to be chosen needs four qualities :

1. *Knowledge of war :*
    (*a*) Pompey has had every chance to acquire it ;
    (*b*) Has proved that he possesses it.
2. *Virtue :*
    (*a*) Chiefly courage ; rapid sketch of his exploits ; results contrasted with previous distress of Rome ;
    (*b*) Other virtues, contrasted with vices of other generals, chiefly disinterestedness.
3. *Authority :*
    (*a*) Important ;
    (*b*) Great in Pompey.
4. *Success :*
    (*a*) A special gift to some ;
    (*b*) That of Pompey extraordinary.
Recapitulation of the whole argument of speech.
6. *Refutation :* appeal from authorities to facts.
    I. *Hortensius objects :*
        1. " Give not all to one man."
    Answer : " It is well we did not follow your advice before."
        2. " At least make not Gabinius his lieutenant " (*digression*) :
            (*a*) As he is a special friend of Pompey ;
            (*b*) As he was lately tribune.
    Answer : " The first is the very reason to appoint him ; the second has often been disregarded."
    II. *Catulus objects :*
        1. " We cannot afford to expose Pompey."
    Answer (jocose) : " If he perish we will take you next."
        2. " Our ancestors avoided innovations."

Answer :

   (*a*) " In peace, yes ; in war, no " : examples ;
   (*b*) " Catulus should not oppose the wisdom
         of the people."
   (*c*) " No one but Pompey is disinterested
         enough."
   (*d*) " Other weighty authorities balance yours."

7. *Peroration :* cheers on Manilius—promises help ;
protests disinterestedness in the matter.

IV. **The speech was successful,** but perhaps unfortunately for Rome. Cicero here aided to make one man too
powerful, unconsciously preparing the way for Cæsar's
ambition and the civil wars in which Cicero himself perished.

This is probably the most regular great speech in existence.

182. **II. Cicero's Oration for Milo.**

For introductory remarks see Book ii. c. i.

Plan.

Introduction : from the circumstances, which were adverse to Milo, but which Cicero interprets favorably, to inspire the judges with confidence ; appeal
   to their firmness and compassion.

Proposition : Acquit Milo, who acted in self-defence.

(*Division* not stated, because Part II. would have created prejudice.)

Refutation. Objection 1 (implied) : horror of all bloodshed.

   Answer :

      (*a*) Violence is often lawful—examples ;
      (*b*) Especially in self-defence—examples ;
           common consent ; wording of the law.

Obj. 2. " The Senate has condemned Milo."

Answer :

    (*a*) Rather the contrary : " they say I rule the Senate."

    (*b*) " It has condemned the violence committed, not the conduct of Milo."

Obj. 3. " Pompey condemns Milo."

Answer :

    (*a*) " Why, then, has he appointed a trial ? "

    (*b*) " The exceptional form of this court is due to the dangerous times."

    (*c*) " Pompey has selected friends of Milo as judges."

Narration (most plausible and skilful) of Milo's departure ; the affray.

Argumentation :

Part I. Clodius waylaid Milo.

Order historical :

    I. Antecedent to meeting :

      1. *Final cause :*

        (*a*) *Cui bono ?*

        (*b*) Clodius hated Milo.

      2. *Antecedents of both rivals*—a majore.

      3. *Journey then and there* necessary for Milo ; rash for Clodius.

    II. Circumstances of meeting ; place, equipment ; objections answered.

    III. Subsequent events :

      1. *Slaves* freed in pure gratitude.

      2. Testimony of *Clodius' slaves* unreliable.

      3. *Milo's* return to Rome.

      4. *Present situation :* Pompey not hostile ; Milo his friend (insinuates that Milo may be needed by Pompey) ; fair trial.

Part II. Even if Milo had killed him wilfully he should be acquitted.

> *Proofs :* 1. *From Effects :* He has freed Rome from a plague (an eloquent prosopopœia).
>
> 2. *From Contrary :* Could Clodius return to life—I see you shrink from the thought (a happy hypothesis); now, a public benefactor merits gratitude.
>
> 3. *From Causes :* Death of Clodius the work of Providence. For there is a Providence, who had reasons to punish Clodius in that very place and manner.

Recapitulation of 2d Part : Clodius, a great plague, could not be resisted except by Milo, who, by destroying him, saved Rome.

Peroration excites mercy for the sufferings of Milo, and admiration for his unflinching firmness.

183. **III. Cicero for Marcellus.**

Remark : Cæsar had just declared in the Senate his willingness to let Marcellus, a former adherent of Pompey, return to Rome, and had called on each senator present for some expression of approbation. Cicero is in turn asked his opinion. He takes this occasion to make one of his most eloquent speeches ; it is not very regular, but very artful and full of noble sentiments beautifully expressed. It is one of the noblest orations of this great orator.

His End is twofold :

1. To acknowledge the favor done to his own friend ;
2. To induce Cæsar to put a stop to all resentment, and repair the evils of the civil war. This he strives to accomplish by two means :
   1. By extolling the present act of clemency above all military glory ;
   2. By explaining the task still remaining.

Excellences:
1. The praise is magnificent, a model of panegyrics;
2. The tact most delicate in lecturing Cæsar.

Plan.

Introduction brief: reasons to speak after a long silence; fully satisfied with the situation.

Part I. Expresses and richly develops his *appreciation of the favor* done to himself, to Marcellus, to all.

Part II. Extols the act of clemency, both to give Cæsar deserved praise and to suggest further leniency.

Proposition: This act is more honorable than all your exploits.

Proofs: 1. It is your own entirely;
2. Most difficult;
3. Excites more admiration and gratitude
4. Is so highly beneficial.

Pathetic recapitulation and amplification:

5. Under the appearance of extolling the favor, he here artfully excuses himself, and Marcellus, and the whole party of Pompey, laying all the blame on some few extremists.
6. Returning to the point, he gives a beautiful common-place on the praise of generosity.

Refutation of Cæsar's fear of treachery; danger improbable among the conquered as well as the conquerors; still, caution is just.

Part III. The task remaining to Cæsar—boldly but delicately told.

Proposition: You have still a great work to do.

Proofs: 1. Description of existing evils;
2. You must save your country;
3. Your glory requires it;
4. Posterity will exact it;

5. There is no further reason for hostility.
Narration.   Still, provide for your safety.

Peroration : Thanks.

184. IV. Speech of Cicero for Murena.

The end intended is to have Murena, consul-elect, ac·quitted from a charge of bribery brought against him by his rival, Sulpicius, who was supported by Cato and Postumius.

State of the question : Did Murena use illegal means to get voters ?

It had been argued by accusers :

1. That he could not otherwise have defeated Sulpicius in the election, being his inferior in moral qualities and in dignity ;
2. That he had actually used bribes.

To refute this, Cicero

1. Disproves his depravity ;
2. Maintains that he was equal to Sulpicius in dignity and more skilled and fortunate in canvassing ;
3. Disproves his illegal proceedings. Cicero had besides to spare the feelings of the prosecutors, and to lessen Cato's influence over the minds of the judges.

The principal beauty of the speech lies in the delicate address with which all this is so happily accomplished that the court was convulsed with laughter, without offence to any one, and the suit was dismissed.

Plan.

Introduction wins benevolence and docility by—

1. A prayer for concord ; homage paid to the judges.
2. Excuses :
(*a*) To Cato ;
(*b*) To Sulpicius, for undertaking the defence.

Arguments:

Part I. Charges against his morals:

1. His sojourn in Asia was for his father's sake, and blameless;

2. The charge that he had disgraced himself by dancing is disproved from his antecedents.

Part II. Respective claims of the two candidates.

Order Historical: 1. Birth—equal enough;

2. Questorship, too;

3. Subsequent career as attorney and lieutenant;

4. Prætorship;

5. Following year;

6. Canvassing for consulship—mistakes of Sulpicius;

7. Election day—conduct of Catiline.

Part III. Bribery.

Order Distributive: 1. Sad lot of *Murena* to come near losing all, and to have such opponents;

2. Charges of *Postumius* and young *Sulpicius* refuted;

3. Reply to *Cato:*

(*A*) Weakens his influence—no great name should sway the judges; Cato's rules are too rigid, owing to his Stoic philosophy, which gets all the blame.

(*B*) Reviews his accusations:

(*a*) In general, declamations against bribery are useless where there was no bribery, no law violated; the senate's decree conditional.

'*b*) As to facts in particular: grand receptions are common, retinues

proper; the shows were not his;
besides, these too are common.

(*c*) Cato's principles are too rigid;
they are useless, unpopular, and
refuted by his own conduct;

(*d*) Consequences of the trial; two
consuls needed now, as great dangers threaten; even Cato is not
safe.   The judges are to determine whether there shall be two.

Peroration : Fear and pity, both aroused by tableaux.

185. **V. Demosthenes' Second Olynthiac** ('Eπì πολλῶν
μὲν ἄν).   The people of Olynthus had asked the Athenians for help against Philip, who threatened to enslave
them.

End intended : to encourage and arouse the Athenians.

Introduction : We may thank the gods for this occasion ;
profit by it.

Part I. To encourage.

Proposition : I will reveal to you Philip's shameful condition.

Proof 1. *Considering his allies :*

(*a*) He has grown powerful by deceit—facts
prove it—hence no one will trust him any -
longer;

(*b*) He cannot keep his allies by main force;

(*c*) Power built on deceit is not lasting.

Hence now is the time for us to act, assisting Olynthus,
sending ambassadors to Thessaly.

But we must act *at once*, else no one will mind us ; and
energetically—this will reveal his weakness.

Proof 2. *His own power is little :*

(*a*) Macedon by itself is weak ;

(*b*) It is weakened by internal discord, as his

subjects share not his ambition, and they are the sufferers by these wars ;

(*c*) Even his army is not what they say, for through jealousy he discards good generals ; honest men cannot bear his dissipation ; hence none but knaves and flatterers surround him—you know some of them ;

(*d*) His first reverses will show all this ; comparison with hidden diseases.

Proof 3. *He is not the favorite of fortune,* which rather favors us.   His success arises :

(*a*) From our neglect and his activity ;

(*b*) From our folly, who do more for others than for ourselves ;

(*c*) From our trifling away precious time.

Part II. To arouse the Athenians to action.

Proposition : We must change our ways.

I. Proofs :

1. The conduct which has ruined all can restore nothing ;

2. We cannot afford to lose any more.

II. Plan proposed :

1. Contribute, march out, etc.,

2. Treat your generals better ;

3. Do away with your party spirit ;

4. Contribute equally ;

5. Hear all alike, then judge.

Conclusion : Do not so much applaud your speaker as act in such a way that you may applaud yourselves.

186. **VI. Demosthenes' First Olynthiac** ('Αντὶ πολλῶν ἂν).

Circumstances similar to preceding.

Introduction : You wish to know what to do ; well, then, listen and judge.

Part I.

Proposition : We must seize the opportunity.

Proofs : 1. Philip is so active that we must be on the spot ;

2. The opportunity is a good one ; for the Olynthians will be firm allies, as they distrust and hate Philip ;

3. We have been putting it off too long already ·

4. The gods invite, we must co-operate ;

5. It is our last chance ; proved by rapid sketch of Philip's encroachments.

Part II.

Introduction : You want to know how ; I am afraid of proposing measures, but I must overlook my danger.

Proposition 1. Send some troops to Olynthus, others to Macedon.

Proof : We must divide his power.

Proposition 2. Provide money, or rather use well what money you have.

Proof : We must have money for this war.

Part III. Enforces these measures by proving :

Proposition 1. Success is certain :

Proofs :

(*a*) Philip would not have advanced if he had expected resistance ;

(*b*) The Thessalonians are unfaithful to him ;

(*c*) The Pæonians and Illyrians are unreliable. Hence set to work ; details.

Proposition 2. Action is necessary.

Proofs :

1. Else the war will come to us, as no one else will resist ;

2. That will be a great calamity.

Conclusion : Let all ranks do their duty.

187. **VII. St. John Chrysostom's speech of Flavian to Theodosius.** The people of Antioch had insulted the emperor during a tumult ; a severe punishment was ordered by the latter. The aged Bishop Flavian, in a speech attributed to his deacon, St. John Chrysostom, pleads for pardon and obtains it.

Introduction allays the emperor's anger :

    (*a*) By exhibiting humility and love ;

    (*b*) By artfully presenting another object for indigna-
    tion ;

    (*c*) By exciting pity for the condemned city.

Proposition (implied) : You should pardon.

Arguments : I. Extrinsic :

    1. Example of God pardoning man. This is
    skilfully treated, showing that in the present
    case, as in the example cited, the evil spirit is
    chiefly to blame, and is punished by the act of
    pardon ;

    2. Example of Constantine ; its glory amplified ;

    3. Example of Theodosius himself, applying a
    wish which he once uttered to the present
    case.

II. Intrinsic :

    1. Glory of pardoning shown from its nature and
    effects ;

    2. Its rewards from God ;

    3. The propriety of granting this to a bishop :

        (*a*) It shows more freedom ;

        (*b*) It argues piety ;

        (*c*) The bishop is a messenger from God, the
        Judge ;

        (*d*) He comes without gifts, inviting the em-
        peror to imitate God.

Peroration : If you do not pardon I will not return to my people.

The chief beauty lies in the art of insinuation and in tenderness and elevation of feeling.

188. **VIII. St. John Chrysostom's Speech on the Disgrace of Eutropius.**

Eutropius, as prime minister, had oppressed the faithful of Constantinople ; disgraced, he had sought refuge in the cathedral ; the indignant populace clamored for his death. St. Chrysostom ascends the pulpit to calm them, to make them forgive and intercede for the fallen minister with the Emperor Arcadius.

It is a **model of insinuation,** as artful as it is noble. He appears at first to insist on nothing but what every one grants—the vanity of honors and riches—thus inspiring pity for a man who had been beguiled by these, and who is already so much punished; thus the orator draws tears from all eyes. Then he ascends to the sublimest sentiments of Christianity, and persuades all to pardon their enemy and intercede for him.

Plan :

    Introduction (*ex abrupto*) *:* Greatness is vanished, the foe is prostrate.

    Prop. I. The vanity of life should be ever remembered, developed by enumeration, description, contrast, hence the fall of one should be a lesson for all.

    Prop. II. Elevation is not only vain, but dangerous.

        Proof : See how the minister is fallen—a tableau to move pity.

    Refutation :

        Obj. 1. " He has insulted the Church."

        Answer : " Therefore God has wished him to feel her power and her mercy."

        Obj. 2. " No glory in pardoning such a wretch."

Answer :

    (*a*) " Such was the harlot pardoned by our Saviour."

    (*b*) " Thus Christ forgave his enemies on the cross."

Peroration contains the main proposition : Let us pray for him and intercede for him with the emperor.

Effect : His life was spared for the present ; some days after, having left the church, he was arrested, banished, and at last executed.

BOOK IV.

DEVELOPMENT OF THOUGHT.

---

189. When the arguments of a speech have been collected and properly arranged, the next task of the orator is to develop all the parts of the plan or synopsis which he has prepared, so that every thought may be presented to the best advantage. In this task he may be much assisted by the precepts which rhetoricians have laid down for the several parts of the oration. We shall consider these parts in the order in which they usually occur.

CHAPTER I.

THE INTRODUCTION.

190. The **Introduction,** or **Exordium,** as Blair remarks, "is not a rhetorical invention.   It is **founded upon nature** and suggested by common sense.   When one is going to counsel another, when he takes upon himself to instruct or to reprove, prudence will generally direct him not to do it abruptly, but to use some preparation, to begin with somewhat that may incline the persons to whom he addresses himself to judge favorably of what he is about to say, and may dispose them to such a train of thought as will forward and assist the purpose which he has in view.   This is, or ought to be, the main scope of an introduction."

191. "Accordingly Cicero and Quintilian mention **three ends,** to one or other of which it should be subservient : *Reddere auditores benevolos, attentos, dociles.*   First, to conciliate the good-will of the hearers—to render them *benevolent,* or well affected, to the speaker and to the subject. Topics for this purpose may, in causes at the bar, be sometimes taken from the particular situation of the speaker himself or his client, or from the character and behavior of his antagonist contrasted with his own ; on other occasions, from the nature of the subject, as closely connected with the interest of the hearers; and in general from the modesty and good intention with which the speaker enters upon his subject.   The second end of an introduction is, to obtain the *attention* of the hearers, which may be done by giving them some hints of the importance, dignity, or novelty of the subject, or some favorable

view of the clearness and precision with which we shall treat it, and of the brevity with which we shall discourse. The third end is to render the hearers *docile*, or open to persuasion, for which end we must begin by studying to remove any particular prepossessions they may have contracted against the cause or the side of the argument which we espouse."

192. "Some one of these ends should be proposed by every introduction. When there is no occasion for aiming at any of them, when we are already secure of the good-will, the attention, and the docility of the audience, as may often be the case, formal introductions may without prejudice be **omitted.** And, indeed, when they serve for no purpose but mere ostentation, they had, for the most part, better be omitted, unless as far as respect to the audience makes it decent that a speaker should not break in upon them too abruptly, but by a short exordium prepare them for what he is going to say. Demosthenes' introductions are always short and simple ; Cicero's are fuller and more artful." (Lect. xxxi.)

193. We may distinguish **two kinds** of Introductions : the *Calm* and the *Passionate.* The latter—the exordium **ex abrupto,** as it is usually called—supposes that not only the speaker but also the hearers are excited by unusual circumstances ; otherwise it would appear unseasonable to begin a speech in a passionate manner. The most familiar example of this species is the Exordium of Cicero's *first Catilinian* oration. In it passion was most opportune. Catiline, a known conspirator against the state, had dared to come into the senate when it had been expressly convoked to defeat his plans. All shrank from him as from a criminal. Cicero addresses him thus :

" How long, O Catiline, wilt thou abuse our patience ? How long wilt thou baffle justice in thy mad career ? To what extreme wilt thou carry thy audacity? Art thou nothing daunted by the nightly watch posted to secure the Palatium? . . . Seest thou not that all thy plots are exposed? that thy conspiracy is laid bare to every man's knowledge here in the senate? that we are all well aware of thy proceedings of last night, of the night before; the place of meeting, the company convoked, the measures concerted? Alas the times! alas the public morals! The senate understands this. The consul sees it. Yet the traitor lives! Lives? Ay, truly, and confronts us here in council; takes part in the public deliberations; marks and destines every one of us as a victim for the impending butchery," etc.

194. The **Calm** Introduction may be of three species: *Simple*, *Solemn*, or *Insinuating*. Of the **Simple**, which is of course, the most common, here is an example: Edmund Burke, speaking on the East India Bill of Mr. Fox, begins thus: "Mr. Speaker, I thank you for pointing to me; I really wished much to engage your attention in an early stage of the debate. I have been long very deeply, though perhaps imperfectly, engaged in the preliminary inquiries, which have continued without intermission for some years," etc. So the First Philippic and First Olynthiac, the Oration on the Chersonesus, of Demosthenes, and most other introductions of this great orator.

195. Of the **Solemn** we have examples in the Oration on the Crown, in that on the Manilian Law, in many of Bossuet's great panegyrics. Webster's Oration at the Laying of the Corner-stone of the Bunker Hill Monument begins thus:

"This uncounted multitude before me and around me proves the feeling which the occasion has excited. These thousands of human faces, glowing with sympathy and joy, and, from the impulses of a common gratitude, turned reverently to heaven in this spacious temple of the firmament, proclaim that the day, the place, and the purpose of our assembling have made a deep impression on our hearts," etc.

196. Of the **Insinuating**, Cicero's speech against Rullus contains a beautiful specimen. We give Blair's comments on the subject. He says (Lect. xxxi.) : " This Rullus was a tribune of the people, and had proposed an agrarian law the purpose of which was to create a decemvirate, or ten commissioners, with absolute power for five years over all the lands conquered by the republic, in order to divide them among the citizens. Such laws had often been proposed by factious magistrates, and were always greedily received by the people. Cicero is speaking to the people ; he had lately been made consul by their interest, and his first attempt is to make them reject this law. The subject was extremely delicate and required much art. He begins with acknowledging all the favors which he has received from the people, in preference to the nobility. He professes himself the creature of their power, and of all men the most engaged to promote their interest. He declares that he held himself to be consul of the people, and that he would always glory in preserving the character of a popular magistrate. But to be popular, he observes, is an ambiguous word. He understood it to import a steady attachment to the real interest of the people, to their liberty, their ease, and their peace ; but by some, he says, it was abused, and made a cover to their own selfish and ambitious designs. In this manner he begins to draw gradually nearer to his purpose of attacking the proposal of Rullus, but still with great management and reserve. He protests that he is far from being an enemy to agrarian laws ; he gives the highest praise to the Gracchi, those zealous patrons of the people, and assures them that when

he first heard of Rullus' law he had resolved to support it, if he found it for their interest ; but that, upon examining it, he found it calculated to establish a dominion that was inconsistent with liberty, and to aggrandize a few men at the expense of the public; and then terminates his exordium with telling them that he is going to give his reasons for being of this opinion, but that, if his reasons shall not satisfy them, he will give up his own opinion and embrace theirs. In all this there was great art. His eloquence produced the desired effect, and the people with one voice rejected the agrarian law."

197. But perhaps the finest masterpiece of insinuation is the supposed speech of Mark Antony over the dead body of Cæsar, as given in Shakspeare's " Cæsar," act iii. sc. 2.

When no advantage is to be obtained by an introduction, none need be used, but the orator may rush "*in medias res*," as is frequently done in deliberative assemblies. Thus Lord Mansfield, On Taxing America, begins thus: " My Lord, I shall speak to the question strictly as a matter of right."

198. For the Introduction, whatever its kind, rhetoricians lay down some excellent **rules.**

The *first rule* is, that the Introduction should be **easy and natural.** The subject must always suggest it. It must appear, as Cicero beautifully expresses it, "*effloruisse penitus e re de qua agitur*"—"to have sprung from the matter under consideration as naturally as a flower springs from the stem." In order to render introductions natural and easy, it will be well to follow the practice of Cicero. " When I have planned and digested all the materials of my discourse," he says, "it is my custom to think in the last place of the introduction with which I am to begin."

A *second rule* for Introductions is that **correctness** should be carefully studied in the expression. The hearers are not as yet occupied with the subject and the arguments ; their attention is wholly directed to the speaker's style and manner.   Still, for the same reason, too apparent art is to be avoided.   *Ut videamur*, says Quintilian, *accurate*, *non callide dicere*—"That we may appear to speak with care, not with craft."

"In *the third place*," says Blair, "**modesty** is another character which it must carry.   All appearances of modesty are favorable and prepossessing.   If the orator set out with an air of arrogance and ostentation, the self-love and pride of the hearers will be presently awakened, and will follow him with a very suspicious eye throughout all his progress.   His modesty should discover itself not only in his expressions at the beginning, but in his whole manner ; in his looks, in his gestures, in the tone of his voice.   Every auditory take in good part those marks of respect and awe which are paid to them by one who addresses them.   Indeed, the modesty of an introduction should never betray anything mean or abject.   It is always of great use to an orator that, together with modesty and deference to his hearers, he should show a certain **sense of dignity**, arising from a persuasion of the justice or importance of the subject on which he is to speak. . . . .   There are cases in which it is allowable for him to set out from the first in a high and bold tone ; as, for instance, when he rises to defend some cause which has been much run down and decried by the public."

Fourthly, The Introduction should usually be carried on in a **calm** manner ; the exception of the exordium *ex abrupto* has already been explained.

Fifthly, It is a rule in Introductions **not to anticipate** any material part of the subject, lest important arguments lose the charm of novelty.

Sixthly, The Introduction ought to be **proportionate**,

both in length and in kind, to the discourse which is to follow, since good taste requires among the parts of any composition a certain proportion both in length and spirit.

199. **In the case of replies** Quintilian makes an observation which is worth inserting here. He says : " An introduction which is founded upon the pleading of the opposite
party is extremely graceful, for this reason : that it appears
not to have been meditated at home, but to have naturally
arisen from the discussion and to have been composed on
the spot. Hence it gives to the speaker the reputation
of a quick invention, and adds weight likewise to his discourse as artless and unlabored, insomuch that, though all
the rest of his oration should be studied and written, yet
the discourse appears to be *extempore.*"

CHAPTER II.

NARRATION AND EXPLANATION

200. **Narration** properly regards facts which should succeed each other. **Explanation** regards a situation, a doctrine, a view of what exists simultaneously. Both are treated as separate parts of speeches when they are made the foundation of subsequent reasoning. Thus the lawyer narrates the facts of his case before he begins to reason on them ; the preacher explains a doctrine before he proves it or applies it to his hearers.

201. As the Narration or Explanation is to be the foundation of subsequent reasoning, this fact, whilst revealing its importance, also determines the rules that should direct it ; for everything is to be adapted to the end intended. Hence we have the following **rules**: "*To be clear and distinct*," says Blair, "to be *probable* and to be *concise*, are the qualities which critics chiefly require in narration : each of which carries sufficiently the evidence of its importance. Distinctness belongs to the whole train of the discourse, but is especially requisite in narration, which ought to throw light on all that follows. A fact or a single circumstance left in obscurity, and misapprehended by the judge, may destroy the effect of all the argument and reasoning which the speaker employs. If his narration be not probable the judge will not regard it, and if it be tedious and diffuse he will be tired of it and forget it. In order to procure **distinctness**, besides the study of the general rules of perspicuity which were formerly given, narration requires a particular attention to ascertain clearly

the names, the dates, the places, and every other material circumstance of the facts recounted. In order to be **probable** in narration, it is material to enter into the characters of the persons of whom we speak, and to show that their actions proceeded from such motives as are natural and likely to gain belief. In order to be as **concise** as the subject will admit, it is necessary to throw out all superfluous circumstances, the rejection of which will likewise tend to make our narration more forcible and more clear."

202. To the three qualities just mentioned we may add two others, *elegance* and *truthfulness*. Of **elegance** the judicious Father Kleutgen remarks (*Ars Dicendi*, n. 379): "That the narration may gain credit by conciliating and moving the heart, it should be embellished with all possible charms; this rule will be modified by the subject. In unimportant matters, as private pleadings generally are, let the style be concise. Let there be great care in the choice of words, that they be expressive and attuned to the sense, a concealed but charming melody; the figures not poetically bold, but varied enough to keep interest alive. For explanation is of itself destitute of all charms, and unless it commend itself by such beauty it will necessarily appear tame and dry. Nor is the hearer ever more attentive; and, therefore, nothing that is well expressed is lost. Besides, some way or other, we believe more readily what is. pleasing to the ear, and pleasure obtains credit."

"But when the matter is more important it will be proper to expose crime with indignation, and suffering in strains of pity, not so as to exhaust these passions, but so as to give the hearers a taste of them, that the main tone of the future speech may at once be understood."

203. That **truthfulness** is required of an honest man on all occasions is a general principle from which no departure is ever allowed. But what if a lawyer defends a cul-

prit whom he knows to be guilty? Is he to proclaim the full truth? No, indeed: the culprit's crime is his own secret, which, for the common good, the law respects until the guilt is proved; and his lawyer is sacredly bound by the duties of his office to protect that secret. When the orator asserts his client's innocence he tells no lie; for his words mean, in the acceptation of men, that the client is innocent before the court, or not legally guilty—that, as the Scotch express it, the crime is *not proven*. But this does not entitle the lawyer to state what is positively and un-equivocally false. His skill will consist in presenting all the facts favorable to him in a clear light, while he throws doubt and an air of indistinctness on the facts alleged against him, and treats all that is not proven as not having happened.

204. A beautiful **model** of this skilful management is found in the narration of Cicero's speech for Milo; every circumstance making it unlikely that Milo waylaid Clodius is distinctly pointed out, while the affray itself is made con-fused enough, with little light thrown except on the palli-ating circumstances. He says: " Milo, after staying in the senate that day till the senate adjourned, went home. He changed his shoes and dress; he waited a little, while his wife was getting ready; then he started at a time when Clodius, if he was to come to Rome at all that day, could already have returned. He is met by Clodius unencum-bered, on horseback, without carriage or baggage, without the Greek companions he was wont to have, without his wife—a rare exception—while this waylayer, who, they pre-tended had planned that journey to commit the murder, was riding with his wife in a carriage, wrapped up in his cloak, attended by a large promiscuous crowd, with a nu-merous suite of women and delicate boys and girls. He meets Clodius before the latter's farm an hour before sun-

down or thereabouts. At once a numerous armed band rush on him from a higher ground; those in front slay his driver; but by the time Milo had thrown off his cloak and jumped from the carriage, and while he was vigorously defending himself, the attendants of Clodius, with drawn swords, ran back to the carriage to attack Milo in the rear, while some, because they thought him already killed, began to slay his slaves who were behind. Of these some, faithful to their master, and preserving their presence of mind, fell in the action; others, seeing the contest around the carriage, and unable to help their master, and hearing from Clodius' own lips that Milo was slain, and believing it to be true, did—I will say it not to exculpate him, but as it happened—the slaves of Milo did, without the orders, or knowledge, or presence of their master, what every man would have wished his own slaves to do under the circumstances."

205. Another admirable specimen of Narration at the bar is found in Webster's Speech in Knapp's Trial, giving the facts of the murder of Mr. White; it is, as the occasion required, more ornate and pathetic than Cicero's.

206. The Narration may be **omitted** if the judge or the audience not only know the facts, but also view them as the speaker desires; and, in general, when no probable advantage will result from its insertion.

207. The Narration is sometimes **divided into parts**; such a division is useful:

1. When the whole truth told at once would offend;

2. When the opponent's narration must be refuted point by point;

3. When the matter is too intricate; it may then be explained by portions. Thus Webster relates separately: (*a*) the murder of White; (*b*) all that proves the existence of a conspiracy; (*c*) the circumstantial evidence of Knapp's concurrence as a principal in the murder. Demosthenes

also, in his speech on the Crown, has made several distinct narrations, the ground-work of separate reasonings. Almost all the rules and remarks which apply to *Narration* are also suited to *Explanation*, on which, therefore, we need not comment any further.

CHAPTER III.

PROPOSITION AND DIVISION.

208. After the Introduction and the Narration or Explanation it is natural and usual for the speaker to state briefly his **Proposition**—*i.e.*, what he undertakes to prove or advocate. This statement is generally useful and often necessary. **It should be made** whenever the hearers do not already know what we are going to maintain, unless there is danger of arousing their prejudices; in this latter case the Proposition may either be deferred till near the end of the speech or be omitted altogether. Thus, in his first Catilinian speech, Cicero defers his proposition, which we take to be this: " The consul commands a public enemy to leave the city. Into exile? I do not command it; but if you consult me, I advise it." In the fourth Catilinian the orator lays down no proposition, as he wishes to shirk the responsibility of condemning the conspirators to death.

209. When made, the statement of the Proposition should be **brief and clear**; it may also be repeated in various terms to impress it on the minds of the hearers. Ornaments of style in expressing it are only proper when they can lead to no ambiguity. Even **when not expressly stated** the Proposition must be clearly and distinctly conceived by the orator in his own mind, because it contains the proximate end of the whole speech, it is the magnetic needle which is to guide him, the target which he is to hit. But this rule, though most important, is too clear to need further explanation.

210. The **Division or Partition,** viewed as a part of the

speech, is the statement of the principal heads of our plan. This statement should be *brief* and *pointed* ; for, if there be any use in making it at all, it should be so worded as to be easily understood and remembered by the audience. Whether the division should be stated or not, will depend on many considerations, and not a little on the taste of the orator and the audience. In general we may say that in argumentative and explanatory speeches, in which the understanding is addressed rather than the heart, the clear statement of the division is very useful, for the hearers are thus enabled to follow and remember more easily our line of thought.

211. There is also considerable **beauty and stateliness** in a clear Division distinctly laid down and faithfully carried out, as appears in the Oration on the Manilian Law. This is, perhaps, the most regular oration in any language, and as such it is well worth the study of learners ; not that they are expected to attain such regularity in all their speeches, but that they may discipline their minds and be able to write a regular oration when the occasion require.

212. **The Division should not be stated:** 1. When its statement would displease ; *e.g.*, by appearing to announce a rather long speech.

2. When some parts seem useless at first, as happens in the oration for Milo.

3. When the statement would interfere with an oratorical suspense or other artifice.

213. The question whether **in sermons** the Division should usually be expressed or omitted is carefully discussed by Blair (Lect. xxxi.) and by Adams (Lect. xix.) Both are in favor of retaining the statement of the Division, while Fénelon would omit it. Blair gives these reasons : 1. It is an established practice ; 2. It arouses attention ; 3. It aids the hearer to understand and remember ;

4. It relieves the fatigue of the hearer, as the milestone does that of the traveller. " The appearance of premeditation it certainly has," says Adams ; " but, without premeditation, to deliver a speech upon a long and complicated argument is not within the compass of human powers."

214. But **when the Division is not expressed** it must, as we have remarked of the Proposition, be clearly conceived by the speaker and carefully remembered.

We may add in this place the following **suggestions to find a good division :**

I. **A Complex Proposition** contains a Division ready made in one of four ways : **1.** Different independent assertions are made on the same subject ; *e.g.*, Washington was a hero and a patriot.

2. A general proposition is united with a special one ; *e.g.*, Engage in the war, and do so vigorously.

3. A theoretical truth, with its practical application ; *e.g.*, We have immortal souls and we should save them.

4. A course of action proposed, with the means recommended, to which is often added the urgency of prompt measures ; *e.g.*, Assist the Olynthians, by the means which I will point out, and do so at once.

II. **A Simple Proposition** may be proved by arguments classed according to the topics which suggest them :

1. The same topic may suggest different heads ; *e.g.*, the definition : the false views, the true view of the subject.

2. Each topic may furnish a point ; *e.g.*, that the French Revolution of 1790 was an anti-religious movement may be proved from its causes and from its effects.

3. The extrinsic topics may furnish one part and the intrinsic another ; *e.g.*, we prove the existence of future rewards and punishments from authority and from reason.

4. Various moral topics afford a classification ; *e.g.*, it is just, necessary, and glorious to defend the oppressed.

III. Divisions are often suggested by the **nature of the cause** or by various **circumstances**; *e.g.*, at the bar each charge may require a separate point to answer it. Thus Cicero for Murena: "I understand that there were three parts to the accusation," etc. He divides his speech accordingly into three parts.

215. Whatever Division is chosen, **these rules** must be observed—viz. (Blair, xxxi.): 1. The parts should be really distinct, one not including another. Lord Hervey sings: "Of Sapphic, lyric, and iambic odes"; but Pope reminds him that lyric include Sapphic and iambic.

2. The Division should be obvious, not forced: "We must divide the subject into those parts into which it is most easily and naturally resolved, that it may seem to split itself, not to be violently torn asunder"—*Dividere, non frangere.*

3. The several members must exhaust the subject—*i.e.*, must exhibit the whole plan.

4. The terms in which our partitions are expressed should be as concise as possible.

5. Avoid any useless multiplication of heads—never more than five, says Adams. "Subdivision," he adds, "may sometimes be graceful, but in general it will produce its effect better by being concealed than disclosed."

216. Of Divisions these **examples** are much admired by French critics: Massillon, on the words of Christ, *consummatum est*—"it is consummated"—says: "This imports the consummation (*a*) of justice on the part of God, (*b*) of wickedness on the part of men, (*c*) of love on the part of Christ."

Bourdaloue, on the words, *My peace I give unto you*, says: "Peace (*a*) to the understanding by submission to faith, (*b*) to the heart by submission to the law."

CHAPTER IV.

ARGUMENTATION—REFUTATION—PATHOS.

217. These three parts are classed together in one chapter because they usually occur blended with each other; for objections are to be refuted where they occur to the minds of the hearers, and pathos is often blended with reasoning and refutation. These three combined form the main body of the speech; the other parts are appendages more or less useful. These three are intended to enforce the proposition so as to obtain the end intended in the oration.

Now, this **end is threefold**: to *please*, to *instruct or convince*, and to *persuade*. These special ends are usually more or less combined in a speech, though one of them is likely to predominate, and sometimes one alone is aimed at. Pleasure is chiefly intended in public lectures, in speeches at annual commencements, Fourth of July orations, panegyrics, etc. Conviction affects the understanding, and is predominant at the bar and in dogmatic and controversial lectures. Persuasion affects the heart and the will; it prevails in speeches before popular assemblies and legislative bodies, in moral sermons. It includes conviction; for it is chiefly through the mind that the heart is reached. We shall now consider the chief ways by which we are to convince, to please, and to persuade our hearers.

ARTICLE I. WAYS TO PRODUCE CONVICTION.

218. The chief ways to produce conviction are Exposition, Reasoning, and Refutation.

§ 1. *Exposition.*

Exposition, or **Explanation,** is of the highest importance in oratory, and is often sufficient by itself to produce conviction, and even persuasion. An adversary often opposes us, or auditors often remain indifferent, simply because they do not understand the case : explain it well, and we have gained our point.

Many great speakers use explanations copiously; others have a predilection for reasoning, according to the bent of their genius. Thus Cicero explains more copiously than Demosthenes ; the latter reasons more. We may select as examples of Exposition **the four Catilinian speeches** of Cicero.

In the first, Cicero in the senate exposes, or lays bare, the facts of the conspiracy ; but he introduces frequent reasoning to defend his own conduct.

In the second, he exposes the conspiracy before the people in the forum.

In the third, also spoken in the forum, he explains the arrest of the conspirators.

In the fourth, he explains, in the senate, the two conflicting opinions concerning the punishment to be inflicted. This speech is like the summing-up of a judge in an address to the jury—calm and clear. In the last three of these speeches we have scarcely anything but Exposition.

219. **Edmund Burke's** cast of mind led him to use Exposition very copiously. "He has left us, indeed," says C. A. Goodrich (*Brit. Eloq.*, p. 240), "some beautiful specimens of dialectical ability ; but his arguments, in most instances, consisted of the amplest enumeration and the clearest display of all the facts and principles, the analogies, relations, or tendencies, which were applicable to the case, and were adapted to settle it on the immutable

basis of the nature and constitution of things. Here again he appeared of necessity more as a teacher than a logician, and hence many were led to underrate his argumentative powers." His explanation of the resources and circumstances of the colonies in his Oration on Conciliation with America is a good instance in point. Of William Pitt, on the other hand, Macaulay remarks that he did not succeed in Exposition.

220. **Cardinal Newman** in this respect appears to us to bear a close resemblance to Edmund Burke. Besides the natural bent of his genius, he has been led to adopt this manner by his position as one of the leading champions of a religion which is still very unpopular in England. Feeling sincerely convinced that the hostility of his countrymen to Catholicity is the effect of rooted prejudices and of a misunderstanding of its doctrines, its history, and its practices, he has incessantly labored, in his speeches and his writings, to explain and expose a multitude of matters, doctrinal and historical, so that his literary productions, so varied and so deservedly esteemed by all parties, abound in Exposition. To point out but one example in a thousand, we may refer to the first of his *Discourses to Mixed Congregations*, and select the passage descriptive of a man who has discarded his religion (pages 8 to 11).

221. In the United States the late eloquent lecturer, **Father Smarius, S.J.**, had for a similar reason adopted the same method, and a collection of his principal lectures, styled *Points of Controversy*, contains many eloquent expositions—*e.g.*, the first half of the first lecture, also a rapid sketch of the variations of Protestantism (pages 82–92) and of the unity of the Catholic Church (pages 187–201).

222. A still more recent orator, the Dominican **Father T. N. Burke**, abounds in powerful Exposition. For in-

stance, in his oration on "The Liberator" he gives a long
and graphic account of the state of Ireland anterior to the
agitation of O'Connell, and of the manner in which the
Catholic Emancipation was obtained (vol. ii. p. 201, etc.)

223. We shall conclude our remarks on Exposition with
an extract from **Wm. Wirt's** Speech in the Trial of Aaron
Burr, showing the innocence of Blennerhasset : "Who is
Blennerhasset ? A native of Ireland, a man of letters,
who fled from the storms of his own country to find quiet
in ours. On his arrival in America he retired even from
the population of the United States, and sought quiet and
solitude in the bosom of our Western forests. But he
brought with him taste, and science, and wealth ; and 'lo !
the desert smiled.' Possessing himself of a beautiful isl-
and in the Ohio, he rears upon it a palace, and decorates
it with every romantic embellishment of fancy. A shrub-
bery that Shenstone might have envied blooms around him.
Music that might have charmed Calypso and her nymphs
is his. An extensive library spreads its treasures before
him," etc., etc. (*Amer. Eloq.*, ii. p. 467).

§ 2. *Reasoning.*

224. By **reasoning** we mean that process of the mind by
which one proposition is deduced from the admitted truth
of another. Formal reasoning is the most ordinary, and
usually the most effective, means to produce conviction.

Its requisites are: 1. That the principles or starting-
points be such as our opponents or our hearers will admit ; 2. That the inference be clearly and logically drawn.
In oratory it is not enough that the reasoning *can* be understood by attentive and intelligent hearers ; it must be so
presented that *no one can avoid understanding it.* Although
such a degree of clearness is necessary in every part of a
speech, it is especially proper to call attention to it here,

as reasoning is harder to follow than anything else. We shall mention the common forms which reasoning usually assumes; the full explanation of them belongs to logic. (See Hill's *Elements of Philosophy:* Logic, p. i. c. iii.)

225. While the arguments explained in logic are fundamentally the same as those employed in rhetoric, the **style** in which they are presented is considerably different. Logic cares little for ornament; rhetoric is fond of clothing itself to the best advantage. "The ornaments and graces in which oratory studiously attires the muscular form of logic are indulgences to human infirmity," says Adams (Lect. xxi.) They are the honey in which the wholesome draught of instruction must be mingled to make it palatable.

226. 1. **The Syllogism** is a form of reasoning consisting of three propositions so connected that from two, which are granted, the third one follows. The two granted are called the *Premises*, the third is the *Conclusion*. Of the premises, the more general is called the *major*, the more particular the *minor*. The force of this argument lies in the fact that the major, which is granted, implicitly affirms the conclusion; while the minor explicitly declares this relation between those two propositions.

"Whoever is first in place ought to be first in valor;

"We are the first in place;

"Therefore we ought to be first in valor."

Here is the same argument arrayed in poetical splendor:

> " Why boast we, Glaucus, our extended reign,
> Where Xanthus' streams enrich the Lycian plain,
> Our numerous herds that range the fruitful field,
> And hills where vines their purple harvest yield,
> Our foaming bowls with purer nectar crowned,
> Our feasts enhanced with music's sprightly sound ?

> Why on those shores are we with joy surveyed,
> Admired as heroes, and as gods obeyed,
> Unless great acts superior merit prove,
> And vindicate the bounteous powers above?
> 'Tis ours the dignity they give to grace;
> The first in valor, as the first in place."
>
> —*Pope's Iliad*, b. 12.

227. **2. The Epichirema**, called the oratorical syllogism, is a syllogism to which is added the proof of the major or of the minor, or of both; *e.g.*, "To prove Roscius guilty of parricide you must prove him most depraved, for this crime supposes all depravity; but you can show in him no depravity whatever," etc. (Cicero). Others call an Epichirema a reasoning condensed into one sentence, thus: "Can you call Roscius a parricide when you cannot detect in him any other crime?"

228. **3. The Enthymeme** is an abridged syllogism, or a syllogism in which one of the premises is not expressed, but understood; it is very common in oratory, far more so than the regular syllogism. Thus Cicero says: "Whoever, impelled by no private resentments, stimulated by no personal injury, instigated by no expectation of reward, undertakes to impeach another before the public tribunals as a criminal of state, ought to weigh well beforehand not only the importance of the immediate task which he assumes, but also the rule of morality by which he voluntarily binds himself for the conduct of his own future life. He who calls to account another man, especially under the profession of having no other motive than the general welfare, imposes upon himself the perpetual obligation of innocence, of purity, of every social virtue." This, with much further development, is the major, from which, omitting the minor, "but I am accusing Verres," Cicero draws the following conclusion: "Thus, by undertaking this im-

peachment, I have prescribed for myself a rule of conduct as directly opposite as possible not only to the deeds and words, but even to those proud looks and that insolent deportment which you have all observed in him."

229. **4.** The **Dilemma** is an argument which presents the adversary with two or more alternatives, and defeats him with any he may choose. Wm. Pitt reasons thus in favor of abolishing the slave-trade : " Do the slaves diminish in numbers ? It can be nothing but ill-treatment that causes the diminution. This ill-treatment the abolition must and will restrain. In this case, therefore, we ought to vote for the abolition. On the other hand, do you choose to say that the slaves clearly increase in numbers ? Then you want no importations, and in this case also you may safely vote for the abolition. Or if you choose to say, as the third and only other case that can be put, and which perhaps is the nearest to the truth, that the population is nearly stationary and the treatment neither so bad nor so good as it might be, then surely, sir, it will not be denied that this, of all others, is, on each of the two grounds, the proper period for stopping farther supplies," etc. (*Brit. Eloq.*, p. 582).

230. **5.** The **Sorites** is an abridged form of a series of syllogisms ; it is a series of propositions so connected that the predicate of the first point becomes the subject of the second, the predicate of the second becomes the subject of the third, etc., till in the last proposition the predicate of the preceding is assigned to the subject of the first proposition. You have a playful example of it in the wise reason which some precocious scientist in ancient times put in the head of a fox : " Whatever makes a noise moves ; what moves is not frozen hard ; that which is not frozen hard is liquid ; liquid will bend under weight ; therefore if, on trying to cross the ice, I hear the sound of the water beneath, it is not frozen and it will not support me."

231. **6. Analogy**, or **Example**, is an argument which makes the hearers admit a point on account of its similarity to other points which are granted ; *e.g.*, " A ship is good, not if nicely painted, but if safe and fast ; a sword is good, not if set with jewels, but if sharp and strong ; so a man is good, not if fair of aspect, but if he lives for that for which he was created."   That this argument may be convincing, the examples quoted must be evidently true and bear a clear resemblance to the case in point. We have admirable examples of this argument in many of the teachings of our Blessed Saviour ; *e.g.*, " Behold the birds of the air, for they neither sow, nor do they reap, nor gather into barns ; and your heavenly Father feedeth them. Are you not of much more value than they ? . . . Consider the lilies of the field, how they grow," etc. (St. Matt. vi. 26, etc.)

Analogy and Examples are not exactly synonymous. In the latter we argue from the similarity of two things ; in the former from the similarity of their relations.

232. **7.** " **Induction** is an argument in which we conclude that because some property or law is true of each individual of a class, or at least of a sufficiently large number of individuals, it is a property or law of the whole class." It is the great lever of the natural sciences, resting on the assumed fulcrum of the uniformity of nature's laws, and is valid as far as this uniformity is real. Rhetoric applies induction rather to the moral order—*i.e.*, to actions dependent on the free-will of man ; hence it is more liable to err. Still, within due limits, it is perfectly reliable ; *e.g.*, witnesses, under certain conditions, afford infallible certainty.

233. To the arguments so far explained we may add the **Argumentum ad hominem.** " This," says the *Art of Extempore Speaking*, " is an enthymeme which overturns an adversary's arguments by his own facts and words. Tubero brought an accusation against Ligarius that he had fought

against Cæsar in Africa. Cicero defended Ligarius, and turned the charge against his accuser : ' But, I ask, who says that it was a crime in Ligarius to have been in Africa ? It is a man who himself wanted to be there ; a man who complains that Ligarius prevented him from going, and one who has assuredly borne arms against Cæsar. For, Tubero, what was that naked sword doing in your hands at the battle of Pharsalia ? Whose breast was its point seeking ? What was the meaning of those arms of yours ? Whither looked your purpose? your eyes? your hand ? your fiery courage ? What were you craving ? For what were you wishing ?' This was the passage which so moved Cæsar that the act of condemnation of Ligarius dropped from his trembling hand, and he pardoned him " (p. 310).

§ 3. *Refutation.*

234. " It has been remarked," says J. Q. Adams (Lect. xxii.), " that very moderate abilities are sufficient to qualify an accuser, but that eminence in defensive practice could be attained only by the brightest endowments of eloquence ; and Quintilian gives it as his deliberate opinion that accusation is as much easier than defence as it is easier to inflict than to heal a wound."

" **Refutation** is equally **used** by both parties to a suit at law ; by all who take a part in public deliberations ; and even by the demonstrative and pulpit orators, although they have no antagonist immediately before them. . . . Confutation is not limited to what the antagonist has actually said. It must often be extended to what he will say, and even to what he may say. . . . A panegyrical orator may often be called in the discharge of his duties to defend the character of his hero against prevailing prejudices."

235. After giving us these views of the difficulties and the general usefulness of refutation, Adams cautions us

against **three chief errors** often committed in this important task. "The first," he says, "may be termed *answering too much ;* the second, *answering too little ;* the third, *answering yourself* and not your opponent."

As to the first error—**answering too much**—he remarks : "If you contend against a diffuse speaker who has wasted hour after hour in a lingering lapse of words which had little or no bearing upon the proper question between you, it is incumbent upon you to discriminate between that part of his discourse which was pertinent and that which was superfluous. Nor is it less necessary to detect the artifice of an adversary who purposely mingles a flood of extraneous matter with the controversy for the sake of disguising the weakness of his cause. . . . This species of management is not easily discovered, though it is one of the most ordinary resources of sophistry. *One of the surest tests* by which you can distinguish it from the dropsical expansion of debility is by its livid spots of malignity. It flies from the thing to the person. It applies rather to your passions than to those of your audience. Knowing that anger is rash and undiscerning, it stings you, that it may take off your feelings, your reason, and your active powers from the part you are defending to your own person." In the letters of Junius there are two remarkable examples of this disingenuous artifice—viz., in the controversies with Sir Wm. Draper and Mr. Horne. The study of these examples, both in those letters and in the comments of Mr. Adams, is as interesting as it is useful.

236. "To avoid the second fault—**answering too little**—it is as essential to ascertain which are the strong points of your adversary's argument as it is to escape the opposite error of excess. . . . If we substitute petulance or scorn for logic the verdict of the jury or the sentence of the court will soon correct our misapprehension. It is in de-

liberative assemblies, when party spirit has acquired an overruling ascendency, that this species of perverseness most frequently makes its appearance."

237. "But the most inexcusable of all the errors in confutation is that of **answering yourself** instead of your adversary, which is done whenever you suppress, or mutilate, or obscure, or misstate his reasoning, and then reply, not to his positions, but to those which you have substituted in their stead."

Unfairness is ever unworthy of an honorable man ; besides, here, as everywhere, honesty is the best policy. Still, we need not state an objection with the same strength as the adversary would state it. For we should not strengthen a falsehood : even in our very statement of an objection we may exhibit its weakness or unsoundness, which was skilfully hidden by our opponent.

238. As to the **order of objections** we may suggest the following directions: 1. Those objections should be first attacked which appear to make the most impression on our hearers ; 2. Those refutations should precede which facilitate those following ; 3. When we cannot refute the strongest objections triumphantly, we may begin with some weaker ones, so as to lessen the credit of our opponent ; 4. When we promise to answer a certain objection later on, we should give a good reason for the delay ; 5. If we can take up the refutation in the same order as the objections were proposed by our adversary, we thereby gain in clearness and earn the confidence of the audience. But we may have stronger reasons to prefer another order. Demosthenes, challenged by Æschines to refute point by point, plainly refuses to do so, claiming his right to follow his own arrangement.

239. There are **three chief ways of refuting**—viz., by *denying*, by *distinguishing*, and by *retorting*, each of which we

shall briefly explain. I. **We may deny** either a statement or a conclusion drawn from it. 1. We can *deny a statement* of an opponent, for we are not usually obliged to believe him on his word. If we can disprove some capital assertion of an opponent, and scatter all his declamation by a clear citation, we gain a telling advantage. Junius writes to Sir W. Draper : " I wish that you would pay a greater attention to the truth of your premises before you suffer your genius to hurry you to a conclusion. Lord Ligonier *did not* deliver the army (which you, in your classical language, are pleased to call a Palladium) into Lord Granby's hands. It was taken from him, much against his inclination, some two or three years before." We need not charge our opponent with wilful falsehood, but in a gentlemanly way we may deny his facts. Even when we do not choose to deny his assertion we may often require a proof and insist on the principle : *Quod gratis asseritur, gratis negatur—* " An assertion unsupported by proof goes for nothing," or " The burden of proof lies on the accuser." We need not prove a denial ; it is enough to assign some plausible reason for denying, and it is reason enough that our opponent has given no proof. 2. We may *deny a consequence—i.e.,* we may grant the statement or allow it to pass, but deny that it proves anything against us. Thus when Cicero charged Verres with having stolen certain articles, and Verres pleaded that he had bought them, Cicero answers by supposing that he did buy them, and then shows that this plea does not clear him, as a Roman governor was forbidden by law to buy such articles while in office.

240. II. **We distinguish** when we grant what is true in the objection and deny what is false. There is usually something true in an objection ; for men, when not entirely blinded by passion, accept a false proposition only on account of the fragmentary truth which it contains. By

drawing the line exactly and clearly between the truth and the falsehood of the objection we are apt to please and convince, conciliating all by granting whatever we can reasonably grant. To deny completely what is only partially false damages our cause. The distinction should be expressed *exactly*, *clearly*, and *strikingly*.

We can recall no clearer **specimen** of an objection solved by distinguishing than the following extract from F. Smarius (Lect. i.) *Objection:* "There is good and evil in all religions; why should I be bound to connect myself with any?"

Answer: "If you mean to say that the principles of all religions are partly true and partly false, you are mistaken; for then there would be no religion at all. Religion comes from God, not from man; and nothing false or evil can come from God, who is the sovereign truth and good. If you mean to say that even false religions have some principles which are good, you are right in the assertion, but wrong in the inference which you draw from it. A religion made up of sheer errors without any basis of truth could scarcely be conceived, much less exist in the world. But it does not follow that a part of the truth is as good to you as the whole, any more than that a quarter of a dollar is of as much value to you as the whole, a maimed limb as good as a sound, a sick body as serviceable as a healthy one, or a little talent as valuable as prominent intellectual gifts or genius. We need the truth in its integrity, not in fragments only; we need the full blaze, not a mere glimpse or gleam. When God reveals he wishes to be believed unreservedly. One word of his is as good as another, one command as binding as another. . . . If you wish to say that in all religions there are bad as well as good men, you must make a distinction. That there are good men in false religions, in the sense that the false religion produces good men, is not true, any more than a fig-tree bears grapes, or the vine figs, or fresh water yields salt.   Men are better than their principles, only when they abandon bad for good principles in practice.   That there are bad men in the true religion cannot be denied ; but they are bad despite, not in virtue of, their religion," etc.

241. III. We **retort** an argument of an opponent when we turn it against him.   Thus Cicero convicts Verres by turning his own defence into a charge : "To this I hold fast, here I stop " (De Suppl, 64), " with this alone I have enough ; I omit and dismiss all the rest—he must fall by his own testimony.   You did not know who he was ? you suspected that he was a spy ? I ask not what suspicion you entertained ; I accuse you on your own admission : he said he was a Roman citizen."   A Roman citizen could not be lawfully crucified.   Verres had no right to set aside the plea of Roman citizenship till it was disproved.

242. There are many **other ways of meeting objections**; *e.g :* **1.** Not minding the objection, we may *attack the objector*, lessening his credit by showing his ignorance or bad faith, as Demosthenes often treats his opponent, Æschines.   Cicero reproaches Rullus with obscurity, Piso with puerility, Anthony with ignorance of the subject, with impropriety of expression, and with insipidity.   O'Connell, in his speech for Magee, made a vigorous onslaught on Saurin, the attorney-general (*Gramm. of Eloq.*, 428).

2. We may *oppose stronger objections.*

3. We may *make the objection ridiculous or odious.* Ridicule, however, is a dangerous, two-edged weapon, but often very efficient.   Cicero uses it to great advantage in his oration for Murena, good-naturedly ridiculing the extravagance of the Stoic philosophers, and thus lessening the authority of Cato and repelling his attacks as unwarranted.

4. We may use the *reductio ad absurdum—i.e.,* point out absurd consequences as following from our opponent's argument.

243. *As specimens of vigorous refutations* we may refer to Grattan's Invective against Corry (Goodrich's *Brit. Eloq.*, p. 397), Chatham's Reply to Walpole (ib. p. 81), Shiel's Reply to Lord Lyndhurst (Speech on the Municipal Corporation Bill).

244. We should not omit pointing out thé **fallacies** which it is important for an orator to unmask in the arguments of his opponent; these are the principal : 1. **Ignoratio elenchi, or mistaking the question.** Prentiss, in his argument before the House of Representatives on the Mississippi contested election—a speech which continued for three days and won enthusiastic applause—makes his exordium by guarding against an *ignoratio elenchi :* " The first use I shall make of the privilege accorded to me will be to set the House right as to the attitude of the question ; for I perceive that many members labor under a misapprehension on this point, and I am anxious that the position I occupy in the matter should be distinctly understood," etc. Webster, in his rejoinder to Hayne, on Foot's Resolution, begins by calling for the reading of the resolution, and then shows that the real question was entirely ignored by his opponent (see *Amer. Eloq.*, ii. p. 370).

245. **2. Petitio principii, or begging the question** instead of proving it—viz., when in the apparent proof the speaker takes that for granted which he ought to be proving. Thus some scientists, to prove that order may be the result of unintelligent forces, argue that the order so conspicuous in all the Creation is the result of the blind forces of nature ; they take for granted the very point denied by common sense—that anything orderly can exist without an intelligent ordainer.

246. The **vicious circle** differs from the *petitio principii* in

this: that the latter proves A by A, the circle proves A by B and B by A.

247. 3. Post hoc, ergo propter hoc, or **non causa pro causa.** This fallacy attributes a fact to a false cause, arguing erroneously that because one thing happened after another, therefore it was caused by the other. Thus the pagans ascribed the calamities that befell the Roman Empire to the rise of Christianity (vide St. Aug., *De Civ. Dei*, l. i.)

248. **4. False analogy, defective induction, incomplete enumeration, false assumption, ambiguity of terms**, are so many. other fallacies, whose very names express their nature sufficiently, and hence need no further explanation.

ARTICLE II. WAYS TO PLEASE OR CONCILIATE.

249. The **pleasure** which the hearers derive from an excellent oration **results from a variety of causes** all harmoniously blended together ; as the beauty of a garden, or a painting, or a group of statuary does not consist in one or two features only, but in the excellence of all the details and the perfect proportion in which the whole is combined. It is the same with all the works of art, and in particular with the productions of eloquence. The beauty of an oration, and consequently the pleasure which it is able to impart, implies great perfection in all particulars— felicity in the invention and choice of proofs ; a happy arrangement or combination of the parts ; richness and clearness of development ; elegant and appropriate expression— so that not only conviction or persuasion is attained where either of these is intended, but their success is accomplished with a certain gracefulness or splendor which cannot but delight the audience. Cicero writes (*De Or.*, 3, 4) : "Those two are easy parts which have just been explained, propriety and clearness ; the others are great, intricate, varied, weighty, in which originate all admiration for genius

and all the glory of eloquence. No one has ever admired an orator because he spoke correct Latin ; if he did not they would laugh at him. . . . What, then, sends a thrill of pleasure through the hearers? on what speaker do they gaze with amazement? whom do they applaud? whom do they look upon as almost a god among men? It is he who speaks distinctly, elegantly, copiously, luminously in thoughts and words, and who pours forth his oration with a certain melody and poetic numbers."

250. Of all sources of pleasure there is probably not one more agreeable to the audience than *beauty of style*. But of style we are to treat in its proper place. Here we wish to consider three other means of pleasing or conciliating our hearers, which we may term respectively *oratorical ornaments*, *politeness*, and *oratorical precautions*.

§ 1. *Oratorical Ornaments.*

251. By **oratorical ornaments** we mean certain passages introduced into a speech for the express purpose of pleasing the hearers. Cicero calls them *Illustrationes*, for which our English term **Illustrations** is not an exact equivalent. Both words imply light and beauty ; but in the Latin term it is *beauty* which is made prominent, and in the English it is *light*. Of these Illustrationes, or oratorical ornaments, rhetoricians usually enumerate seven—*similitudes, examples, fables, parables, aphorisms, digressions*, and *pleasantry*. Of most of these enough was said when we treated of the topics. We shall here add a few remarks on Digressions and Pleasantries, to which we shall add some suggestions on Transitions.

252. By **Digressions** we sometimes mean such passages as deviate from the main subject or purpose of the speech to gain some present advantage aimed at for its own sake. In this meaning Digressions are not ornaments ; they are ora-

torical licenses, rather tolerated on account of usefulness than admired for their beauty. Thus Demosthenes, while speaking on other matters, often inveighs against the Macedonian party in Athens, letting pass no occasion of branding them with infamy.

But a Digression is an ornament when it departs from the subject for the sake of pleasing the audience, with a view to gain more readily the precise end intended in the whole oration. Thus Cicero, on the Manilian Law, leaves aside for a while the praise of Pompey to extol Lucullus, and thus gain the support of his adherents. These Digressions often consist in elegant descriptions or **word-paintings**, and their immediate effect is an increase of attention and a relief of the weariness of the audience. When the thoughts thus introduced are as noble as the style, these are like the gems adorning the golden chain of argument, adding little to its solidity, no doubt, but much to its beauty. Such is the praise of *Liberty* by Macaulay : " Ariosto tells a pretty story of a fairy who, by some mysterious law of her nature, was condemned to appear at certain seasons in the form of a foul and poisonous snake. Those who injured her during the period of her disguise were for ever excluded from participation in the blessings which she bestowed. But to those who, in spite of her loathsome aspect, pitied and protected her she afterwards revealed herself in the beautiful and celestial form which was natural to her, accompanied their steps, granted all their wishes, filled their houses with wealth, made them happy in love and victorious in war. Such a spirit is Liberty. At times she takes the form of a hateful reptile. She grovels, she hisses, she stings. But woe to those who in disgust shall venture to crush her ! And happy are those who, having dared to receive her in her degraded and frightful state, shall at length be rewarded by her in the time of her beauty and glory."

253. **Pleasantries** gain favor : (*a*) By putting the hearers in good-humor ; (*b*) By showing the speaker to advantage as a man of quick wit ; (*c*) By discomfiting an opponent, often despatching with a laugh objections which it would be irksome to answer seriously.

Pleasantry may be of **two kinds**—witty sayings, or *witticisms, and ridicule ;* the latter raises a laugh at the expense of some person or thing. The matter of ridicule should be confined to the minor faults or follies of men who are neither specially beloved, nor unfortunate, nor highly criminal. Great care should be taken not to wound those for whom the blow was not intended ; else we might fare like the lawyer who ridiculed the diminutive stature of his opponent, not remembering that the judge was still more diminutive. Besides, whoever ridicules others must be prepared to be ridiculed ; the dart is often shot back, as it was to the archer who had written on his arrow, " To the right eye of Philip." Nor should an orator ever stoop to the buffoonery of a clown in vulgar jests or postures ; he should show his modesty by hinting rather than developing what is ridiculous.

254. A **Transition** is a sentence or two used to pass naturally from one argument or part of speech to another. " The same natural aversion of mankind to abruptness at the commencement or close of an oration, which has established the custom of opening with an exordium and of ending with a peroration, has erected these bridges over the various inlets which intersect the different regions of the province." " Transitions, fully displayed, contribute to perspicuity, and Cicero employs them the most formally upon those orations where he was most solicitous to make his meaning clear and his discourse memorable to all his hearers—in his first oration at the bar, that for Quinctius, and his first oration to the people for the Manilian Law " (Adams, Lect. xxiii.)

255. The transitions of a speech should be **varied**; some-

times they explicitly refer to both parts, which they unite ;
e.g., "Sir, the honorable gentleman having spoken what
he thought necessary upon the *narrow* part of the subject, I have given him, I hope, a satisfactory answer. He
next presses me, by a variety of direct challenges and ob-
lique reflections, to say something on the *historical* part. I
shall therefore, sir, open myself fully on that important and
delicate subject" (Edmund Burke on American Taxation).

Sometimes transitions refer to one point only ; *e.g.,* " The
revenue act formed the fourth period of American policy "
(ib.) " I pass, therefore, to the colonies in another point of
view—their agriculture " (On Conciliation with America).

Variety is obtained by the use of various figures ; *e.g.,* by
correction, preterition, objection, etc. We add a few examples : " Ah ! but Bonaparte has declared it as his opinion
that the two governments, France and England, cannot
exist together " (Fox). " Perhaps, however, my honorable
friends may take up another ground, and say," etc. (Pitt).
" And what were the explanations they offered on these
different grounds of offence ? " (id.) " Since I have spoken
of the nature of the war, I will say a few words on its mag-
nitude " (Cicero).

Adams quotes with much admiration these poetical transitions from Milton :

> " The angel ended, and in Adam's ear
> So charming left his voice that he awhile
> Thought him still speaking, still stood fixed to hear;
> Then, as new waked, thus gracefully replied."
>
> —*Par. Lost,* vii. 1.

> " As one who in his journey bates at noon,
> Though bent on speed, so here the archangel paused
> Betwixt the world destroyed and world restored,
> If Adam aught perhaps might interpose;
> Then, with transition sweet, new speech resumes."
>
> —Ib. xii. 1.

§ 2. *Politeness.*

256. **Politeness** on the part of the orator, besides removing whatever could prejudice or alienate the hearers, has many **positive advantages.** It secures: 1. A polite attention ; 2. Respect for all the orator's just claims ; 3. Deference to his opinion in return for the deference he shows to others ; 4. Docility, arising from a sense of his superiority. For we all feel respect for a perfect gentleman, and we allow ourselves more easily to be convinced and persuaded by one whom we have learned to esteem and love.

257. In this accomplishment, as in most other matters, **Cicero is a distinguished model** for imitation ; he sometimes seems almost to overdo it by showing what might appear excessive regard for the prejudices and weaknesses of his hearers. But, provided we commit no moral wrong, as false praise or flattery would be, we are not apt to be misled by imitating so great a master. In particular we may call attention to several passages of his plea for Murena, §§ I., II., III., V., VI., X., XI., XII., XIII.

In his oration for Marcellus the first part resembles flattery, and we wonder at first how so noble a character as Cicero can stoop to such eulogy of Cæsar, whom he had opposed on principle ; but the second part abundantly atones for this apparent fault by a polite but masterly remonstrance against all further prosecutions : he reads Cæsar a lesson which needed such an introduction.

258. **Politeness,** or good manners, implies a proper mixture of respect for self and respect for others. Cicero has **defined** it : *Scientia earum rerum quæ agentur aut dicentur suo loco collocandarum* (*De Off.*, i. 40)—" The art of doing and saying things seasonably." It regards all situations in life, and it should guide the orator in all the departments

of his art. *Caput artis est decere, quod tamen unum arte tradi non potest* (*De Or.*, i. 29)—" The chief point of his art is tact, and this one point art cannot teach."

259. **Politeness contains two parts,** one *natural* and one *conventional.* The **conventional** part can be acquired by all, and should be carefully studied as far as is expected from each one's station in society. It is usually called Etiquette. Its application to oratory is limited : it requires that the speaker should have regard for the reasonable customs prevailing in the place where he speaks, such especially as imply respect for his audience : for instance, to be properly introduced, if he is a stranger ; to address officials by their proper titles, a promiscuous assembly in the approved fashion of the place ; to observe in an organized assembly the general rules of order or parliamentary law, as laid down in *Jefferson's Manual, Cushing's Manual, Roberts' Rules of Order*, etc.

260. The **natural part** consists in a certain tact by which a person sees or feels instinctively, as it were, what will conciliate others, and what may in the least ruffle their feelings. It is inborn, being a part of judgment, and exists in different persons in different degrees of perfection. It is very capable of improvement, especially in early years.

261. Even in later years **it may be much improved:** 1. By the exercise of the **social virtues,** chiefly of universal kindness, which will at least prevent many offences ; and of modesty, which keeps a man in his proper place, avoiding forwardness and sallies of ill-nature or of vanity. Cicero's habit of self-gratulation would be insupportable in a Christian who professes to act for higher motives than mere earthly glory ; but even Cicero takes care, while exalting himself, never to humble his hearers. For, after all, the secret of the pleasure produced by politeness lies in the respect shown for the feelings of those present ; the defe-

rence and modesty of a gentleman are a delicate compliment to his audience.

262. **2. By attention to polite manners and address in private life.** The best rule is to avoid doing whatever we notice to be offensive in the conduct of others: *Fit enim, nescio quomodo, ut magis in aliis cernamus, quam in nobismet ipsis si quid delinquitur* (*De Off.*, i. 41)—" For, some way or other, it happens that we notice mistakes in others more than in ourselves."

263. **3. By observance of these precepts for public speaking** :

(*a*) Never overdo anything. *Magis offendit nimium quam parum* (Or. 22)—" Excess is more offensive than defect "

(*b*) Consider what becomes your age, condition in life, etc. Thus a priest should speak in the pulpit, a judge in his chair *sicut potestatem habens*—as one having power—but never unkindly, overbearingly, or rudely. Nor should any one assume such superiority as the hearers do not most willingly concede to him ;

(*c*) Have a proper regard for the weaknesses, and even for the prejudices, of your hearers ;

(*d*) See what suits the place and the time.

264. Many striking **specimens of Christian politeness** are found in the Epistles of St. Paul. These are couched in the language of fervent zeal, tempered by an admirable modesty and charity ; he praises freely what is right, thus making his reproofs more acceptable. We may refer in particular to Philippians i. 1–19 ; 1 Corinthians i. 1–14 ; 2 Corinthians ii. 1–9.

Among the moderns the very mention of the word politeness recalls to mind the accomplished and graceful Lord Chesterfield, the skilful diplomatist, whose chief power, and the source of no unimportant service rendered to his country, lay in his exquisite politeness. Chesterfield's *Letters to* *his Son* are unfortunately disfigured, as Goodrich remarks (*Brit. Eloq.*, p. 45), by a profligacy of sentiment which has cast a just odium on his character. In the letters of Cicero, the correspondence of George Washington, of which some choice selections are found in Irving's *Life of Washington*, there are exquisite specimens of politeness. In oratory we shall find numerous examples in any of our great orators, especially in the exordiums of their speeches; for instance, in the Introduction of Webster's address on occasion of a reception tendered him at Boston, in which the modesty of the distinguished orator is no less charm·ing than the warmth of his affection.

§ 3. *Oratorical Precautions.*

265. **Oratorical Precautions** are such special precautions as the orator uses to avoid giving offence in circumstances of peculiar delicacy.

266. 1. When we are compelled by necessity **to blame our hearers,** (*a*) We redouble our kindness; (*b*) We put the most favorable construction on their actions and their in-tentions; (*c*) We limit the blame to as few persons as pos-sible; (*a*) We blame with evident reluctance.

267. **2.** When we are to speak of **a public misfortune** we should never seem to rejoice; but we enter into the senti-ments of the hearers and yield only to necessity. Thus Cicero, in his oration on the Manilian Law, wishing to show how complete was the defeat of Lucullus, effects his ob-ject most strikingly by a single phrase, which he adorns with the figures of omission and simile. "Allow me in this place," he says, "to do like the poets, and say no-thing of our calamity, which was so great that the news of it was brought to the ears of Lucullus, not by a messen-ger from the field of battle, but by a vague rumor."

268. **3. With regard to opponents,** we should remember

that we can never hope to persuade those whom we offend, nor their friends and followers. A skilful speaker rarely gives reasons for offence, even to his enemies, much less to any others. Thus Cicero, in defending Murena, had to oppose Cato and Sulpicius; but he knew how to refute them, even causing the court to be convulsed with laughter at their expense, and yet without offence. Still, there are cases in which it is a duty to break entirely with men and parties, and to treat them unsparingly, as Cicero does with Verres, Catiline, Antony, and the Clodians; with these he considered that any milder course would have been unmanly and unpatriotic. In such cases we cannot hope to influence them except by fear; but we may gain our audience to sympathize with us in our opposition.

269. **4. The pulpit orator** must attack error and vice fearlessly, as it is his sacred office; but he must do it prudently. Hence when he deals with common errors and vices he can safely be bold and strong; though even then it is easy to exceed by condemning totally what can partly be excused. But when the errors or vices belong to certain distinct classes of men he must use the greatest caution. In particular he must not seem to apply to the whole class what may be the fault of only some individuals. Particular persons should not, under any circumstance, be attacked from the pulpit, though their arguments may be refuted if it be thought proper. The errors of pernicious sects may be, and often must be, exposed; but the persons belonging to those sects should not be sweepingly accused of bad faith or want of intelligence, nor be held up to ridicule, though their leaders may be often deservedly chastised.

270. **5. When adverse passions** animate the hearers one way is to overawe them; but this is rarely possible, except with persons of little intelligence. The other way is to

enter partly into their sentiments, then either to turn the same passion against a different object, or change the passion itself into another, as St. Chrysostom did in his masterly oration for Eutropius. Or we may do both together, as the same orator did in the speech of Flavian to Theodosius.

271. **6. When the hearers are·determined to remain un-moved**, say to pity, they may be thrown off their guard by working on some other passion to which they are prone. Thus Cicero, wishing to move Cæsar to pity Ligarius, and knowing he was determined not to pardon, began his attack on the heart of Cæsar through the passion of self-complacency.

272. **The discourses of St. Chrysostom** are exquisite specimens of eloquence, and particularly suited to exemplify the use of oratorical precautions. Eutropius had persecuted the Church when prime minister of Arcadius ; disgraced by the emperor and in danger of death, he had fled for refuge to the cathedral of Constantinople. The people demanded his death. The bishop attempts to appease them, and even to prevail on them to intercede with the emperor for the pardon of the fallen minister. He begins by entering into the feeling of his hearers—viz., of joy at the fall of their persecutor—but he gradually works on their pity and on their Christian principles, saying : " Believe me, I relate not this to insult and triumph over his fall, but that I may soften your hearts' rough surface, may infuse one drop of pity, and persuade you to rest satisfied with his present anguish. Since there are persons in this assembly who even reproach my conduct in admitting him to the altar, to smooth the asperity of their hearts I unfold the history of his woes. Wherefore, O my friend ! art thou offended ? Because, thou wilt reply, the Church shelters the man who waged an incessant war against it. But this is the especial reason for which we should glorify our God, be-

cause He has permitted him to stand in so awful a necessity as to experience both the power and clemency of the Church—the power of the Church, because his continued persecutions have drawn down this thunderbolt on his head; and her clemency, because, still bleeding from her wounds, she extends her shield as a protection, she covers him with her wings, she places him in an impregnable security, and, forgetting every past circumstance of ill, she makes her bosom his asylum and repose," etc. After a while Chrysostom noticed that tears were flowing freely from the eyes of his auditors; then he added: "Have I excited your compassion? Yes, those tears that are flowing from your eyes sufficiently attest it. Now that your hearts are affected and an ardent charity has melted their icy hardness, let us go in a body to cast ourselves at the feet of the emperor, or rather let us pray that the God of mercy may appease him, that he may grant an entire pardon." The people were appeased for a time.

273. When **Flavian**, Bishop of Antioch, appeared before the Emperor Theodosius to beg pardon for his people, who were then under sentence of death for having dragged the emperor's statue through the mud in mutiny, he begins by confessing the whole guilt without any excuse; he mourns over the blindness and the present distress of his people; he describes the triumph of Satan in ruining so noble and so beloved a city, and does not speak of pardon till Theodosius has been moved to compassion and generosity. His success was complete.

274. It happens not rarely that able and well-meaning speakers and writers needlessly pain their friends, and make themselves many enemies, by an ignorance or a disregard of these oratorical precautions. On the other hand, a delicate regard for the feelings and the prejudices of their very opponents exhibited by such illustrious men as

Cardinals Wiseman, Manning, and Newman has largely contributed to the veneration in which they are so deservedly held by the English-speaking world, and to the powerful influence which their speeches and writings have exercised even on their bitterest adversaries. As an example of this I may refer to the conclusion of **Cardinal Manning's Reply to Gladstone's** attack on the Vatican Council: "And now there only remains to me the hardest and saddest part of my task, which has not been sought by me, but has been forced on me. A few months ago I could not have believed that I should have written these pages. I have never written anything with more pain, and none of them have cost me so much as that which I am about to write. Thus far I have confined myself to the subject-matter of Mr. Gladstone's pamphlet; but before I end I feel bound by an imperative duty to lay before him, in behalf of his Catholic fellow-countrymen, the nature of the act which he has done," etc. (*Battle of the Giants*, p. 210).

275. It is as instructive as it is painful to read the account given by Goodrich (*British Eloquence*, pp. 232–234) of the **breach between Edmund Burke and Fox**, which was brought about in the British Parliament by the latter's neglect of the precepts just given—an occurrence which severed the bonds of friendship between these two statesmen so totally that even on his death-bed Burke refused the interview which Fox solicited in the kindest terms.

ARTICLE III. WAYS TO MOVE OR PERSUADE.

276. We are now entering on the consideration of **a matter in which the power of a speaker is chiefly to be exerted**; by conspicuous success in this particular he is properly denominated an *orator*. *Probare necessitatis est, delectare suavitatis, flectere victoriæ.*—"To convince is a matter of necessity, to please is the part of refinement, to

move is the triumph of eloquence." And again : " Since, among all the attributes of eloquence, the greatest by far is the power of firing the minds of the auditors and of bending them at pleasure in any direction, who will not grant that the speaker who is destitute of this power is wanting in the most important element of success ?" (Cic., *Brutus*, 80).

The same is the view of Quintilian (*Inst.*, vi. 2) : " Let the orator direct all his exertions to this point; let him fasten most obstinately upon it, without which everything else is slender, feeble, and ungracious. So true it is that the strength and the soul of a pleader's discourse centre in the passions."

277. However, when we come to examine with a critical eye the reasons why the ancients were so enthusiastic in their praise of impassioned eloquence, we cannot fail to perceive that, with them, **the field open to pathos was far more extensive** than it is with us. Every orator must adapt himself to his own circumstances of time and place ; and in the matter of pathos circumstances among the moderns have made some very important changes. Without detracting in the least from the praise of impassioned discourse whenever it is admissible, and while maintaining that admiration for this kind of eloquence is rooted in human nature, and therefore common to all phases of civilization, we must point out **two characteristic differences** on this subject between ancient and modern times. Attention to these variations is of the highest importance, especially to classical students, who, to the great advantage of modern literature, seek for inspiration from the masterpieces of Greek and Roman eloquence.

278. The first difference affects the very **nature of ancient pleadings at the bar,** as compared with those of modern times. Among the ancients judicial pleadings offer as

wide a scope for impassioned discourse as any other species of orations.   In fact, we find that Quintilian had judicial oratory chiefly in his mind when he wrote the praises
of pathetic language.   He says (*Inst.* vi. 2): " There is
perhaps nothing so important as this in the whole art of
oratory.   An inferior genius, with the aid of instruction and
experience, may succeed and appear to great advantage in
all other parts.   You can easily find men able to invent arguments and proofs, and even to link them together in a
chain of deduction.   These men are not to be despised.
They are well qualified to inform the judges, to give them
a perfect insight into the cause—nay, to be patterns and
teachers of all your learned orators.   But the talent of delighting, of overpowering the judge himself, of ruling at
pleasure his very will, of inflaming him with anger, of melt-
ing him to tears—that is a rare endowment indeed.   Yet
therein consists the true dominion of the orator ; therein
consists the power of eloquence over the heart.   As for arguments, they proceed from the bosom of the cause itself,
and are always the strongest on the right side.   To obtain
the victory by means of them is merely the success of a
common lawyer ; but to sway the judge in spite of himself,
to divert his observation from the truth when it is unpropi-
tious to our cause—this is the real triumph of an orator. . . .
No sooner does the judge begin to catch our passions and
to share our hatreds and friendships, indignations and fears,
than he makes our cause his own.   And as lovers are ill-
qualified to judge of beauty, because blinded by their passion, so in like manner the judge, amidst his perturbations,
loses the discernment of truth.   The torrent hurries him
along, and he gives himself up to its violence," etc.

279. Who does not feel that this view of the matter is **incompatible with our idea of legal justice ?**   Happily our
laws are far more perfect than those of the ancient pagans;

this is one of the many departments of modern civilization in which the influence of Christianity has produced the most beneficial results. What rhetorician would think, at present, of teaching any artifice which should make "the judge catch our passions, share our hatreds and friendships, indignations and fears, so that he shall make our cause his own "?

"Our judges," as Adams remarks (Lect. xvi.), "are sworn to administer justice according to the law. Our juries are under oaths equally solemn to give their verdicts according to the evidence; and even the attorneys and counsellors practising in all the courts are under like engagement to do no wrong, and to suffer none knowingly to be committed. That which Quintilian tells us to be the most splendid triumph of the art would, therefore, now be a high misdemeanor, and the judge who should suffer his sentence to be diverted from the truth, and should join in the hatreds and friendships of one party against another, would soon get himself removed by impeachment."

280. There certainly are, and always will be, in judicial oratory occasions when the most impassioned eloquence is as appropriate and desirable as it ever was or as it can be in any orations. For innocence must be defended and important rights must be maintained against unjust assailants. Such cases will and must inspire the orator with earnestness, and even passion, as warm as it is sacred and efficacious. But such circumstances are now comparatively rare. Even when they do present themselves the tone of the modern pleader will differ considerably from that of ancient advocates. They appealed directly to the heart of their judges; he must ever presume, or at least appear to feel convinced, that judge and jury look at nothing but the justice of the cause, and in his warmest passion he must **seem to aim at nothing but conviction.** The few points which

are really left to the judge or jury's discretion will be afterwards considered in our chapter on Judicial Oratory.

281. The second difference is thus referred to by Quincy Adams : " The Christian system of morality has likewise produced an important modification of the principles regarding the use of the passions. In the passage (above quoted from Quintilian) no distinction is made between the **kindly and malevolent passions.** Neither does Aristotle intimate such a distinction. Envy, hatred, malice, and indignation are recommended to be roused, as well as love, kindness, and good-will. The Christian morality has commanded us to suppress the angry and turbulent passions in ourselves, and forbids us to stimulate them in others. This precept, like many others proceeding from the same source, is elevated so far above the ordinary level of human virtue that it is not always faithfully obeyed. But although perhaps not completely victorious over any one human heart, the command to abstain from malice and envy and all the rancorous passions has effected a general refinement of manners among men."

282. We should not, however, understand Adams to condemn all manner of anger, for he tells us in another place that this passion has its proper uses. But speaking of vicious emotions, this judicious rhetorician adds : " Addresses to the malevolent passions are not necessary to the highest efforts of eloquence. To convince yourselves of this truth **compare the oratorical compositions of Burke with the letters of Junius.** They have been sometimes ascribed to the same author, and there are many particulars in which the resemblance between them is remarkable. They are both writers of ardent passion and high vehemence. But in regard to the motives and feelings which they strive to excite they differ as widely as possible. Burke was upon principle and conviction a Christian. He had examined its

evidences, and compared its moral system with every other known theory of ethics. The result of his investigation was a conviction of the truth of Christianity, and its laws of general benevolence and charity appear in every page of his writings. The blaze of passion, the bolt of indignation, flash with incessant energy from his controversial speeches and publications, but the tone and character of his sentiment is invariably generous and benevolent. All his maxims of wisdom, all his remarks upon life and manners, beam with humanity, with good-will to men. Junius was probably infected with the shallow infidelity of the French Encyclo-pédists. He seldom suffers an opportunity for a sarcasm upon religion to escape him ; and he always speaks of piety with a sneer, as if it conveyed to his mind no image other than that of hypocrisy. Yet he dares not avow his infi-delity, and, when directly charged with it, shuffles with the dexterity of a rope-dancer, and cavils with the subtlety of a sophist, to disclaim an offence which at the same moment he repeats. It is obvious from the general tenor of his letters that Christian principles were as foreign from his heart as Christian doctrines from his understanding. His eloquence is unshackled by any restraint of tenderness for his species. He flatters the foulest prejudices. He pan-ders to the basest passions," etc.

283. Still, after all proper allowances are made for the difference between the ancient and modern uses of passion in oratory, we find that the importance of this subject is very great for the practical purposes of eloquence in all ages ; and the matter is as difficult as it is important. In explaining it we shall consider : 1. The *passions* of the human heart in themselves ; 2. The chief *means* which may be employed to arouse them, and through them to affect the will of the hearers ; 3. The *expression* of excited pas-sion.

§ 1. *On the Passions in Themselves.*

284. The thorough study of the passions belongs to Philosophy (see Rev. W. Hill's *Moral Philosophy,* p. i. c. iv.); we shall view them here in as far only as they are at the service of the orator. **The passions,** according to Aristotle's *Rhetoric* (ii. 1), are " emotions on which pleasure or pain are consequent, and by which men are influenced in their decisions." In English the term passion is usually confined to *strong feelings prompting to action,* as Webster's Dictionary expresses it ; and the same authority adds : " When any feeling or emotion completely masters the mind we call it passion." But the ancients comprised under the term passions (Quintilian, vi. 2) not only the more **violent emotions,** which they called πάθη—whence our term *pathetic*—but also the **gentler feelings,** or Ἤθη, by which they meant those social virtues and habits of politeness which we have treated in a former paragraph. We shall here consider the stronger emotions only, taking the word passion in its ordinary English meaning.

285. The pleasure and the pain of which Aristotle speaks as consequent upon these emotions arise from the apprehension of *good* and *evil;* for a man tends instinctively to what his imagination presents to him as good, and he shrinks from what it presents as evil. Hence come immediately six passions, viz.:

From the apprehension of good arises complacency or *love ;*

From the apprehension of future good arises a wish or *desire ;*

From the apprehension of present good arises pleasure or *joy ;*

From the apprehension of evil arises dislike or *hatred ;*

From the apprehension of future evil arises flight or *aversion ;*

From the apprehension of present evil arises pain or *sadness.*

These six passions proceed directly from our instinctive longing (concupiscentia) for good and instinctive shrinking from evil. Hence they are called the **concupiscible passions**; but this term does not here imply anything inordinate.

Together with the apprehension of good and evil, we often apprehend *difficulty* in attaining good and avoiding evil. With respect to such difficulty man experiences a second set of passions, called the **irascible passions.** These are five in number :

From the apprehension of attainable good arises *hope ;*

From the apprehension of unattainable good arises *despair ;*

From the apprehension of evil that is difficult to avoid arises *fear ;*

From the apprehension of evil that is not difficult to avoid arises *courage ;*

From the apprehension of present evil arises *anger.*

(St. Thomas, *Summa*, 1ª 2ᵃᵉ, q. 23.)

These eleven may be considered as **simple passions**; all the others take their rise from them. For instance : intense pleasure becomes *delight ;* intense hatred, *horror* or *abomination ;* intense sadness, *dejection ;* sorrow over another's evil is *pity ;* over another's good, *envy ;* hope and courage when excessive become *presumption* and *rashness ;* fear becomes *cowardice ;* anger changes into *fury* and *madness.*

Aristotle devotes the first seventeen chapters of his second book on *Rhetoric* to a thorough and most ingenious examination of various passions, considering in what classes of persons and under what circumstances they are apt to arise and by what process they may be enkindled.

The passions with which **the orator is chiefly concerned** are enumerated by Cicero as follows (*De Or.*, ii. 51): love, hatred, anger, envy, pity, hope, joy, fear, and displeasure.

286. The orator should carefully consider whether his subject will admit of passion. The **gentler emotions** are always appropriate, not in public speaking only, but in all kinds of literary compositions. Even scientific treatises rise to the dignity of literature when they are permeated with proper sentiments: witness the philosophical writings of Plato and Cicero, which are as soothing to the heart as they are instructive to the mind; while a mere text-book from which all sentiment is excluded must derive all its interest exclusively from intellectual sources.

But the **stronger emotions** or passions must not be employed on every subject. They are, of course, inopportune in trifling matters, and they can rarely be used to advantage before hostile hearers. For there is nothing more absurd than for a speaker to give himself up to passion when his hearers do not share his emotion. Even when the violent passions find a proper place they should be **tempered with gentler feelings.** You must "use all gently," as Hamlet instructs the players to do; "for in the very torrent, tempest, and, as I may say, the whirlwind of your passion, you must acquire and beget a temperance that may give it smoothness." "Oh ! it offends me to the soul," he adds, and the warning is not out of place for orators, "to hear a robustious, periwig-pated fellow tear a passion to tatters, to very rags," etc. Still, we may add with Shakspeare : " Be not too tame either; but let your own discretion be your tutor." The rule of tempering the stronger with the gentler emotions had, long before Shakspeare's time, been laid down by Cicero in his treatise *De Oratore* (ii. 53).

§ 2. *The Chief Ways of Arousing the Passions.*

287. As the passions arise from what appears good or evil, it is the task of the orator, when he desires to arouse any passion in his hearers, to **present the good or the evil strikingly** to the minds of his auditors. His chief talent will lie in this, to make his hearers apprehend vividly the good or the evil, so as to arouse the proposed passions. For the passions, though to some extent under the control of the will, usually act instinctively, and to a certain extent necessarily, on the apprehension of their proper objects. " To every emotion or passion," says Blair (Lect. xxxii.), " nature has adapted a set of corresponding objects, and without setting these before the mind it is not in the power of any orator to raise that emotion. I am warmed with gratitude, I am touched with compassion, not when a speaker shows me that these are noble dispositions and that it is my duty to feel them, or when he exclaims against me for my indifference and coldness. He must describe the kindness and tenderness of my friend ; he must set before me the distress suffered by the person for whom he would interest me ; then, and not till then, my heart begins to be touched, my gratitude or my compassion begins to glow."

288. Now, there are **three ways** in which persons may be made to apprehend a thing—viz., by presenting it, I. *To their senses ;* II. To their *imagination ;* or III. To their *understanding.*

I. The orator will rarely be able to **present objects to the senses.** In poetry we have an instance of such use in the speech of Mark Antony over the dead body of Cæsar, where he holds up the mantle of Cæsar with the rents made by the daggers :

> " If you have tears, prepare to shed them now.
> You all do know this mantle : I remember
> The first time ever Cæsar put it on ;
> 'Twas on a summer's evening, in his tent,
> That day he overcame the Nervii.
> Look ! in this place ran Cassius' dagger through :
> See what a rent the envious Casca made :
> Through this the well-belovèd Brutus stabbed ;
> And as he plucked his cursèd steel away,
> Mark how the blood of Cæsar followed it."

Thus among the Romans advocates produced in court persons or things that might move the judges to compassion ; *e.g.*, the innocent children of the culprit or of the victim. But we shall return to this subject when treating of judicial oratory.

289. II. Things are **presented to the imagination** by means of vivid descriptions, which the French call *Tableaux*, the Latins, *Visiones*. Our term *Vision* is applied in rhetoric to only one species of tableaux—viz., to the vivid imagining of an absent object, describing it as if present.

Tableaux abound in eloquent speeches, especially in those addressed to the less educated, as the readiest way to reach their hearts is through the imagination. But there is no audience, no matter how intellectual, with whom they are not welcome and effective. As **examples** of powerful descriptions of this kind we may refer to three parallel passages intended to arouse terror and indignation ; these passages are found in three speeches, of Demosthenes, Fox, and Edmund Burke. The three tableaux are compared together and criticised by C. A. Goodrich in his *British Eloquence*, p. 346. Brief quotations here could not do justice to the subject ; and, besides, the work referred to is found in every library.

290. There is a speech of **Spartacus to the Gladiators**, by Kellogg, which is familiar to most students of oratory, and

which affords excellent opportunities of studying the proper method to stir up the passions, and the power of Tableaux to effect this purpose. Spartacus strives to arouse his fellow-gladiators to rebellion against their cruel masters, the Romans.

First he gains their *love* and *admiration* by an exhibition of his prowess. "Ye call me chief ; and ye do well to call him chief who for twelve long years (Tableaux:) has met upon the arena every shape of man or beast the broad empire of Rome could furnish, and who never yet lowered his arm. If there be one among you who can say that ever in public fight or private brawl my actions did belie my tongue, let him stand forth and say it." (Exhibition to the senses :) "If there be three in all your company dare face me on the bloody sands, let them come on." (*Pity* or *sympathy :*) "And yet I was not always thus—a hired butcher, a savage chief of still more savage men." (Tableaux of innocence :) "My ancestors came from old Sparta and settled, among the vine-clad rocks and citron-groves of Syrasella. My early life ran quiet as the brooks by which I sported ; and when, at noon, I gathered the sheep beneath the shade and played upon the shepherd's flute, there was a friend, the son of a neighbor, to join me in the pastime. We led our flocks to the same pasture and partook together our rustic meal." (Tableaux of injury:) "That very night the Romans landed on our coast. I saw the breast that had nourished me trampled by the hoof of the war-horse, the bleeding body of my father flung amidst the blazing rafters of our dwelling !" "To-day I killed a man in the arena, and when I broke his helmet-clasps, behold ! he was my friend. He knew me, smiled faintly, gasped, and died— (Tableaux of innocence :) the same sweet smile upon his lips that I had marked when, in adventurous boyhood, we scaled the lofty cliff to pluck the first ripe grapes and bear them home in childish triumph." (To excite *indignation, wrath :*) " I told the prætor that the dead man had been my friend, generous and brave "—(Tableaux of humiliation:) " and I begged that I might bear away the body to burn it on a funeral pile and mourn over its ashes. Ay ! upon my knees amid the dust and blood of the arena I begged that poor boon "—(Tableaux of outrageous cruelty:) " while all the assembled maids and matrons, and the holy virgins they call Vestals, and the rabble shouted in derision, deeming it rare sport, forsooth, to see Rome's fiercest gladiator turn pale and tremble at sight of that piece of bleeding clay. (Tableaux of insult:) And the prætor drew back, as I were pollution, and sternly said, ' Let the carrion rot ; there are no noble men but Romans !' (*Fear :*) And so, fellow-gladiators, must you, and so must I, die, like dogs."

(**Direct Pathos**—Apostrophe :) (No. 293.) " O Rome ! Rome ! thou hast been a tender nurse to me. Ay, thou hast given to that poor, gentle, timid shepherd lad, who never knew a harsher tune than a flute-note, muscles of iron and a heart of flint " ; (Tableaux:) " taught him to drive the sword through plaited mail and links of rugged brass, and warm it in the marrow of his foe ; to gaze into the glaring eye-balls of the fierce Numidian lion, even as a boy upon a laughing girl." (Direct Pathos :) " And he shall pay thee back until the yellow Tiber is red like frothing wine, and in its deepest ooze thy life-blood lies curdled ! "

(*Wrath*—by irony ; Tableaux :) " Ye stand here now like giants, as ye are. The strength of brass is in your toughened sinews ; but to-morrow some Roman Adonis, breathing sweet perfumes from his curly locks, shall with his lily fingers pat your red brawn and bet his sesterces upon your blood. Hark ! hear ye yon lion roaring in his den ? 'Tis three days since he tasted flesh ; but to-morrow he shall break his fast upon yours—and a dainty meal for him you will be. If ye are beasts, then stand here like fat oxen waiting for the butcher's knife. (*Hope:*) If ye are men, follow me ! Strike down yon guard, gain the mountain passes, and there do bloody work, as did your sires at old Thermopylæ."

(Patriotism :) "Is Sparta dead ? Is the old Grecian spirit frozen in your veins, that you do crouch and cower like a belabored hound beneath his master's lash ?"

(Direct Pathos :) "O comrades ! warriors ! Thracians ! If we must fight, let us fight for ourselves ! If we must slaughter, let us slaughter our oppressors ! If we must die, let it be under the clear sky, by the bright waters, in noble, honorable battle ! "

291. **Poetry** deals extensively in the production of Tableaux ; all poetry is full of them. It is constantly forming lively conceptions and painting them on the fancy of the reader, as it "bodies forth the forms of things unseen, and gives to empty nothing a local habitation and a name " (Shakspeare). Hence Fénelon has said that poetry is the soul of oratory. This is one of the chief reasons why the study of poetry has always been considered as an important feature in the formation of an orator.

But in oratory great care must be taken, in the drawing of pictures, that no mere play of the fancy be indulged which would amuse the mind rather than move the heart. **Oratorical Tableaux must be**: (*a*) *Vivid*, therefore precise, without useless details, a few bold strokes, no vagueness ; (*b*) *Appropriate* to excite the particular passion wanted ; (*c*) *Trim—i.e.*, free from excessive ornaments, which only weaken passion by delighting the fancy.

292. III. The third means of arousing the passions, and the noblest of all, is powerful, clear **reasoning** ; this is best suited to the educated, and it may be very effective with all classes of auditors, as we see in the speeches of Demos

thenes. But with any audience, reasoning, to arouse passion, must not be obscure or abstract, but clear and vivid. Very often it is mixed with brief pictures, and then it is most powerful. We shall quote some passages from great models.

From the First Philippic of Demosthenes : " When, then, O my countrymen, when will you do your duty ? What are you waiting for ? Some calamity, or dire necessity ? What, then, do you call our present situation ? For myself, I can conceive of no necessity more urgent to freemen than the pressure of dishonor. Tell me, is it your wish to go about the public squares, here and there, continually asking : ' What is the news ? ' Alas ! what more alarming news could there be than that a Macedonian is conquering Athens and lording it over Greece ? ' Is Philip dead ? ' ' No ; but he is sick.' And what if he were dead ? If he were to die your negligence would cause a new Philip to rise up at once, since this one owes his aggrandizement less to his own power than to your inertness."

From the Eighth Philippic : " Indeed, should some god assure you that however inactive and unconcerned you might remain, yet in the end you should not be molested by Philip, yet it would be ignominious—be witness, Heaven ! —it would be beneath you, beneath the dignity of your state, beneath the glory of your ancestors, to sacrifice to your own selfish repose the interests of all the rest of Greece. Rather would I perish than recommend such a course ! Let some other man urge it upon you, if he will ; and listen to him, if you can. But if my sentiments are yours—if you foresee, as I do, that the more we leave Philip to extend his conquests the more we are fortifying an enemy whom, sooner or later, we must cope with—why do you hesitate ? " etc.

Lord Chatham's speech against search-warrants is full cf

such impassioned reasoning ; *e.g.*, " The learned gentlemen were next pleased to show us that the government were already possessed of such power as is now desired.   And how did they show it ?   Why, sir, by showing that this is the practice in the case of felony, and in the case of those who are as bad as felons—I mean those who rob the public or dissipate the public money.   Shall we, sir, put our brave sailors upon the same footing with felons and public robbers ?   Shall a brave, honest sailor be treated as a felon for no other reason than because, after a long voyage, he has a mind to solace himself among his friends in the country, and for that purpose absconds for a few weeks in order to prevent his being pressed upon a Spithead, or some such pacific expedition ? " etc.

§ 3. *Of the Expression of Excited Passions.*

293. Tableaux and vivid reasonings intended to arouse the passions are often called **the indirect pathetic,** while the utterance of excited emotions is pathos proper, or **the direct pathetic.**

Once a passion has been aroused it may be proper to indulge it and dwell upon it by exclamations and other strong expressions of excited emotions.   This manner of development is what the ancients called **Amplification**—*i.e.*, to enforce pathos by copious treatment, so as to keep the minds and hearts of the hearers occupied with the aroused passion.

294. The ancients had **two species of amplification :** the δείνωσις consisted in accumulating kindred thoughts ; the αὔξησις accumulated various expressions of the same thought.   The one is copious in thoughts, the other in expressions.

Of the former this passage of Cardinal Newman (*Ser-*

mons, p. 218) may serve as a sample: "Such is the great God, so all-sufficient, so all-blessed, so separate from creatures, so inscrutable, so unapproachable. Who can see him? who can fathom him? who can move him? who can change him? who can even speak of him? He is all-holy, all-patient, all-serene, and all-true. He says and he does; he delays and he executes; he warns and he punishes; he punishes, he rewards, he forbears, he pardons, according to an eternal decree, without imperfection, without vacillation, without inconsistency." Another example of δείνωσις occurs in Cicero's Defence of Milo, where the orator deplores the sufferings brought on the Roman people by the excesses of Clodius, which he takes occasion to enumerate: " Dura mihi medius fidius," etc., n. 32.

Of the latter we have an example in the speech of Regulus to the Roman Senate (*Standard Speaker*, p. 106): "Conscript Fathers! there is but one course to be pursued. Abandon all thought of peace. Reject the overtures of Carthage! Reject them wholly and unconditionally! What! give back to her a thousand able-bodied men, and receive in return this one attenuated, war-worn, fever-wasted frame—this weed, whitened in a dungeon's darkness, pale and sapless, which no kindness of the sun, no softness of the summer breeze, can ever restore to health and vigor! It must not, it shall not be!"

An eloquent αυξησις is found in the first Catilinian, where Cicero makes Catiline gloat over the disgraceful revels which he will enjoy in the camp of the conspirators.

295. In connection with amplification we may call attention to its opposite, **Extenuation**, which accumulates belittling ideas or expressions. Perhaps the most striking instance of such an inverted δείνωσις is found in Shakspeare's well-known description of Queen Mab:

> " She comes
> In shape no bigger than an agate-stone
> On the forefinger of an alderman,
> Drawn with a team of little atomies," etc.

296. The chief requisite in the utterance of excited feelings is usually expressed in the words written by Horace as a rule for the action of tragedians :

> *Si vis me flere, dolendum est*
> *Primum ipsi tibi.*

" If you wish me to weep, you must first be afflicted yourself."

Certainly the spectators of a drama will not be moved to tears if the actors on the stage remain cold and unconcerned. The same rule will hold in the case of those who listen to a public speaker. But the rule applies directly to those passions that are **aroused by sympathy.** As Quincy Adams remarks, in order to arouse shame the orator need not feel that passion himself, but he will "sound the trumpet of unblemished honor." "Would you strike terror," he adds, "be intrepid ; and in general remember that if it is the nature of some passions to spread by contagion, it is equally characteristic of others never to kindle without collision." This remark is undoubtedly correct ; but we think this distinguished rhetorician errs in the application of his rule when he says : "Would you inflame anger ? Be cool." Did not Spartacus burn with anger when he strove to arouse the same passion in his fellow-gladiators ? Did not Cicero when he denounced Verres and Antony ? All that can be claimed in favor of Adams' view is that anger must be restrained so that it do not overpower the orator ; but the same holds of all the passions : the speaker should always maintain full command of himself, while the actor on the stage may appear to be overcome by his sorrow or other passion.

Allowing for a few special exceptions, the old rule, that **passion must be excited by contagion**, remains true ; and it is emphatically declared by all the great rhetoricians to be most important. Cicero expresses himself thus (*De Or.*, ii. 45): " For as no fuel is so combustible as to kindle without the application of fire, so no disposition of mind is so susceptible of the impressions of the orator as to be animated to strong feeling, unless he himself approach it full of inflammation and ardor." Here it is that natural gifts of no common kind are required for the formation of a truly great orator. What we stated in our introductory chapter here finds its chief application : *Pectus est quod disertos facit, et vis mentis*—" It is the heart that makes men eloquent, and their mental power."

297. Though the language of passion is less subject to definite precepts than any other parts of an oration, still it may not be useless to point out, after the example of the old rhetoricians, some **sources of amplification** to which great orators have frequent recourse.

298. **1. Accumulation**; *e.g.*, of definitions, consequences, causes, effects, circumstances, parts, etc. These are usually displayed in the figures of *vision, personification, interrogation, answer, exclamation*, etc. Sheridan, on the Begum charge, exclaims : " *Filial Piety!* It is the primal bond of society. It is that instinctive principle which, panting for its proper good, soothes unbidden each sense and sensibility of man. It now quivers on every lip. It now beams from every eye. It is that gratitude which, softening under the sense of recollected good, is eager to own the vast, countless debt it never, alas ! can pay, for so many years of unceasing solicitudes, honorable self-denials, life preserving cares. It is that part of our practice where duty drops its awe, where reverence refines into love. It asks no aid of memory. It needs not the deductions of

reason.   Pre-existing, paramount over all, whether moral law or human rule, few arguments can increase and none can diminish it.   It is the sacrament of our nature ; not only the duty but the indulgence of man.   It is his first great privilege.   It is among his last more endearing delights, when the bosom glows with the idea of reverberated love," etc.

Another specimen of the kind is found in Webster's address at Bunker Hill (*Am. Eloq.*, vol. ii. p. 364): " But—ah ! Him ! the first great martyr in this great cause ! Him ! the premature victim of his own self-devoting heart ! Him ! the head of our civil councils and the destined leader of our military bands, whom nothing brought hither but the unquenchable fire of his own spirit ; him ! cut off by Providence in the hour of overwhelming anxiety and thick gloom ; falling ere he saw the star of his country rise ; pouring out his generous blood like water before he knew whether it would fertilize a land of freedom or of bondage ! How shall I struggle with the emotions that stifle the utterance of thy name ! " etc.

299. **2. Comparison**; *i.e.*, examples and anything similar, dissimilar, or contrary adduced to heighten passion. Byron thus gives utterance to his passionate love of liberty :

> " Still, still, for ever ;
> Better, though each man's life-blood were a river,
> That it should flow, and overflow, than creep
> Through thousand lazy channels in our veins,
> Dammed like the dull canal with locks and chains,
> And moving as a sick man in his sleep,
> Three paces, and then faltering—better be
> Where the extinguished Spartans still are free,
> In their proud charnel of Thermopylæ,
> Than stagnate in our marsh ; or o'er our deep
> Fly, and one current to the ocean add,
> One spirit to the souls our fathers had,
> One freeman more, America, to thee ! "

300. 3. "**Climax**," as Adams remarks (Lect. xxiv.), "is the universal key to all oratorical composition. It applies to the discourse as a whole ; it applies to every sentence as a part. The ideas of the audience should be kept in a constantly ascending state, though it is not always necessary that the ascent should be made by regular and artificial steps." Pathos especially should go on increasing in depth and intensity ; for, as Quintilian remarks (*Inst.*, vi. 1), "whatever does not add to the passion detracts from it." As a peculiar manner of amplification, climax is exemplified in the following extracts : " It is a crime to put a Roman citizen in bonds ; it is the height of guilt to scourge him ; little less than parricide to put him to death. What name, then, shall I give to the act of crucifying him ? " (Cicero *In Verr.*)

" Gentlemen, if one man had anyhow slain another, if an adversary had slain his foe or a woman occasioned the death of her enemy, even these criminals would have been capitally punished by the Cornelian law ; but if this guiltless infant, who could make no enemy, had been murdered by its own nurse, what punishments would not then the mother have demanded ? With what cries and exclamations would she have stunned your ears ? What shall we say, then, when a woman guilty of homicide, a mother guilty of the murder of her innocent child, has comprised all those misdeeds in one single crime—a crime in its own nature detestable, in a woman prodigious, in a mother incredible, and perpetrated against one whose age called for compassion, whose near relationship claimed affection, and whose innocence deserved the highest favor ? " (McKenzie).

301. 4. **Reasoning** or **Inference**—*i.e.*, when the orator dwells on a matter that enkindles the passions not directly, but indirectly and by implication, as Cicero does when, in

his discourse on the Manilian Law, he dwells feelingly on the prostration of the Roman power during the war of the Pirates, thus keeping alive admiration in the hearts of his hearers for the prowess of Pompey, who defeated these enemies of the republic. " Quis enim toto mari locus," etc., Nos. 11 and 12.

Thus, too, Milton amplifies the person of Satan by a description of his weapons :

> " His ponderous shield,
> Ethereal temper, massy, large, and round,
> Behind him cast ; the broad circumference,
> Hung on his shoulders like the moon, whose orb
> Through optic glass the Tuscan artist views
> At evening from the top of Fesolé
> Or in Valdarno to descry new lands,
> Rivers, or mountains on her spotty globe.
> His spear, to equal which the tallest pine,
> Hewn on Norwegian hills to be the mast
> Of some great admiral, were but a wand
> He walked with."

. By these and like means pathos may be continued for some time and with great effect ; for a momentary excitement leaves no lasting impression, while a prolonged feeling of any passion is apt to decide the action of the will.

302. Still, it must be remembered that violent excitement cannot last long—*violenta non durant*—and the rhetorician Apollonius remarks that "nothing dries up more quickly than tears." Hence the orator must be careful not to sustain any passion when the audience begins to tire of it ; and he must remember that when the hearers cease to share his feelings they will at once begin to criticise and find fault with himself or his subject. He can do one of two things : he may either conclude his speech when excitement is at its highest, so as to leave a powerful impression on his hearers, provided he can do so naturally without offensive abrupt-

ness ; or he may descend from the high tone of his passion through gentler feelings, so as to find a natural transition to the calm reasoning that is yet to follow.

The following is the **transition** used by Edmund Burke after the pathetic passage above referred to (No. 289) : " These details are of a species of horror so nauseous and disgusting ; they are so degrading to the sufferers and the hearers ; they are so humiliating to human nature itself, that, on better thoughts, I find it more advisable to throw a pall over this hideous object and to leave it to your general conceptions."

Fox, after his brilliant pathos, simply says : " Sir, I have done ; I have told you my opinion." Then he passes on to some calm but earnest conclusions, and prepares to finish his speech.

303: The orator in a pathetic passage may arouse *various passions* at once or in close succession, as one passion will usually help another ; but he must carefully *avoid mixing* anything foreign with his passions : (*a*) Anything abstruse or erudite ; (*b*) Cold details, no matter how pretty ; (*c*) And. in general all ornament evidently labored ; for these things, besides showing that he is not full of his subject, also fill the minds of his hearers with images at variance with passion.

Finally, the orator must be careful not to carry the pathetic too far—that is, beyond the measure of what is natural and becoming. Cicero was undoubtedly guilty of this mistake when, in his prosecution of Verres, he thus concluded a most pathetic passage : " Were I pouring forth my lamentations to the stones and rocks in some remote and desert wilderness, even those mute and inanimate beings would, at the recital of such shocking indignities, be thrown into commotion." This is not genuine passion, but strained declamation.

CHAPTER V.

CONCLUSION OR PERORATION.

304. As it would appear inelegant and harsh under ordinary circumstances to enter upon a discourse without at least a brief Introduction, so likewise it would usually be unsatisfactory to stop abruptly without at least a **brief Conclusion or Peroration.**

But besides avoiding harshness, as the Introduction aims at positive advantage by preparing the audience to receive favorably the views and sentiments of the speaker, so the Peroration aims at impressing those views and sentiments upon their minds by a last and well-directed effort.

Hence if the speech has been chiefly argumentative the Conclusion ought either to insist upon some one important consideration which the orator desires to be best remembered, or to recapitulate the most weighty arguments. If the point is to be carried rather by moving the heart than by convincing the understanding, the whole power of pathos may be appropriately exerted in the Conclusion. No general rule can be laid down but this : that the speaker should manage his Conclusion in such a manner that the end come not unexpectedly on his hearers, and, on the other hand, that it do come when they expect it. He may select for the concluding sentence any argument or feeling or image which will enable him to retire, leaving on his auditors a favorable impression of his subject and no unfavorable one of himself. Nothing is more unpleasant in a Peroration than to see the orator continue when every one expects and wishes him to stop. It is better to conclude in any manner than remain hunting for a good conclusion.

When the **recapitulation** occurs in the Peroration it may be set off to advantage by the use of well-chosen terms, striking figures, and variety in the way of introducing it ; *e.g.*, Cicero against Verres puts one recapitulation in the mouth of Verres' own father, while another is embodied in an address to the gods whose temples have been plundered.

305. **As examples** of happy Conclusions we may quote the following : **Bossuet** concludes his funeral oration on the Prince of Condé thus : " Accept, O prince, these last efforts of a voice which you once knew well. With you all my funeral discourses are now to end. Instead of deploring the death of others, henceforth it shall be my study to learn from you how my own can be blessed. Happy if, warned by these gray hairs of the account which I must soon give of my ministry, I reserve solely for that flock which I ought to feed with the word of life the feeble remnants of a voice which now trembles, and an ardor which is now on the point of being extinct."

Bayard, on the Judiciary, thus : " We are standing on the brink of that revolutionary torrent which deluged in blood one of the fairest countries of Europe. France had her National Assembly, more numerous and equally popular with our own. She had her tribunals of justice and her juries. But the legislature and her courts were but the instruments of her destruction. Acts of proscription and sentences of banishment and death were passed in the cabinet of a tyrant. Prostrate your judges at the feet of party, and you break down the mounds which defend you from this torrent. I am done. I should have thanked my God for greater power to resist a measure so destructive to the peace and happiness of the country. My feeble efforts can avail nothing. But it was my duty to make them.

The meditated blow is mortal, and from the moment it is struck we may bid a final adieu to the Constitution."

As a last specimen of an appropriate Peroration we shall quote the words with which **J. Q. Adams** concludes his first course of Lectures on Rhetoric (Lect. xxiv.) : " While I am treating of the conclusion of a discourse, one-half of the audience to whose instruction my services are devoted is brought to a conclusion of their academic career. Accept my thanks, gentlemen, for the attention with which you have uniformly favored me, and the punctuality with which you have performed the duties of which the superintendence has been allotted to me. As you pass from this to a theatre of higher elevation for the pursuit of science, I cannot but feel a sentiment of regret at your departure, though mingled with that of cordial felicitation upon your advancement.' Henceforth you are to unite the study of living man with that of ages expired ; the observation of the present with the meditation upon the past. And so rapid is the succession of years that you will soon feel the balance of your feelings and of your duties pointing with an irresistible magnet to futurity, and the growing burden of your hopes and wishes concentrated in the welfare of your successors upon this earthly stage ; of yourselves upon that which must succeed. Go forth, then, with the blessing of this your intellectual parent. Go forth according to the common condition of your nature, to act and to suffer ; and may He in whose hands are the hearts as well as the destinies of men be your guide for the one and your staff for the other. May he inspire you at every needed hour with that fortitude which smiles at calamity ; may he at every fortunate occasion fire you with that active energy which makes opportunity success, and that purity of principle which makes success a public and a private blessing."

CHAPTER VI.

ON THE STYLE OF SPEECHES.

306. It is not here intended to write a treatise on style, but simply to explain those qualities which should characterize the style of speeches as distinguished from other compositions.

The **importance of style** in oratory is such that without it all our arguments, no matter how skilfully invented and arranged, no matter how ably developed, remain ineffectual, like a good sword hidden in a scabbard. "By polish and embellishment of style," says Quintilian (viii. 3, 2), "the orator recommends himself to his auditors in his proper character; in his other efforts he courts the approbation of the learned, in this the applause of the multitude." . . . "This grace of style may contribute in no small degree to the success of a cause; for those who listen with pleasure are both more attentive and more willing to believe, . . . and are sometimes carried away by admiration " (ib. 5).

307. The first quality of the oratorical style is **Perspicuity.** This quality, necessary to a great extent in all manner of compositions, ought to be so perfect in oratory that the hearers not only *can* easily understand what is said, but cannot help understanding it, as we see the sun on a clear day without looking for it. Without such perspicuity speakers may tickle the ears of the vulgar with fair words and empty sounds; but such eloquence is contemptible and such triumphs are not worthy of a good and earnest man.

Of this quality it is useless to give any example ; it is the very essence of the proper style for public speaking. Any passage of an oration that will not illustrate this quality of style is evidently defective, no matter what other good qualities it may combine. But it may not be useless to give an example of the absence of this perspicuity. Mazzini, addressing the young men of Italy, says : " Love, young men, love and reverence the ideal ; it is the country of the spirit, the city of the soul, in which all are brethren who believe in the inviolability of thought and in the dignity of our immortal natures. From that high sphere spring the principles which alone can redeem the peoples. Love enthusiasm, the pure dreams of the virgin soul, and the lofty visions of early manhood ; for they are the perfume of Paradise, which the soul preserves in issuing from the hands of the Creator."

This is fine language ; but what does it all mean ? What, for instance, does the speaker mean by " the inviolability of thought"? In this example the want of perspicuity is not the result of dulness or carelessness in the orator, but he appears to use language to conceal his thoughts. This is called an art, but it is one no honest man would recommend ; the use of it is a stain upon the character of a speaker. Of obscurity resulting from dulness or negligence examples are readily found in many speeches ; none need here be quoted.

308. The second and distinguishing quality is **Directness.** The speaker should constantly address the hearers as if conversing with them ; this keeps their attention alive and causes the orator to adapt himself to their understanding. If we compare distinguished with inferior speakers we find that the former are ever conversing, as it were, with their hearers, while the latter often seem to be reading a page of a book to them.

309. The third quality is **Appropriateness** of the style **to the thoughts.** As style is nothing else than that sort of expression which our thoughts naturally assume, it will, of course, vary with the varying characteristics of the thoughts themselves. Now, thoughts will vary with the aim for which the orator conceives them. He may aim at pleasing, at convincing, or at persuading ; and as he will adapt his selection of thoughts to the special aim presently intended, so likewise will he adapt the expression of them to the same purpose. This difference of style has been pithily express-ed by Cicero in these words : *Subtile in probando, modicum in delectando, vehemens in flectendo.* His meaning is that the style of an orator should be plain and simple when he de-sires to impart conviction, modest when he aims at plea-sure, and forcible when he strives to persuade. Since one or other of these three aims will be predominant on any particular occasion, some one or other character of style will prevail in a discourse. Still, even within the same oration there will naturally arise varieties of style, according to the different aims of the separate parts. Thus in the *Introduction* modesty and dignity are usually blend-ed ; the *Narration* will be plain and very clear, "almost in the style of daily conversation," says Cicero ; an *Exposition* or *Explanation* requires leisure and repose ; *Reasoning* must be close and brisk, usually in short and pointed sen-tences—*incisim et membratim*, as Cicero calls it ; *Pathos* should be poured forth with "richness, variety, and even copiousness of language" (*De Or.*, ii. 53). It admits of all the figures of word and thought, all the oratorical re-sources of speech, provided that everything be kept within the limits of common sense and gentlemanly refinement.

310. The fourth quality is **Appropriateness to the audi-ence.** A book is written for all ; its style may and should differ with its subject-matter. But it cannot so easily adapt

itself to the age and condition of the reader ; the style of a speech can and should be so adapted. Not that an orator who is refined with the refined should ever be. vulgar with tne vulgar, but he should, without stooping too low, adapt his language to the understanding of his audience. It is beautiful to observe how great men have often stooped to the taste of children, and lofty minds to the common thoughts of the uneducated.

As an **example** of the latter we may quote the introduction to the first of Cardinal Newman's sermons : " When a body of men come into a neighborhood to them unknown, as we are doing, my brethren, strangers to strangers, and there set themselves down, and raise an altar, and open a school, and invite or even exhort all men to attend them, it is natural that they who see them and are drawn to think about them should ask the question, What brings them hither ? Who bid them come ? What do they want ? What do they preach ? What is their warrant ? What do they promise ? You have a right, my brethren, to ask the question. Many, however, will not stop to ask it, as thinking they can answer it for themselves. Many there are who would promptly and confidently answer it, according to their own habitual view of things, on their own principles, the principles of the world," etc.

It may not be unprofitable to compare, or rather to contrast, the style of this extract with the introduction to a letter of Junius addressed to the Duke of Grafton : " If nature had given you an understanding qualified to keep pace with the wishes and principles of your heart, she would have made you, perhaps, the most formidable minister that ever was employed under a limited monarch to accomplish the ruin of a free people. When neither the feelings of shame, the reproaches of conscience, nor the dread of punishment form any bar to the designs of a minister, the people would have too much reason to lament their condition, if they did not find some resource in the weakness of his understanding. We owe it to the bounty of Providence that the completest depravity of the heart is sometimes strangely united with a confusion of the mind which counteracts the most favorite principles and makes the same man treacherous without art and a hypocrite without deceiving." These are three well-balanced periods, each very beautiful in sound and harmony, and certainly not devoid of meaning. But the whole passage is strikingly unsuited for oratory. No skilful speaker would use such style with any manner of audience.

311. The fifth quality is **beauty or ornament**: this should not be confined to the pathetic parts, but affect the entire composition, as blood permeates the whole human body. It should be manly, strong, and chaste; not effeminately smooth and affected, but shining with the beauty of a healthy, manly form. "True beauty of style is not one thing and utility another," says Quintilian. "Nor is it enough," he adds, "that the language be clear and pure; there should be a choice of proper words even on common matters, but in important ones no ornament should be spared unless it obscure the sense." Figures may add as much to clearness as to elegance, as when Cicero says that "the laws are silent in the midst of arms," and that "the sword is handed to us by the laws themselves." But the figures should be ornaments, not impediments.

312. The sixth quality. Perspicuity and beauty combined make a style **popular**—that is, such as the people love to hear; it is the perfection of the oratorical style. To attain to it the orator must study to discern what points the people wish to have explained or proved, and what they are willing to accept on his word. He must know what illustrations will suit their minds. For these

purposes he must know his audience, their circumstances and predilections, their weaknesses and their virtues, their views and their prejudices, their interests and their aspirations. Above all, he must **know the human heart.** The knowledge of the heart of man cannot be acquired from the mere precepts of a teacher, nor the writings of philosophers, nor by the extensive perusal of literary works. These means will help, no doubt, to that purpose; but it is by intercourse with his fellow-men, and especially by self-introspection and the scrutiny of his own heart, that a man will acquire a knowledge of human nature which no books can teach, and which will discover to him the secret springs of human actions. He is apt to understand others best who understands himself best; the old oracle spoken to Crœsus, " Know thyself," is applicable to all men, but particularly to those who are ambitious to become the guides of others.

313. A seventh quality is **copiousness of treatment.** In reading a book a person can read over a second time what he failed to understand the first time; but it is not so when he listens to a speech. Hence everything important must be fully presented, even presented more than once, but in different terms, so that it does not appear to be a repetition. There are parts of the speech that may be more concise; but the general characteristic of the oratorical style is fulness, copiousness, rather than brevity. Skilful speakers dwell long on the same thoughts, if important, presenting them now in plain, then in figurative language; now by reasoning, then by illustration; now in general, then in particular examples, etc.

We have a fine **specimen** of copious style in this well-known extract from a speech of Patrick Henry; it will be noticed that every thought is expressed more than once: " Mr. President, it is natural for man to indulge in the illusions of hope. We are apt to shut our eyes against a painful truth and listen to the song of the siren till she transforms us into beasts. Is this the part of a wise man engaged in a great and arduous struggle for liberty ? Are we disposed to be of the number of those who, having eyes, see not, and, having ears, hear not, the things which so nearly concern our temporal salvation ? For my part, whatever anguish of spirit it may cost, I am willing to know the whole truth, to know the worst and to provide for it," etc.

As *models* in English of the oratorical style we may mention Chatham, Fox, Edmund Burke, Pitt, Cardinals Wiseman and Newman, Father Tom Burke, Webster, Calhoun, Clay, Everett, Patrick Henry, etc.

314. The language of an orator, especially in extemporaneous efforts, will in great part depend upon his **style in ordinary conversation.** Young men should therefore accustom themselves to converse in correct and cultivated language, most carefully avoiding all rude and faulty expressions and all kinds of slang terms. On the other hand, they should avoid affectation, and even the use of words that may be correct enough but not generally used ; many recommend the use of words of Saxon origin, as being more familiar to all and often more expressive. Pedantry is always improper ; but it cannot be called pedantic in a man of education to avoid vulgar words and such constructions as violate the well-known rules of grammar. "This advice," says Quintilian (*Inst.*, x. 7), "is approved by Cicero, that no portion of even our common conversation should ever be careless, and that whatever we say, on any occasion, should be, as far as possible, excellent in its way."

BOOK V.

315. The composition of a discourse has now been explained with sufficient fulness; but as a jewel, after it is completely formed and polished to perfection, must next be properly set to display it to the best advantage, thus an oration must be committed to memory, and so delivered as to make the most favorable impression. Hence we find that to the parts of oratory so far explained, treating respectively of the invention, arrangement, and development of arguments, Quintilian adds two other divisions (*Inst.*, iii. 3), viz.: *Memory*, and *Action or Delivery.* We shall briefly consider these two subjects, treating: 1. Of memorizing; and 2. Of the delivery of an oration.

CHAPTER I.

ON MEMORIZING THE ORATION.

316. I. The first question that presents itself under this head is whether, supposing the oration to have been written, it is always necessary to commit it to memory. **Is it not enough to read it?** This question was not discussed by the ancients: they never read their speeches. They always aimed at perfection in every art ; and there is no doubt that the perfection of eloquence is impeded by those trammels which the reading of a discourse imposes on the orator. Even if he should have great dexterity in using his manuscript, there is in his very glance at the written page an interruption to the flow of soul which marks real eloquence.

"The practice of reading sermons," says Blair (Lect. xxix.), "is one of the greatest obstacles to the eloquence of the pulpit in Great Britain, where alone this practice prevails. No discourse which is designed to be persuasive can have the same force when read as when spoken. The common people all feel this, and their prejudice against this practice is not without foundation in nature. What is gained hereby in point of correctness is not equal, I apprehend, to what is lost in point of persuasion and force."

317. Still, there are occasions when a written speech is not altogether out of place. Thus lectures on scientific subjects, delivered before highly intellectual audiences, may sometimes be read to advantage. But even in such cases it is desirable that the lecturer almost know his composi-

tion by heart, so that, under the modest appearance of a reader, he may exert all the influence of an orator. When a lecture is thus read, not spoken, we **expect in it certain qualities** which may atone for the absence of oratorical power—viz., (*a*) more solidity than usual, (*b*) more calmness and deliberation, and (*c*) more correctness and refinement of expression.

318. II. A second question is, **Should the speech, if memorized, be learned word for word?** There is a great advantage in doing so, as the speaker will thus reap the full fruit of all his preparation, and not lose a single one of the figures and the constructions which he has carefully selected. All orators should begin with this laborious exercise of their memories and continue it for many years. In later life they may find it sufficient to write their orations and read them over once or twice. But, as a rule, those who stop laboring stop improving. Some who cease to read their speeches still continue to write them, and find no little profit in thus reducing their thoughts to written expression. In delivering their orations, thoughts more forcible and more elegant may occur to them than those which they had conceived during their hours of quiet preparation, and practised speakers will know how to profit by them. Whatever method they find most useful to themselves, let them adopt it, for they are masters of the art. The precepts of this book are written for pupils, and for these undoubtedly the fullest and most careful preparation is the most desirable.

319. III. These, then, should memorize their discourses word for word. For this purpose they should study how to improve their memories. Now, **How can the memory be improved?** No faculty is more capable of improvement; and the means is *practice, exercise.*

Rule 1. Young people should be made to **learn by heart**

daily. "If any one asks me," says Quintilian (*Inst.*, xi. 2), "what is the greatest, nay, the only art of memory, my answer is. Exercise, labor, much learning by heart, much meditation, and, if possible, daily repeated; this is worth all the rest. Nothing thrives so much by industry; nothing perishes so much by neglect. Let, then, the practice be taught and made frequent in childhood; and whoever, at any period of life, would cultivate his memory must submit to the distasteful work of going over and over again what he has written and already many times read. The habit of learning by heart, when acquired in early youth, gives ever after a readiness which disdains paltry indulgences. No prompter, no looking on the paper, then should be endured, for it encourages negligence; and when we have any fear of failing in our recitation we shall scarcely succeed in hiding our embarrassment. Hence the course of delivery will be interrupted, a hesitating, stammering mode of speech will be formed, and all the grace of the most elegant writing be lost in the continual confession that, instead of speaking, we are reading a written composition."

Rule 2. Let young people **learn that only which is worth remembering.** "There is perhaps as much failure of excellence arising from the misapplication of this faculty to frivolous or irrational objects as from its utter neglect" (Adams).

Rule 3. Let all **beware of whatever is apt to impair the memory.** "The memory is impaired," says Adams (Lect. xxxv.), "by all the diseases which the vices of men bring upon them, and by some which are merely the visitations of Heaven. It is occasionally suspended for a time by sensual excesses, and particularly by intoxication. It is gradually corroded and consumed by long-continued habits of intemperance. All the violent passions, for the time while they exercise their dominion over the mind, en-croach upon the memory. . . . A firm and conscientious regard to truth is a quality very material to the memory; and hence the deficiency of that power in persons whose veracity is feeble has in all ages been proverbial."

320. IV. **What devices may assist** to learn a discourse by heart ?

1. Learn in the quiet hours of the evening, and repeat the task in the calm of the early dawn.

2. In the manuscript distinguish the heads of the oration by marks that catch the eye and thus seize on the ima-gination.

3. Learn the speech by parts, according to those same divisions.

4. Learn from the same manuscript, so as to derive as-sistance from the local memory.

5. Learn aloud, so that the ear may aid the mind.

321. V. **Is extempore speaking ever advisable ?**

If by *extempore* speaking is meant speaking without careful preparation, without having formed clear ideas on the matter discussed, it were rash ever to attempt it. "Eloquence," says Quintilian, "derides those who thus insult her ; and those who wish to appear learned to fools are decidedly pronounced fools by the learned" (*Inst.*, x. 7). But extemporaneous speaking is usually understood to have a different meaning, and to consist in the delivery of an oration the matter of which has been thoroughly studied and arranged, but not reduced to written sentences. It differs from the full preparation in this one point, that the words are not written ; but the plan is usually drawn up, and even the words are passed over in the mind, and sometimes the introduction at least is written out. "It is the general practice," says Quintilian, "among plead-ers who have much occupation, to write only the most essential parts, and especially the commencements, of their speeches; to fix the other portions, that they bring from home, in their memory by meditation, and to meet any unforeseen attacks with extemporaneous replies" (*Inst.*, x. 7).

322. Even such manner of extemporizing is advisable for those only who cannot prepare in full. For persons so circumstanced we shall add a few **suggestions** culled from Quintilian (*Inst.*, x. 7).

1. "If any chance shall give rise to such a sudden necessity for speaking *extempore*, we shall have need to exert our mind with more than its usual activity; we must fix our whole attention on our matter, and relax for the time something of our care about words, if we find it impossible to attend to both. A slower pronunciation, too, and a mode of speaking with suspense and doubt, as it were, gives time for consideration; yet we must manage so that we may seem to deliberate, and not to hesitate. . . . Afterwards, as we proceed on our course, we shall fill our sails. . . . This will be better than to launch forth on an empty torrent of words, so as to be carried away with it, as by the blasts of a tempest, whithersoever it may wish to sweep us."

2. "There is also another kind of exercise, that of meditation upon whole subjects, and going through them in silent thought (yet, so as to speak, within ourselves)—an exercise which may be pursued at all times and in all places, when we are not actually engaged in any other occupation."

3. "Speak in the hearing of several persons, especially of those for whose judgment and opinion you have much regard; for it rarely happens that a person is sufficiently severe with himself. Let us, however, rather speak alone than not speak at all."

4. "As to writing, we must certainly never write more than when we have to speak much *extempore ;* for by the use of the pen a weightiness will be preserved in our matter, and that light facility of language which swims, as it were on the surface, will be compressed."

CHAPTER II.

ELOCUTION OR DELIVERY.

323. **By Elocution or Delivery** we mean the art of regulating the voice and the gestures. But the ancients included style as a portion of elocution, and what we call delivery they denominated **Action.** We read of Demosthenes that, after failing of success in one of his earliest orations, he walked away disconsolate, a picture of despair. He was met by a friend, a distinguished elocutionist, who, on learning the cause of his disconsolate looks, walked home with him, and there declaimed some portions of the orator's manuscript in such a way that Demosthenes wondered at the power exhibited in his own production when perfectly rendered. Henceforth he devoted himself with redoubled ardor to the study of delivery; and later in life, when he was asked what was the chief point in oratory, he replied *action;* and what the second? *action* again; and the third? *action* once more. So thoroughly did he feel convinced that almost the whole efficacy of oratory depends upon elocution. Cicero and Quintilian quote this conviction of Demosthenes with approbation. Adams suspects that in modern times delivery is of less importance. This may be true enough in judicial oratory, owing to the altered character of our courts; and it may hold, to some extent, in representative bodies. For it now often happens that a discourse is expected to appear in the public press immediately after it is spoken, and that more importance is attached to the impression it will make on the readers of it throughout the land, than to its immediate effect on the

hearers in the legislative halls. But when discourses are spoken before a popular audience with a view to present results, then the power of delivery is as great as it ever was, for it flows from the very constitution of human nature.

Thus Shakspeare, who knew mankind so well, makes the Duchess of York thus impeach the sincerity of her husband :

" Pleads he in earnest ? Look upon his face ;
His eyes do drop no tears, his prayers are jests ;
His words come from his mouth, ours from our breast ;
He prays but faintly and would be denied ;
We pray with heart and soul."

324. **Elocution** cannot be taught to perfection by precept alone ; more than any other branch of oratory it requires the assistance of a teacher ; but we may refer to the most important directions usually laid down by rhetoricians on this subject. We shall divide the matter into its two natural branches of *pronunciation* and *gesture.*

ARTICLE I. PRONUNCIATION.

325. A member of a popular assembly, as Adams remarks, is said to *make a speech ;* a lawyer at the bar *argues a cause ;* the orator of a festival *delivers an oration*, and a clergyman *preaches a sermon.* The management of the voice in all these species we denominate **Pronunciation.** Now, the functions of the voice are twofold—*to transmit words to the ears* of the audience, and *to convey emotions to their hearts.*

326. I. **To transmit words to the ears** the speaker must attend to : 1. *Loudness ;* 2. *Distinctness ;* 3. *Slowness ;* and 4. *Pauses.*

1. The **Loudness** should be such that the orator shall

be easily understood by all whom he addresses ; excess is unpleasant. The voice has **three pitches**: the *high*, for calling to some one at a distance ; the *low*, for whispering ; and the *middle*, for ordinary conversation.

This last should generally be used in public speaking. It alone can be properly modulated and long supported. The high pitch soon pains the speaker, and whatever is felt to pain the speaker at once pains the hearers. All this should be remembered by those especially who speak in the open air. Finding that the voice does not come back to them, as it does in a hall, they readily imagine that they do not speak loud enough. This may be true or not, but taking a higher key will not mend it ; it will only make them hoarse and prevent them from being understood at all. Every man's voice has a certain limit of power, beyond which it is useless to strain it. That power is exerted to the best advantage in the middle pitch. All that can be done is to manage the voice judiciously.

2. For this purpose **Distinctness** of pronunciation is of the greatest importance. The teeth must cut every syllable sharply and precisely, so that every sound be produced perfect in its kind and carried to the ear separately from every preceding and every following sound. A weak voice speaking with distinct articulation will be far better understood than a strong voice without it. Even a whisper well articulated can be made to fill a vast hall. When a resonance exists, even in a smaller room, this distinctness becomes absolutely necessary.

3. A proper degree of **Slowness** is required, both that the words may not run into each other, and also that no more sound be given out than the speaker can conveniently utter at one breath. But, that he may not run into the opposite defect of a drawling manner, he will do well to seek the direction of a discreet friend.

4. The **Pauses** that mark the sense should be attended to. As distinctness of pronunciation keeps the syllables from running into one another, so the pauses should keep apart groups of words. Sentences are perfect groups, each of which makes a full sense. A larger pause will separate these. Within the sentences are smaller groups, which should be separated by minor stops, even when no marks of punctuation are written. Now, the voice should be so judiciously managed as to keep together all the words that are grouped into a common construction, and to separate those that are to a degree independent of one another. These pauses will, if carefully managed, allow the speaker to take breath and prevent him from feeling fatigued.

327. II. **To convey emotions to the heart,** whether the gentler feelings that please or the stronger passions that arouse, attention must be paid to emphasis and to the tones.

1. Emphasis is a special stress laid on some words more than on others. It is often used to distinguish the sense, as will be readily noticed by pronouncing a sentence like this, " Do you ride to town to-day ? " different times with different emphasis. Emphasis becomes a vehicle of emotion when the stress is prompted by the feelings of the speaker rather than by the bare requirements of the sense, as when the following lines of Byron, describing the " Dying Gladiator," are feelingly pronounced :

> " He heard it, but he *heeded* not ; his eyes
>   Were with his *heart*, and that was *far away ;*
> He *recked* not of the *life* he lost, nor prize,
>   But where his *rude hut* by the Danube lay :
> *There* were his *young barbarians* all at play ;
>   *There* was their *Dacian mother*—he, *their sire,*
> *Butchered* to make a Roman *holiday*—
>   *All this* rushed with his blood. Shall he expire,
>   And *unavenged ? Arise,* ye Goths, and *glut* your ire ! "

2. Tones are the peculiar modulations of sound which nature has adopted to express various feelings. Sheridan has said that "words express ideas, tones emotions" (*Art of Reading*). To utter different feelings in one and the same tone is like using one word to express different ideas. The prevalence of one only tone in a speech produces monotony, which is as unpleasant as it is lifeless. The right management of the tones is the most impressive element in moving the heart. Now, if we remember that the power to move the heart is what properly denominates a man an orator, we shall readily understand how important is the study of the tones. Unfortunately, paper instructions are powerless to teach the tones. Nature must dictate them, and the living voice may help to suggest them to imitative youths. But no one can explain on paper the peculiar modulations of voice with which a feeling heart will pour forth sorrow like this:

> "Alas, my noble boy ! that thou shouldst die !
>   Thou who wert made so beautifully fair !
> That death should settle in thy glorious eye,
>   And leave his stillness in this clustering hair !
> How could he mark thee for the silent tomb,
>   My proud boy, Absalom !
>
> "Cold is thy brow, my son ! and I am chill,
>   As to my bosom I have tried to press thee '
> How was I wont to feel my pulses thrill,
>   Like a rich harp-string, yearning to caress thee,
> And hear thy sweet ' My father ! ' from those dumb
>   And cold lips, Absalom ! "   —*Willis.*

Still, these **suggestions** may be useful : 1. The speaker must feel every emotion keenly. Here applies the maxim : *Si vis me flere, dolendum est primum ipsi tibi.* It is not enough that he has a tender heart ; he must himself vividly realize the situation. This power of conceiving passion can be developed by judicious training in the declaiming of pathetic passages in prose and verse. Boys have wonderful power of imitation in this regard. 2. Let speakers guard against such tones as are not prompted by real sentiments. There exists in various localities a sort of *sing-song*, the outgrowth of mannerisms. Such are certain pulpit tones. The preacher, it is true, occupies a peculiar position. As ambassador of Christ, from whom he has a mission, he is entitled to speak with special authority, *sicut potestatem habens*—"like one having power." But there is no reason why he should be unnatural. Like the Apostle, "let him weep with those that weep, and rejoice with those that rejoice, and become all things to all men."

ARTICLE II. GESTICULATION.

328. **Gestures** are motions of the body intended to add grace or expression to speech. Like tones, they are the language of nature—a language not equally developed in different nations and in different individuals, remarkably varied and expressive among the races of southern Europe, and as remarkably scanty and unmeaning among more northern peoples. The warning of Shakspeare, " Do not saw the air too much with your hand, thus," would be pointless among Italians, whose variety and expressiveness of gesture are almost as perfect as the music of their spoken language. It appears to have been the same with the ancient Romans : the figures painted in the Vatican copy of Terence represent the very attitudes and gestures familiar to this day among the modern inhabitants of the Eternal City. Among these, gestures are plentiful, even in common conversation ; children acquire the use of them as they acquire their mother-tongue. (See on Italian gesticulation one of Cardinal Wiseman's *Essays*, vol. iii. p. 531, or *Dublin Review* for July, 1837.) Among those nations

that speak the English language the faculty of gesticulation needs careful training, and we may say with Cardinal Wiseman : "We do think that our pulpit eloquence would be greatly improved by Italian gesture ; a species of action not considered as a poising of limbs alternately or by given laws, the stretching out of the right hand at one member of a sentence and of the left at another, as silly books on elocution describe, but of action considered as language addressed to the eyes, which as definitely conveys ideas through them as the words do through the ears, and which consequently rivets the spectator as much as the auditor, and makes men long to *see* the orator."

But **gesture should be taught by living masters.** Vandenhoff, an accomplished elocutionist and a successful teacher of his art, says : "I know of no means of teaching gestures by written instructions ; nor do I think that much assistance can be gathered from plates of figures representing different actions and attitudes."　Still, he proceeds to lay down some general directions which substantially agree with those taught by all modern writers on the subject, and with the minute rules formulated by Quintilian (*Inst.*, xi. 3).　Nor is this agreement to be wondered at, since gestures are a language of nature, and therefore must be radically the same among all men.

329. **To gesticulate properly** an orator must have acquired a great facility to adopt all manners of attitudes and motions which are elegant and expressive.　In particular he should be taught :

1. **A dignified bearing of the body,** not stiff, but firm, manly, and free, with head erect but not bolt-upright, chest expanded, feet not far apart.

2. **A great variety of motions with his arms,** not starting from the elbow, as Adams strangely recommends, but from the shoulders, as elocutionists generally teach.　Now

the right arm will move alone; now, but rarely, the left one by itself; often the two in unison. All the motions should be made in curves, for the curve is the line of beauty. The arms themselves must be extended in a curve, rarely straight at full length; and when they hang down they must be in a natural posture of rest.

3. A great flexibility about the wrists and hands. There are comparatively few speakers "who have ever realized the wonderful life, vigor, and expression which lurk within a shapely and facile hand" (Potter, *Pastor and People*). "There is an extraordinary character in the palm of a well-shaped, nervous hand; and this is equally evident, whether it be employed in the downward gesture of forbidding, crushing, or destroying, or whether it be turned toward the object addressed with the action of aversion, rejection, or repulsion. The action of the hands when they are closed or clenched in strong passion is wonderfully vivid and expressive" (ibid.) Hence Quintilian remarks: "The action of the other parts of the body assists the speaker, but the hands, I could almost say, speak themselves." What a pity, then, that many persons appear to be at a loss what to do, during their discourse, with such awkward appendages as their hands seem to be!

330. All these elements of declamation can, with proper training, be acquired by most speakers. Once possessed, they can readily be adapted to any particular discourse, provided proper judgment guide them. Judgment or common sense will direct them to the **twofold end of all elocution**—*elegance* and *power*. **Elegance** requires that some gesture or other be used to relieve sameness in the appearance of the speaker's person, and it will suggest such motions as are in unison with the sounds of the periods uttered. But the **power of expression** is the chief aim of gestures, whether these help to express the sense—as when

they point to the spot where the object spoken of is im-
agined to be, or they imitate the motions referred to—or
whether, as is more usual, the gestures express the feelings
of the soul. This latter kind of gestures is instinctive, like
the tones : it expresses desire, aversion, anger, rebuke, sup-
plication, horror, hope, dejection, despair, etc., etc., by
very different motions, not of the hands only, but especially of the countenance, and, above all, of the eyes, those
mirrors of the soul. Expression of features can, of course,
not be subjected to rules, nor can the motions of the hands
be directed by rule alone. The soul must speak through
the body, with which it constitutes one complete being.

331. Let the aspiring orator be taught in youth by a truly
able master how to **declaim** properly some select pieces of
prose and verse. Let him practise before some judicious
friend on the proper application of tones and gestures to
some of his early discourses. Then through life, provided
he feels intensely the passions to which he gives utterance,
and provided he is possessed of such social virtues as gen-
tleness, modesty, etc., which will give the passions smoothness, he will be a graceful and a forcible speaker.

332. We scarcely see the necessity of adding further particulars on the subject of gesture, unless it be to call attention to some **minor details**.

1. The hands should seldom be closed. Their usual
form is open, but not stiff ; with the fingers joined and
slightly curved, except the index finger and the thumb,
which are straight.

2. Shrugging the shoulders, or any such ungraceful motion, and all grimaces should be carefully avoided. No
buffoonery is ever allowed.

3. The gestures should be appropriate to the subject and
the circumstances. Copious gesticulation is out of place
in a familiar address ; wide gestures are ill-suited to trifling

matters, narrow ones to important thoughts. Modesty dictates the use of fewer gestures on starting out.

4. The eye must follow the direction of the hands.

5. The hands may somewhat anticipate the words to which they refer, but never linger behind them.

6. The hands are not usually to be raised above the eyes, nor to gesticulate below the waist.

7. The body should not swing like a pendulum.

8. The speaker should rise and come forward with dignity, and not begin his discourse abruptly, but when all are ready to hear him.

9. Practising before a mirror is often recommended, and it has advantages ; but a judicious friend or an able teacher is better than all the looking-glasses in the world. For a man may be blind to his own faults and mistake his oddities for beauties. However, he might make use of a mirror to correct those defects to which others have called his attention.

BOOK VI.

THE DIFFERENT SPECIES OF ORATORY.

333. The **purpose** of dividing oratory into certain species must, of course, be to assist the orator in attaining the end or object for which he discourses. Now, this object is persuasion—*i.e.*, influencing the minds of his hearers ; therefore the various species of oratory ought to be distinguished with reference to *the minds of the hearers.*

" But the hearer," says Aristotle (*Rhet.*, i. 3), " must necessarily be either an unconcerned hearer ($\theta\epsilon\omega\rho\acute{o}s$) or one who is expected to decide ($\varkappa\rho\iota\tau\acute{\eta}s$) ; and he is to decide either on things past or on things to come. Some, then, decide on things to come, as do the members of a popular assembly ; others on the past, as a judge in a court of justice ($\delta\iota\varkappa\alpha\sigma\tau\acute{\eta}s$) ; while others decide respecting excellence ($\delta\upsilon\nu\acute{\alpha}\mu\epsilon\omega s$), as does the unconcerned hearer. Thus there will result three kinds of orations : the *deliberative*, the *judicial*, and the *epideictic*. Cicero, in his *Partitiones*, calls the same " deliberationis, judicii, exornationis."

In the epideictic, more usually called by its Latin equivalent, *demonstrative*, the hearer is to judge of *excellence ;* not of the excellence of the discourse alone, but also, and chiefly, of the excellence of the person or thing that is the subject-matter of the discourse. Some rhetoricians misunderstand this term, and consider demonstrative oratory as idle declamation. Webster's Dictionary, on the other hand, makes it "seek to persuade by full amplification." These are misconceptions.

The distinction of species laid down by Aristotle is *radical* and exhaustive ; every discourse that has real unity belongs to one of these three kinds. The reason is that the hearer is necessarily in one of the three conditions stated above.

334. After laying down the **essential** difference between the species, Aristotle points out some **accidental** or secondary differences. *Deliberation*, for instance, deals with exhortation and dissuasion ; it regards a future measure, viewed usually as expedient or inexpedient. *Forensic* rhetoric, on the other hand, is concerned with accusation and defence ; it regards a past fact as just or unjust. *Demonstration* is employed in praising or blaming persons for what is honorable or disgraceful ; it usually regards the present, for qualities presently possessed are wont to make a man admirable or contemptible.

Aristotle calls all these differences *accidental*. Thus the demonstrative may incidentally dwell on what is just or what is honorable in the person praised ; the deliberative may consider the justice or the honorable character of the measure proposed, etc. But many modern rhetoricians confound what is accidental with what is essential, and suppose that whenever praise and blame are dwelt upon there is demonstrative eloquence.

Even J. Q. Adams, one of the most correct of modern critics, says (Lect. x.) that "the panegyric of Pompey interwoven by Cicero into his oration on the Manilian Law, that of Cæsar in the oration for Marcellus, that of literature in the oration for Archias, . . . and Cicero's invectives against Antony in his Philippics, against Piso, Catiline, Clodius, and Verres in many others of his orations, are applications of the demonstrative manner in certain parts of deliberative or judicial discourses." An important distinction is here overlooked by Mr. Adams. Not all passages praising or blaming a person belong to demonstrative oratory, but such only as are addressed to the unconcerned hearers, θεωροί, as Aristotle calls them—that is, to men who are not actually engaged in making up their minds about a case or a motion. We have on a former occasion explained digressions (252) as passages in which the orator departs for a while from his subject for some special purpose. They resemble episodes in epic poetry. In this way demonstrative passages may be introduced in deliberative or judicial orations by way of digressions ; and the praise of poetry in Cicero's oration for Archias is a case in point. But, in most of the instances here mentioned by Adams, praise and blame are intended by the speaker to produce definite effects on the present decision of judges or deliberative bodies. This constitutes them in different species of oratory, and brings them under the control of different laws of composition.

335. The ancients, in laying down their logical divisions of oratory, viewed the mind of the hearer as variously conditioned ; but in all those varieties they considered the hearer as deciding or speculating on *natural* principles alone—natural justice, natural usefulness, natural honor.

The moderns must add a fourth species of oratory to suit the peculiar state of mind of a hearer who views things in a *supernatural* light. This is **sacred** oratory, for which the ancients had no equivalent. We shall, therefore, treat in so many chapters of these four species : the deliberative, the forensic, the demonstrative, and the sacred.

Dr. Blair scarcely does justice to this distinction, which, as he nevertheless acknowledges, runs through all the ancient rhetorics and is followed by many moderns (Lect. xxvii.) He proposes what he calls a " more useful division, taken from the three great scenes of eloquence—from popular assemblies, the bar, and the pulpit." But, as Adams remarks, " we must reinstate demonstrative oratory in the place from which Dr. Blair has degraded it."

CHAPTER I.

DELIBERATIVE ORATORY.

336. **Deliberative oratory,** as has just been explained, supposes hearers who are expected to decide on a particular measure. The orator is to aim at *persuasion or dissuasion.* Now, either of these implies not only the conviction of the auditors' understanding, which is the task of forensic rhetoric as well, but also the moving of their will. Here, then, is a field which affords the speaker room for the display of all the resources of his art. And as the audience is usually either very numerous or, if small, highly intellectual, and the subjects may be of the greatest importance, the deliberative is evidently a most noble species of oratory. Cicero, while assigning to forensic eloquence the place of the highest difficulty, has assigned to the deliberative that of the greatest importance.

337. It is especially **important** in all lands in which the government is in whole or in part of the representative kind, and in none more than in the United States : " From the preponderance of democracy in the political constitutions of our country, deliberative assemblies are more numerous, and the objects of their deliberations are more diversified, than they ever have been in any other age or nation. From the formation of a national constitution to the management of a turnpike, every object of concern to more than one individual is transacted by deliberative bodies. National and State conventions for the purpose of forming constitutions, the Congress of the United States, the Legis-

latures of the several States, are all deliberative assemblies. Besides which, in our part of the country, every town, every parish or religious society, every association of individuals, incorporated for the purposes of interest, of education, of charity, or of science, forms a deliberative assembly, and presents opportunities for the exhibition of deliberative eloquence " (Adams, Lect. xi.)

338. In the precepts so far laid down for oratorical compositions in general, we have made frequent applications to the eloquence of popular assemblies ; we shall now add some further explanations. Quintilian suggests an appropriate **division of the subject**: " In persuading and dissuading three particulars are chiefly to be regarded : what is the subject of deliberation, who are those who deliberate, and what is the character of him who would influence their decision " (iii. 8). We shall treat these three particulars in as many articles, and add a fourth on the style suited to various classes of deliberative assemblies.

ARTICLE I. THE SUBJECTS OF DELIBERATION.

339. The **subjects of deliberation**, no matter how various in other respects, all agree in this one point : that they consider particular measures proposed for adoption. Here applies all that has been said (b. i. c. 1) on the *subject*, the *question*, the *state of the question*, etc. ; attention to those precepts cannot be inculcated with too much care. Having formed a clear idea of the motion before the meeting, of the measures to be advocated or opposed, the speaker must next consider by what arguments he can influence his hearers. For this purpose he may apply all the topics explained above ; in particular he will attend to the following points :

1. The **legality** of the measure discussed. We shall let

a statesman (J. Q. Adams) explain this matter : " The argument of legality must always be modified by the extent of authority with which the deliberative body is invested. In its nature it is an argument only applicable to the negative side of the question. It is an objection raised against the measure under consideration, as being contrary to law. It can, therefore, have no weight in cases where the deliberative body itself has the power of changing the law. Thus in a town meeting it would be a decisive objection against any measure proposed that it would infringe the law of the State. But in the Legislature of the commonwealth this would be no argument, because that body is empowered to change the law. Again, in the State Legislature a measure may be assailed as contrary to the law of the Union, and the objection, if well founded, must be fatal to the measure proposed, though it could have no influence upon a debate in Congress. There, however, the same argument may be adduced in a different form, if the proposition discussed interferes with any stipulation by treaty or with the Constitution of the United States. The argument of illegality, therefore, is equivalent to denial of the powers of the deliberating body. It is of great and frequent use in all deliberative discussions ; but it is not always that which is most readily listened to by the audience. Men are seldom inclined to abridge their own authority, and the orator who questions the competency of his hearers to act upon the subject in discussion must be supported by proof strong enough to control their inclinations as well as to convince their reason " (Lect. xi.)

2. The **possibility.** This also chiefly concerns the negative. For if it can be proved that a measure is impracticable, incompatible with a necessary advantage, out of the question, absurd, or stultifying to the body deliberating, etc., this would defeat the motion altogether. We may

remark, that which is very difficult or very unreasonable is usually treated as impossible.

3. Necessity, on the other hand, is an argument for the affirmative side ; if the measure is proved to be necessary or of extreme importance to the welfare of the public, it is thereby made imperative on the assembly to vote for it at any cost.

4. Utility or **expediency,** and the opposite quality of uselessness or inexpediency, if less decisive than the preceding topics, are far more frequently available. Comparatively few measures proposed in any assembly are either illegal, impossible, or absolutely necessary ; most of them are to be decided according to the preponderance of their advantages or disadvantages. Utility, therefore, is the topic most frequently to be consulted, and therefore Aristotle calls it the characteristic argument of deliberative oratory.

5. Justice or injustice, **honor** or disgrace, the peculiar topics of judicial and demonstrative eloquence, may often suggest powerful arguments in deliberation. They are then considered as special kinds of usefulness, as advantages which recommend the adoption or rejection of the motion.

6. Facility and difficulty of execution are likewise important factors towards persuasion or dissuasion ; the consideration of these is rarely to be neglected, as the auditors are readily influenced by these motives.

7. Lastly, the argument of **contingency** is sometimes available ; we mean the reflection that, whether one or other consequence shall follow, in either case a real advantage will be the result of the course which we recommend. Thus Cardinal Wolsey advises Cromwell :

> " Still in thy right hand carry gentle peace,
> To silence envious tongues. Be just, and fear not ;
> Let all the ends thou aim'st at be thy country's,
> Thy God's, and truth's ; then if thou fall'st, O Cromwell,
> Thou fall'st a blessed martyr."

Article II. The Characters of the Hearers.

340. Among the motives which may influence an audience, the consideration of *duty* is certainly the most sacred, and it should be the most powerful with all classes of men ; but, unfortunately, the reverse is the case with many. It is generally the least welcome and often the least effective with the hearers ; while *passion*, which should be the weakest motive, is generally the strongest, especially with coarser minds. *Honor* and *interest* occupy a middle region, the former being the nobler, the latter usually the more powerful.

341. But motives that will be most effective with one class of auditors will be of little avail with another. The orator must, therefore, **study the characters of his hearers,** that he may discriminate judiciously, and insist chiefly on such arguments as will act most powerfully on their minds and hearts.

No better suggestions can be given in this matter than the following instructions of Cicero to his son : " The discourse must be accommodated not only to the truth but to the taste of the hearers. Observe, then, first of all, that there are two different descriptions of men : the one rude and ignorant, who always set profit before honor ; the other polished and civilized, who prefer honor before everything. Urge, then, to the latter of these classes considerations of praise, honor, glory, fidelity, justice—in short, of every virtue. To the former present images of gain, emolument, thrift ; nay, in addressing this kind of men you must even allure them with the bait of pleasure. Pleasure, always hostile to virtue, always corrupting by fraudulent imitation the very nature of goodness herself, is yet most eagerly pursued by the worst of men, and by them often preferred not only to every instigation of honor, but even to the dictates of necessity. Remember, too, that mankind are more anxious to escape evil than to obtain good; less eager to acquire honor than avoid shame. Who has ever sought honor, glory, praise, or fame of any kind, with the same ardor that we fly from those most cruel afflictions, ignominy, contumely, and scorn ? Again, there is a class of men naturally inclined to honorable sentiments, but corrupted by evil education and corrupt opinions. Is it your purpose, then, to exhort or persuade, remember that the task before you is that of teaching how to obtain good and eschew evil. Are you speaking to men of liberal education, enlarge upon topics of praise and honor ; insist with the keenest earnestness upon those virtues which contribute to the common safety and advantage of mankind. But if you are discoursing to gross, ignorant, untutored minds, to them hold up profit, lucre, money-making, pleasure, and escape from pain. Deter them, also, by the prospect of shame and ignominy; for no man, however insensible to positive glory, is made of such impenetrable stuff as not to be vehemently moved by the dread of infamy and disgrace."

Of course in the same audience there may be persons of very different characters ; all classes are to be supplied with arguments suited to each.

342. In connection with diversity of audiences we may refer to Edmund Burke's speech at Bristol previous to the election of 1780. It is considerably different in style from his discourses in Parliament. Goodrich says of it (*British Eloquence,* p. 292): " This is, in many respects, the best speech of Mr. Burke for the study and imitation of a young orator. It is more simple and direct than any of his other speeches. It was addressed to merchants and business men ; and while it abounds quite as much as any of his productions in the rich fruits of political wisdom, and has occasionally very bold and striking images, it is less ambi-

tious in style and less profluent in illustration than his more elaborate efforts in the House of Commons. . . . Never was there a more manly and triumphant vindication." All this is certainly true. Why, then, did the orator fail of success? Because his arguments were too noble for his constituents, who could not appreciate his exalted motives. He might have stooped to their level and succeeded in persuading them. He preferred to lose the election, and his speech did him honor. But his failure confirms our precepts.

343. It is proper here to remark that the **consideration of utility** or expediency is far from being unworthy of the noblest minds, especially when, as representatives of the people, they are in duty bound to provide for the public welfare, and for the interests of their constituents particularly.

As **no unjust measure** is to be advocated, so neither is a **depraved motive** to be urged in support of any project. The end does not justify the means. Besides, even Cicero, without the light of Christian revelation, understood and taught his son that nothing is of solid advantage to the hearers but what is just and virtuous. Still, no one is in duty bound to aim on all occasions at the highest good nor to act upon the noblest motives.

344. **A great difficulty** often presents itself to the statesman in our day which was less formidable in past times. Parties have always existed in free states, and the decisions of the assemblies have usually been influenced by party spirit, irrespective of the arguments adduced. But in modern times the action of parties is probably more systematized in representative bodies. Legislators have their minds fully made up to stand by their leaders ; they come to the meetings to vote, not to deliberate. Many may well say with Sheridan : " I have heard speeches that have made

me change my opinion, but my vote never." Even in such circumstances a strong, *manly protest* may often be as efficient of good results as it is honorable to the speaker, though it may not influence the present vote. Thus Fox, by his eloquent oration against the rejection of Napoleon's overtures, totally refuted the arguments of Pitt, who was then prime minister ; the ballot after Fox's speech stood 265 against 64, in favor of Pitt, and it looked as if the discourse had been a total failure. But it was not : the House could not then afford to vote against the premier, but in a very short time the whole policy of England on this question was reversed. The two discourses of Fox and Pitt here referred to are masterpieces, and afford an excellent opportunity to study the handling of either side of an important question (see Goodrich, *Brit. Eloq.*)

ARTICLE III. THE ORATOR HIMSELF.

345. In our Introductory Chapter we explained what natural talents an orator should possess, and what mental and moral qualities he should have acquired ; all those endowments are of especial importance in deliberative eloquence.

The **knowledge** required of the speaker in this department is as varied as the classes of subjects on which he may have occasion to discourse. If he is a statesman he should thoroughly understand the philosophical principles which support the whole social fabric. Wild theories, novel experiments, peculiar notions, bold speculations will only jeopardize the public weal. Strong common sense, confirmed by the experience of ages, enlightened by the soundest philosophy, and irradiated by the supernatural light of Christian revelation, is absolutely needed to provide for the welfare of the people, especially in this age of restless social agitation. An extensive knowledge of history, enlightened political economy, constitutional law and jurisprudence, will be of great assistance.

346. **Virtue** is no less necessary for the popular orator. "What stands highest in the order of means," says Blair (Lect. xxxiv.), "is personal character and disposition. In order to be a truly eloquent or persuasive speaker nothing is more necessary than to be a virtuous man. This was a favorite position among the ancient rhetoricians: 'Non posse oratorem esse nisi virum bonum.' To find any such connection between virtue and one of the highest liberal arts must give pleasure; and it can, I think, be clearly shown that the connection here alleged is undoubtedly founded in truth and reason."

The *first* reason he assigns for this is that a speaker who is known to be honest, candid, and disinterested enjoys the confidence of his hearers and gains their sympathy for the side he espouses, while the corrupt and crafty politician is distrusted.

Secondly, virtue is most favorable to the prosecution of honorable studies; it inures the mind to industry, frees it from bad passions, and removes it from mean pursuits. For, as Quintilian remarks, "nothing is so violently torn and shattered by conflicting passions as a depraved heart. Amidst the distractions which it produces, what room is left for the cultivation of letters or the pursuits of any honorable art? No more, assuredly, than there is for the growth of corn in a field that is overrun with thorns and brambles."

Thirdly, and chiefly, from the fountain of real and genuine virtue are drawn those sentiments which will ever be most powerful in affecting the hearts of others. Bad as the world is, nothing has so great and so universal a command over the minds of men as virtue.

347. The virtues especially needed in this department of eloquence are : 1. Unflinching *fidelity to principles*, both moral and religious.

2. Sincere *patriotism—i.e.,* devotion to the true honor and real happiness of the country.

3. *Magnanimity*, disdaining whatever is at all objectionable in means and ends.

4. Conscientious *respect for the rights* of all men, even of the lowest.

5. Civil or *moral courage*, which is as noble as military courage and far less common.

348. There is a conspicuous **example** of this in a speech of Lord Mansfield, spoken before a mob that strove to overawe him in his court of justice: "Give me leave to take the opportunity of this great and respectable audience to let the whole world know all such attempts are vain. . . . We must not regard political consequences, how formidable soever they may be. If rebellion was the certain consequence we are bound to say, ' Fiat justitia, ruat cœlum !' . . . I wish popularity, but it is that popularity that follows, not that which is run after. It is that popularity which, sooner or later, never fails to do justice to the pursuit of noble ends by noble means. I will not do that which my conscience tells me is wrong upon this occasion to gain the huzzas of thousands, or the daily praise of all the papers which come from the press. I will not avoid doing what I think is right, though it should draw on me the whole artillery of libels. . . . The threats go farther than abuse—personal violence is denounced. I do not believe it. It is not the genius of the worst of men in this country, in the worst of times. But I have set my mind at rest. The last end that can happen to any man never comes too soon, if he falls in the support of the law and liberty of his country," etc. (*Brit. Eloq.*, p. 154).

It was by such qualities as we have enumerated that Demosthenes and Cicero, Chatham and Burke, O'Connell and Grattan, Webster and Calhoun, reached that high eminence of influence and renown which no amount of skill or elegance of style could of themselves have secured. Of Chatham in particular Macaulay remarked: "That which gave most effect to his declamation was the air of *sincerity*, of vehement feeling, of *moral elevation*, which belonged to all he said" (*Essays*, "Chatham").

ARTICLE IV. THE STYLE.

349. As **style** is the peculiar manner in which a writer or speaker expresses his thoughts, it will, of course, vary with the circumstances of the orator, with the nature of his subject, and especially with the character of the audience to which he is laboring to communicate his views. Severely exact in his discussion of law before learned judges, rich and magnificent in demonstrative orations, the speaker before deliberative assemblies will adapt himself to the varieties of his subjects and of his hearers. It will, therefore, be useful to consider style in connection with these different circumstances.

§ 1. Speeches before Promiscuous Assemblies.

350. To this class belong especially addresses at mass-meetings, at political gatherings, and the better class of such as are called stump-speeches.

The **leading qualities** of all these should be:

1. *Sound sense*, solid thought, no trifling with the common sense of the hearers, nor idle display of oratorical beauties, especially on very grave occasions, when men are too earnest to be pleased by ornaments

2. Striking *clearness*, no intricate reasonings, but facts, comparisons, anecdotes, ready wit, all expressed in lucid, forcible, pictured language.

3. *Warm feelings*, but only such as the audience can be made to share. Popularity is most readily achieved by expressing in more apt language than would occur to the listener himself thoughts and emotions already lurking in his mind. Thus we win first, and next lead, our hearers. The more a promiscuous crowd is composed of the rude and uneducated the more it will be swayed by passion and sympathy. Still, even a mob will admire striking exhibitions of courage and firmness, and despise cowardice, in those whose duty it is to restrain its violence and maintain public order and peace. But whether severe measures or a prudent forbearance be determined upon, a calm tone and imperturbable good-nature, with a seasoning of humor and the absence of all bitterness, are powerful aids for the popular orator.

4. *Boldness and power*, even of lungs, gesture, tone, and style, are necessary in addressing numerous popular meetings. Moreover, only strong arguments, too, are appreciated on such occasions. "Not a voice like a flute, a narrow breast, a dwarfish stature, philosophical gestures, and eyes modestly cast down will enrapture the masses in the open air. The people do not appreciate eloquence and genius except under the emblems of power," says the French rhetorician Cormenin. But boldness does not mean arrogance ; a mob expects more deferential manners in its orator than a senate does.

351. An English lawyer, Mr. E. W. Cox, gives some useful hints on what he calls "the Oratory of the Platform" (*The Arts of Writing, Reading, and Speaking*). He is of opinion that the first of the above rules is of minor importance when ladies make up the bulk of the audience.

Pathos, beautiful language, a pleasing voice, refined manner, and a graceful appearance he declares to be sufficient with such hearers. Even if this were all that such hearers would appreciate, it is not all that his sense of duty will require of the speaker. Besides, Mr. Cox's view is hardly plausible.

§ 2. Speeches before Select Audiences.

352. We refer here especially, but not exclusively, to legislative bodies, such as the British Parliament, the Congress of the United States, the Legislatures of the several States, etc. Of speeches made in such bodies we may distinguish **three classes**: 1. *Reports* of committees, and all such writings and addresses as are supposed to convey important information ; presidential messages belong to this division ; 2. *Formal speeches* on any measure discussed ; 3. Mere *business remarks*.

353. Those of the **first kind** should be especially prudent, exact, moderate in tone, concise, lucid. Those of the **second kind** should be :

(*a*) *Telling*, by hitting the precise point, which is often done by laying down clearly the real state of the question.

(*b*) *Fresh, lively, and rapid*, to relieve tedium, except on occasions of unusual gravity. Comparatively few men can command the attention of such an audience during a long speech. Even of Edmund Burke it is said that he often spoke to empty benches, for this very reason, that his orations were not lively and rapid ; but they were lectures of the didactic kind and wearied his hearers. Especially let no one bring an argument a thirtieth time, nor even a second time, after it has been handled by a much abler speaker.

(*c*) *Ready and pliable*, as various circumstances may require. This does not exclude most careful preparation, even writing the discourse, as all should do who have not had much practice in public speaking; but it requires a certain readiness in adapting the prepared speech to the new phases of the debate.

(*d*) *Discreet*, so as not to speak on every question, nor refute every objection at full length, nor become pathetic on trifles.

(*e*) *Parliamentary*, observant of the rules of the parliamentary code—*i.e.*, of such approved customs as have obtained the force of law in organized meetings.

(*f*) Above all, *solid and sound* in facts and reasonings.

354. **Speeches of the third kind**—*i.e.*, mere business remarks—constitute a most important part of deliberative eloquence. They may appear easy and unworthy of attention, but they are just the reverse. Much of the most important work of political bodies is transacted by means of such business remarks; and he who succeeds in this manner of eloquence becomes a power in a legislature. To succeed in this, (*a*) never attempt a *speech* when a pointed remark will do; (*b*) combine great brevity with great clearness; (*c*) never quibble or cause useless delays; (*d*) be sure to offend no one, nor to humble any by unnecessary corrections and criticisms. In connection with this precept we may quote these few words of Henry Clay's reply to John Randolph in the House of Representatives, 1824: " Sir, I am growing old. I have had some little measure of experience in public life, and the result of that experience has brought me to this conclusion : that when business, of whatever nature, is to be transacted in a deliberative assembly or in private life, courtesy, forbearance, and moderation are best calculated to bring it to a successful conclusion," etc. (*Amer. Eloq.*, ii. 318). (*e*) Be not anxious to secure every little advantage, reserving yourself for more important oc-

casions ; (*f*) never rise but when you can do some clear good.

Still, it must be acknowledged that, to become a great debater, **copious practice** is of the utmost importance. "Scarcely any person," says Macaulay (*Essays*, "Chatham"), "has ever become so without long practice and many failures. It was by slow degrees, as Burke said, that the late Mr. Fox became the most brilliant and powerful debater that ever Parliament saw. Mr. Fox himself attributed his own success to the resolution which he formed when very young of speaking, well or ill, at least once every night. 'During five whole sessions,' he used to say, 'I spoke every night but one ; and I regret that I did not speak on that night, too.' Indeed, it would be difficult to name any great debater, except Mr. Stanley, whose knowledge of the science of parliamentary defence resembles an instinct, who has not made himself a master of his art at the expense of his audience."

355. **Models** of speeches before select audiences abound ; *e.g.*, Cicero's First Philippic, his oration for Marcellus, Lord Chesterfield's speech against licensing gin-shops, and most of the speeches of Chatham, Grattan, Fox, and Pitt collected by Goodrich in his *British Eloquence ;* also many speeches of Webster, Calhoun, Clay, Patrick Henry in *American Eloquence.* For brief extracts see *Sargent's Standard Speaker*, part iii., Senatorial.

356. One of the best means by which young men may prepare themselves for the practice of deliberative oratory are well-conducted **debating societies.** On these Dr. Blair makes some very sensible observations. " The meetings," he says (Lect. xxxiv.), "which I have now in my eye are to be understood of those academical associations where a moderate number of young gentlemen, who are carrying on their studies and are connected by some affinity in the fu-

ture pursuits which they have in view, assemble privately in order to improve one another and to prepare themselves for those public exhibitions which may afterwards fall to their lot. As for those public and promiscuous societies in which multitudes are brought together, who are often of low stations and occupations, who are joined by no common bond of union, except an absurd rage for public speaking, and have no other object in view but to make a show of their supposed talents, they are institutions not merely of an useless but of an hurtful nature. They are in great hazard of proving seminaries of licentiousness, petulance, faction, and folly. They mislead those who, in their own callings, might be useful members of society into fantastic plans of making a figure on subjects which divert their attention from their proper business and are widely remote from their sphere of life.

" Even the allowable meetings into which students of oratory form themselves stand in need of direction in order to render them useful. If their subjects of discourse be improperly chosen ; if they maintain extravagant or indecent topics ; if they indulge themselves in loose and flimsy declamation which has no foundation in good sense, or accustom themselves to speak pertly on all subjects without due preparation, they may improve one another in petulance, but in no other thing, and will infallibly form themselves to a very faulty and vicious taste in speaking. I would, therefore, advise all who are members of such societies, in the first place, to attend to the choice of their subjects ; that they be useful and manly, either formed on the course of their studies or on something that has relation to morals and taste, to action and life. In the second place, I would advise them to be temperate in the practice of speaking ; not to speak too often, nor on subjects where they are ignorant or unripe, but only when they have proper materials for a discourse, and have digested and thought of the subject beforehand. In the third place, when they do speak they should study always to keep good sense and persuasion in view rather than an ostentation of eloquence ; and for this end I would, in the fourth place, repeat the advice which I gave in a former lecture, that they should always choose that side of the question to which, in their own judgment, they are most inclined, as the right and the true side, and defend it by such arguments as seem to them most solid. By these means they will take the best method of forming themselves gradually to a manly, correct, and persuasive manner of speaking."

CHAPTER II.

FORENSIC ORATORY.

357. In deliberative and demonstrative oratory the masterpieces of the ancients are still in our day perfect models for the imitation of aspiring youths. It is not so in matters of forensic oratory. For a vast change has come over tribunals since Christianity has enlightened the world on the dignity and the rights of every individual man. It will be useful to point out some differences thence arising.

358. 1. Among the ancients the pardoning power was vested in the judges; the amount of the punishment was left to their discretion. Hence a principal aim of forensic orators was to move the court to pity the defendant; **appeals to the passions** of the judges were frequent and vehement; the accused appeared in mourning, surrounded by his sorrowing family, and humbled himself to the dust even while most loudly protesting his innocence. All this is changed now. The power of pardoning has been transferred to the executive, to the governors of our States; the jury in criminal cases has only one question to decide—viz., Is the accused guilty or not guilty? The judge, on their verdict, awards the sentence. In cases less than capital he may have some discretionary power to proportion the penalty to the degree of the offence; but even this power is limited. In cases of life and death the judge is only the living voice of the law. Adams compares the administration of justice to a strict syllogism, of which the written law forms the major proposition, the verdict of the jury the

minor, and the sentence of the court the conclusion. The
law says that the wilful murderer shall suffer death ; the
jury decides that A. is a wilful murderer ; the judge condemns him to suffer death.

The obvious consequence of this change in our courts is
that the modern lawyer has little occasion to appeal to the
passions ; in criminal cases he must manage his pleadings
upon principles not only different from those followed by
the ancients, but often altogether opposite. He must appear to be fully convinced (even should he on any particular occasion have strong doubts on the subject) that the
court looks to nothing but the justice of his case, and he
must direct all his attention to establish this point. That
difference concerns chiefly the advocate for the defence.

359. **2.** A second difference affects more directly the
prosecution. Among the ancients the accuser had full scope
to bring up against a culprit any crime of his whole life.
With us he must confine himself to **the indictment**; he cannot advance a step beyond the written accusation, planned
with technical accuracy. Every charge must be precise
and specific. Cicero accumulates against Verres all his
misdemeanors of fourteen years. In our courts most of
his charges would have been inadmissible, or not within the
indictment. His official misconduct would have been cog-
nizable by one tribunal, his acts of cruelty by another, his
thefts by a third.

ARTICLE I. THE SUBJECTS OF CONTROVERSY.

360. The controversies that may be brought before a
court of justice are necessarily either *of individuals among
themselves,* or *between individuals and the public power.* By
public power we do not mean the state as the owner of
property, for as such it is treated as an individual before the

courts ; but we mean the right of the state to punish of-
fenders in sanction of the law.

Every individual man, woman, and child has certain in-
alienable rights held from the Creator Himself independent-
ly of any social organization. There are, besides, civil
rights which result from social union. The state guards
and protects both these classes of rights by her *civil code* of
laws. When individuals are interfered with in the enjoyment of these rights by other individuals a **private wrong**
is thus committed, and the person's thus injured may call
upon the state for aid in obtaining redress of the wrong.
The state answers this appeal through her *civil courts*.

But a wrong committed against an individual may often
be injurious to the state itself, to that public order essential
to its existence. The state protects herself against such
public wrongs by her *criminal code*, by which she forbids
certain acts as crimes or misdemeanors, and appoints punishments, which she inflicts through her *criminal courts*. A
breach of promise, a non-payment of debt, is a private
wrong ; the state may be called upon to redress it, provided
the plaintiff first prove its existence by bringing suit in his
own name and at his own risk before the competent tribunals. But in public wrongs the cause is adopted as that
of the nation, and the punishment of the offender is prose-
cuted in the name of the sovereign power. Select bodies
of men are from time to time appointed to inquire into all
such offences committed in their vicinity, and to present them
to the competent courts for trial. The accusation drawn
up by this *grand jury* is called a *bill of indictment*, and the
prosecution is managed by a permanent public officer. The
person accused is then arraigned, and usually pleads that
he is *not guilty* of the offence charged against him. It is
then for the attorney-general, or the person conducting the
prosecution, to prove both the fact and the law—*i.e.*, to prove

that the culprit committed the act, and did so in violation of the criminal code. If the accusation fail in the proof of either the accused is acquitted (Adams, Lect. xii., xiii.)

361. Civil and criminal wrongs require from the orator at the bar very **different methods of proceeding.**

In civil suits the court is treated as absolutely impartial between the parties litigant : justice holds an even balance. Written testimony and the evidence of the complainant himself are received, while they are rejected in criminal suits ; everything is done to discover on which side is the better claim.

In criminal suits the process is very different ; the chief care of the law is that no innocent person shall be punished. Criminal justice holds an uneven balance ; unlike the blind pagan divinity, she throws the weight of mercy into the scale of the accused. She jealously excludes from the other scale all that is of a doubtful nature ; for she prefers that ten guilty should escape rather than that one innocent person should suffer. She directs juries to disregard strong probability and yield to nothing but certainty in finding a verdict against the culprit.

362. Hence the task of the **attorney for the prosecution** is much more difficult than that of the advocate for the defence. The former must establish every point to a certainty ; he must confine himself to matters of fact ; he cannot travel out of the case to consider the antecedents of the accused ; he cannot go a step outside of the indictment.

The ancients directed both parties to study the facts, the will and the power of the accused. The prosecution is to deal with the facts alone. But **the defence** may draw arguments from all these topics. On the question of *fact* the advocate may adduce everything that may throw doubt on the proofs of the prosecution ; for a real doubt of guilt is equivalent to a vindication of innocence. Considering the *will* of his client, he may plead his peaceful and virtuous antecedents, and show that he had no interest in committing the crime. From the topic of *power* he may attempt to prove an *alibi*, and thus decide the acquittal. But he must establish it clearly ; for this plea is so often abused that it is generally looked upon as a desperate refuge of an all but convicted felon, who uses his friends and accomplices to save him by false testimony from the hands of justice.

Public wrongs are distinguished into two classes, *personal* and *official*, tried by distinct tribunals, as will be explained in the next article.

ARTICLE II. VARIOUS TRIBUNALS.

363. We have referred in the preceding article to *civil* and *criminal* courts or tribunals. The functions of both may be combined in the same persons, as they actually are in our supreme courts ; but even then the distinction explained is of the highest importance, as the union of the same jurisdictions in the same tribunal does not affect the differences pointed out in the rules of the evidence, in the maxims of law, and the modes of practice peculiar to each.

364. **For official wrongs**—that is, for wrongs committed by officers in their official capacity—the *Senate* of the United States, or of the particular State against which the wrong is committed, is the proper tribunal. In both cases the lower House originates the impeachment ; the Senate judges, and, when the guilt is proved, removes the culprit from office and disqualifies him from holding any office of honor, trust, or profit ; but it goes no further. The same person may be afterwards tried by indictment before another court, for the same crime for which he has been condemned on impeachment.

Impeachments are rare occurrences, but they must be here noticed, as subject to special laws. In the lower House the question whether the impeachment shall be resolved upon is deliberative, and not judicial. Great care has to be taken that impeachments be not made the engines of party. If the impeachment is voted, a committee of the House is usually appointed to manage the prosecution. The Senate sit as judges both of law and fact ; two-thirds of the members must concur to condemn. The principles of ordinary criminal jurisprudence are modified on such occasions. The judges are less rigorously bound to confine themselves to the prescriptions of the law.

" Moral and political considerations may contribute, to some degree, to the formation of their judgment," says Adams, which is correct if interpreted in favor of the defendant. These motives can, of course, not be urged to procure a condemnation as long as the guilt is not fully proved. In the impeachment of Warren Hastings the English Parliament determined to adhere to the strict rules of legal evidence, thus making an important change in English justice.

365. In the **ordinary courts,** whether criminal or civil, the judicial powers are divided between the *judge* and the *jury*. The radical distinction of the common law is that the jury decides upon the fact and the judge upon the law. But fact and law are often inseparably united. For instance, when the question is to be decided whether the culprit is guilty of libel, this involves the question, What is libel in the sense of the law ? After the parties have argued the case, the judges are in the constant practice of addressing the jury, and stating to them the law, with its application to the facts upon trial. The judge in doing so cannot always avoid giving his opinion on the facts. The jury decides not only whether the culprit has uttered cer-

tain words, but also whether those words, under the circumstances, constitute what the law designates as *libel*. Thus
they give their verdict upon *law and fact*. The following
is given by Adams as an unequivocal rule to direct the
lawyer in the management of his cause (Lect. xii.) : " If
any question of fact is involved in the controversy the
cause must go to the jury. But if the parties have no dis-
pute upon the facts, and 'their contest is merely upon the
operation of the law, it is within the exclusive province of
the judge." Still, he adds : " Hence the parties often have
it at their option whether they will take a trial by the court
or by the jury ; and there are certain forms of pleading
suited to produce an *issue in law*, and others that are adapted to an *issue in fact*." The **pleas** or pleadings here spoken
of are the parts of a lawsuit which are written—the charge
and the answer, drawn up before the case is orally discussed
in the court. By means of these papers the exact point is
settled on which the parties disagree, or *join issue*, as it is
called. The pleadings, in the popular sense of the term,
are the speeches made by the counsels.

366. In an **argument to the court** the orator must give a
disquisition on law ; in a **speech to the jury** a discussion of
the evidence. Both aim at conviction, not persuasion, but
by different means. To the bench is suited profound and
accurate reasoning ; to the jury copious elucidation. To
the judge results are presented ; to the jury principles may
have to be unfolded. The counsel must remember that the
judges are a learned and the jury not a learned body of
men. In fact, all the learned professions are either exempt-
ed or excluded from serving on juries.

367. Much of the skill of the lawyers in a case before a
jury will be employed in **sifting the evidence**. The examination and cross-examination of witnesses is of itself
one of the severest tests of a counsel's talents and ability,

Sometimes witnesses are unwilling to reveal the truth ; at other times they try to put their own gloss upon the facts ; again, though perfectly honest, they are prejudiced against either side ; or they are too ignorant to state what they know and what they are willing enough to reveal. In criminal cases all the testimony is oral ; the truth must be gathered on the spot, and little or no time can be taken to prepare a speech. Not only the wording but even the plan of the whole pleading must be extemporaneous. The very state of the question may have to be determined on the spot.

368. These circumstances make the oratory of the bar at present the most difficult department of eloquence, while among the ancients its especial difficulty arose from the management of the pathetic. There are other **sources of embarrassment** peculiar to forensic pleading in all ages. The demonstrative orator stands alone without antagonist, takes his own time to prepare, and is usually listened to by friends and sympathizers. The deliberative speaker stands one among many in defence of his position ; he usually commands the sympathies of a numerous party ; his defeat is not to be a personal disgrace ; even if he fails to obtain the vote of his hearers he may be honored by the course of subsequent events. The lawyer has none of these advantages : the property, liberty, reputation, and even the life of his client depend mainly on his effort ; his own honor depends on the same ; a sharp-sighted adversary watches all his movements ; an assertion, a denial, a concession, may be fatal to his cause ; learned and able judges, jealous of their own honor, quick to detect a flaw in his argument, fastidious to trivial declamation, must be thoroughly convinced of the justice of his cause. The client's unreason- able prejudices in his own favor are sure to aggravate the difficulties of the situation ; success looks like the natural

course of justice, and defeat like the conviction of incompetency. Still, this incessant collision sharpens all the faculties of the orator; it draws a sharp line of demarcation between spurious and genuine merit, and in the course of time leaves, not the intriguing party, but the truly able counsel, undisputed master of the admiration and the patronage of the public.

369. Diversity in the character of the courts will require diversity in the **style** of the orator addressing them.

1. To a court consisting of **one or more judges** he must speak with the respect due to superiors; he may use technical terms; he should avoid all appearance of declamation, speaking usually with simplicity and directly to the point. Still, on occasions of special importance he may well rise with his subject and show himself possessed of genuine eloquence. For an instance in point we may refer to Webster's Speech on Girard's Will (vol. vi. p. 132). The speech made a deep impression upon the public at the time; in some portions the orator reaches a lofty tone of eloquence. (See pp. 153 to 163.)

2. Before **a court of unusual solemnity,** as in the case of a political impeachment, all the resources of oratory find an appropriate field for their fullest exhibition. Of this species of eloquence no grander specimens can be cited than the speeches of Æschines and Demosthenes on the Crown among the Greeks, of Cicero against Verres among the Romans, of Edmund Burke against Warren Hastings in England. This last oration has been characterized as the greatest intellectual effort made before the British Parliament. See the oration and the judicious remarks of Goodrich in his sketch of Edmund Burke (*Brit. Eloq.*)

3. To a **jury** the lawyer should talk kindly and politely, as to equals. He should carefully weigh their amount of intelligence and information, which is often rather limited.

In such a case he must make matters very clear to them, carefully avoiding the use of technical terms, and seeking the aid of familiar comparisons. He should rather talk *with* his jury than *at* them, making himself, as it were, the thirteenth man of their body; light, lively, plain talk, without frivolity, is often the most effective (see Cox's *Art of Reading, Writing, and Speaking*, pp. 264, etc.) Of course cases of special importance will require a special elevation in the style. Webster's speech in Knapp's trial on the murder of Captain Joseph White (vol. vi. p. 42) is probably the most brilliant and thorough specimen of this kind in the history of the American bar. Erskine's speeches in the case of Paine's *Age of Reason*, and his plea in behalf of Lord Gordon, are distinguished models. His speech on the Rights of Juries may be read to advantage in connection with this matter.

ARTICLE III. THE ORATOR HIMSELF.

370. As justice is administered in modern times, the principal **sources of a lawyer's success** are a character for probity, a thorough knowledge of the law, and an untiring devotedness to the labors of his profession.

371. I. **Probity.** No honorable man will maintain that money-making is the only or chief object of a lawyer's career. It would fare ill with a country if such gain were the highest aspiration of the legal profession. True, even in such a land some might be honest, on the principle that honesty is the best policy; and they would not be disappointed, for the confidence of their clients would be to them a great advantage. But when honesty is pursued simply as a policy and for no higher motive, it will not be a sufficient security for many against the numberless temptations to unfair dealing which beset the lawyer's path. And still his probity is to be one of the chief protections of

his fellow-citizens. Whether, then, we consider his own welfare or the public interest, probity is of the highest importance in the forensic orator.

372. This virtue imposes upon him some important duties : 1. With regard to **his acceptance of the cases** on which he is consulted, he must remember that he is never allowed to co-operate in any injustice.

(*a*) *In criminal matters* he may advocate the cause of any culprit, however guilty ; and, once he has undertaken a case, he must give his client the benefit of his earnest exertions to save him from the hands of the law. For he assumes this obligation in virtue of the implicit contract existing between client and advocate ; and the public good requires that the guilty shall not be punished by any private man, but only by the regular course of public justice. But no lawyer is justified in acting the part of an accuser against a person known to be innocent, unless it be for the purpose of promoting the vindication of such innocence.

(*b*) *In civil cases—i.e.*, when property or titles are disputed—if the claim is doubtful the lawyer may advocate either side, so that the court may decide the matter. But if he knows for certain that the claim of his client is invalid he cannot promote it, for he would thus injure the lawful claimant. He cannot even justly lend his assistance to obtain a compromise, unless this be the less of two unavoidable evils ; but he must urge his client to abandon his unjust claim altogether. As far back as A.D. 1274 a law was made by Philip III., of France, requiring of lawyers an oath " to undertake the management of none but just causes, to defend these with diligence and fidelity, and to abandon them as soon as their injustice became apparent." Our attorneys and counsellors practising in all the courts of the United States are under like engagement to do no wrong and to suffer knowingly none to be committed. Our judges, too, are sworn to administer justice according to the law, and our juries to give their verdict according to the evidence.

373. **2. Justice to his client** requires from the lawyer that he shall—

(*a*) Use ordinary diligence to defend all his rights ;

(*b*) Use all proper expedition, so as not unnecessarily to protract the suit ;

(*c*) Put him to no unnecessary expense ; *e.g.*, by holding out deceitful hopes ;

(*d*) Keep his secrets.

374. **3. Justice to the adversary** requires that—

(*a*) The lawyer shall use no fraud nor allow any to be used in the case, such as false witnesses, forged documents, misquotations of laws, etc. ;

(*b*) He shall cause the adversary no expense which cannot be of benefit to his own client.

If a counsellor has, by unjust practices, deliberately violated the rights of any party, he is bound in honor and justice to see that the wrong be redressed, even at his own expense, if necessary ; and this though he may not have derived any personal profit from his injustice.

375. II. **A thorough knowledge of law.** As the legal profession constitutes in every land a most influential body of men, it is of the highest importance to the nation that the level of their intellectual attainments be placed as high as circumstances allow. In older countries a considerable degree of proficiency in classical studies is required before students can enter on the study of law ; and thus none but well-disciplined minds are admitted to this important field of labor. The same rule is observed with the leading members of the civil service and with all the learned professions. The higher studies, too, are extensive and thorough

in proportion. In our republic, while, owing to various unavoidable causes, the legal requirements are very limited, much has been done by private exertion and by public patronage to supply aspirants to the professions with all the advantages for mental culture which older communities inherit from remote ancestors. The consequence has been that many of our statesmen and jurists have attained to the most honorable eminence in their departments. Others with inferior opportunities of study, but with uncommon talents and untiring labor, have also gained great distinction.

But all men will acknowledge that, whether attained by uncommon industry or by favorable opportunities, a thorough knowledge of jurisprudence is a first requisite for success at the bar ; any one who fails to obtain this knowledge cannot reasonably hope for distinction in his profession. As the *common law* forms the foundation of our jurisprudence, and is itself founded upon the intimate knowledge of the natural rights of man, lawyers should be masters of the science of *Ethics.* Now, this study supposes a clear apprehension of the most important portions of *Metaphysics* and a thorough understanding of all that *Logic* can teach to direct reasoning and discover fallacies. In all these acquisitions classical studies provide the best preparation that mankind has yet been able to discover. The use which a lawyer may make, in his profession, of the Latin and Greek languages is inconsiderable compared to the mental training which classical studies afford as a preparation for higher pursuits. (See *Amer. Catholic Quarterly Review* for January, 1885, p. 18, etc., p. 140, etc.)

376. III. Untiring **devotedness to the labors of his profession.** Genius has often been defined as the power of concentrating all one's attention on a matter. This definition, though not altogether correct, is at least suggestive of

much truth. Without such application no great success can ever be achieved ; this general rule holds in particulaɪ for forensic practice. But the most devoted laborers sometimes fall into an error which frustrates all their efforts. They overload themselves with business, and cannot do justice to what they undertake. They bring ruin upon their clients and dishonor upon themselves ; they remain superficial in their views, unreliable in their knowledge. "Thus some," says Cicero (*De Or.*, ii. 24), "while they would have people believe that their practice is very extensive and that they are hurried from one case to another, attempt to plead causes which they do not understand. . . . Now, no one can fail to disgrace himself by speaking of subjects which he does not know ; and thus while he makes little account of being called ignorant, which in reality is the greater fault, he incurs at the same time the reproach of incompetency, which he is most anxious to avoid."

377. **To study a particular case** the lawyer may take some useful hints from what Cicero says of his own practice (*De Or.*, ii. 24): "It is my custom to have every client explain to me his own case. I see to it that no one else be present at the interview, so that he may speak with perfect freedom. Then I take his opponent's part, to make him defend his own ; and thus I get from him all the information he can give After he is gone I conceive myself in three characters with perfect impartiality, putting myself in my own, in my opponent's, and in the judge's place. Whatever argument seems to present more advantage than disadvantage I select for treatment. What I find to contain more harm than good I leave alone and determine to shun with care. Thus I gain this advantage, that I choose my arguments at one time and develop them at another, while most speakers, relying on their own talents, attempt

to do both at once." Every document bearing upon the case should be carefully scrutinized; the places themselves connected with disputed facts should be visited by the advocates in person; legal authorities should be diligently read; precedents should be found and compared in detail with the case in hand, etc., etc. But such matters belong to a course of law studies rather than to rhetorical precepts.

CHAPTER III.

DEMONSTRATIVE ORATORY.

378. The relation which **demonstrative** bears to the other species of oratory is analogous to that which poetry bears to the other kinds of literature. In literature poetry regards most directly the beautiful, and less directly the useful. It is the same with demonstrative oratory. While all oratory belongs to the liberal arts, the demonstrative species belongs to them pre-eminently. To despise it implies an absence of good taste ; a man might as well despise poetry, music, and painting. Like all these, it is intended for the *contemplative* mind ; by this characteristic quality it is distinguished from forensic and deliberative speaking, which are intended to lead minds to a logical and desired conclusion.

ARTICLE I. AN HISTORICAL SKETCH OF DEMONSTRATIVE ORATORY.

379. The **ancient Greeks and Romans,** who appreciated so keenly the beautiful, held demonstrative eloquence in high esteem. They composed panegyrics upon the gods, upon illustrious benefactors of their countries, upon those who had bravely fallen in battle, and even upon cities and countries which had achieved renown. To praise departed relatives and friends was so honored a custom that even Roman emperors have discoursed on such occasions. It was but natural that those who were devoted to this cultivation of rich encomium should occasionally introduce passages of this species, as *digressions,* in elegant

orations of the deliberative and the forensic kinds. Thus Cicero, in his plea for his old professor, *the poet Archias,* pronounces an elaborate panegyric on poetry. He openly tells his judges in his introduction that he is going to depart from the usual course of pleading, and assigns as his reasons for doing so the peculiar character of his client, the literary taste of the prætor himself, who presided, and the unusual concourse of literary men attracted by the occasion. He first proves by legal argument that Archias had become a citizen, and then enters upon his eulogium in a very different strain.

Demonstrative oratory continued to flourish during the **decadence** of classical taste, and produced some masterpieces worthy of the golden era. Such were the panegyric of Trajan by the younger Pliny, and the magnificent discourses of St. John Chrysostom on St. Ignatius, on SS. Maximin and Juventin, etc.

380. **In modern times** panegyrical eloquence has been carried to its highest perfection—higher far than among the ancients—by such orators as Bossuet, Fléchier, Massillon, and Bourdaloue **in France.** By these it was applied to proclaim the praise of God, his angels and his saints, and the illustrious dead. Besides, the French Academy and other learned bodies require orations of this species from their new members, and they have sometimes proposed such compositions for honorable competition among the learned of the land, awarding a rich prize to the successful competitor. But demonstrative oratory, with its tropical flowers, never took root in the colder soil of **England.** There the saints and angels had been dethroned by the Reformation from their exalted dignity, or, as Adams expresses it, " The Protestant communities know too little of those 'orders bright,' those supernatural intelligences, to honor them with that panegyric to which, by their rank and

dignity in the scale of being, they may, perhaps, be entitled." "The funeral oration," ne remarks, "is the only oratorical form in which they (the English) have been accustomed to utter eulogy, and even that discourse has rather been devoted to soothe private sorrow or to gratify friendship than to testify public gratitude or admiration . . . The British poets, indeed, have often spoken, with exquisite pathos and beauty, the language of eulogy ; but In the whole compass of English literature there is not one effusion of eloquence which, like those of Isocrates, Cicero, and Pliny in Greece and Rome, or those of Bossuet, Fléchier, Massillon, and Thomas in France, immortalize at once the speaker and his subject, and interweave in one immortal texture the glories of achievement with those of celebration." It is no wonder, then, that Blair has entirely omitted to treat of demonstrative oratory, and has thus degraded, as Adams expresses it, this noble species of literature. Still, the germs of panegyrical eloquence are sown by nature in the heart of man, and we are not surprised to find in the speeches of Edmund Burke, Chatham, and others many a bright flower of praise springing, as it were, unbidden from the flooded spring of their rich imaginations. Such are Burke's eulogy of Howard, of Lord Bathurst, of Charles Townsend, of Sir George Saville, and, above all, of the American people, which last Adams calls "the fairest and most glowing tribute of panegyric that was ever uttered in their honor" (Lect. x.)

381. But the more genial soil of the **United States** has restored vigor to the germs which never took deep root in England. "On the anniversary of our independence," says Adams, "every city and almost every village of this Union resounds with formal discourses, strictly belonging to the demonstrative class of the ancients. There are many other occasions, public and private, upon which we are accus-

tomed to assemble in churches and hear orations of the demonstrative kind. Many of the performances at all our public commencements are of the same description. Funeral orations, as distinct from funeral sermons, are very common amongst us ; and in general the public taste for this species of public oratory is a distinguishing feature in our character." Since Adams' time another variety of such orations has grown into general favor and become an important feature in our national habits. I refer to elegant lectures given in public halls, to select or promiscuous audiences, on all sorts of historical, philosophical, literary, and scientific subjects. Scarcely a speaker has of late years attained to distinction among us who has not appeared upon this popular stage of eloquence; and some distinguished writers of England have come to this country to give courses of such entertainments to an appreciative public.

ARTICLE II. PANEGYRICS.

382. While demonstrative oratory embraces all discourses addressed to unconcerned hearers, it has most generally been applied, by ancients and moderns alike, in praise of deserving parties at the most solemn meetings of an admiring people. Hence has arisen the name of **panegyrics**, from the Greek term πανήγυρις, which designated an assembly of the whole people for a solemn festival, as was the gathering at the Olympic games. It is true that *blame* as well as *praise* is always mentioned as proper matter for this oratory, but we apprehend that it is so mentioned for the philosophical reason that *contrariorum eadem est ratio*— "contraries bear the same relations"—than for the sake of much practical application. Blame is rarely capable of rich development, nor is it in the spirit of Christian eloquence to dwell on blame for any but such necessary

practical purposes as at once transfer the speech to another kind of oratory.

383. An obvious question here presents itself : What is the **practical usefulness of panegyrical orations ?** We have said before that they possess the same advantages as all the other productions of the most elegant arts, of poetry, music, painting, sculpture, etc.; but they have an immediate and special usefulness of a very exalted nature. Besides the honor which they enable us to pay to those to whom honor is due, in itself a most worthy purpose, they contribute powerfully to maintain in a nation a lofty standard of public and private worth, and in particular of heroic virtue. It was the maintenance of this high esteem for real merit, more, perhaps, than anything else, that raised the Greeks and Romans to the lofty eminence which they hold and ever will hold among the nations ; and it was when that standard was lowered that both countries began to decline.

Heroism is unselfish ; it seeks the good of others rather than its own, public rather than private advantages (Arist., *Rhet.*, i. 9). But to make the sacrifice of selfishness man needs encouragement of a lofty nature. The approbation, the applause of their fellow-men has always been felt to be among the most precious rewards which prompt exalted spirits to deathless achievements. Panegyrical orations eminently and directly provide this applause, and as such are highly useful.

384. Meanwhile it is of the highest importance that the **standard or rule by which exalted virtue is estimated** should be of the purest kind, free from base alloy. "I know of no function," said Mr. Windham in his speech on Pitt's Funeral, "requiring to be discharged under a sense of more solemn obligation than that which relates to the adjudication of national honors." And still in this same speech he furnishes a striking specimen of a wrong stand-

ard, which appears the more debased when contrasted with the lofty standard advocated by Demosthenes. It had been moved in the House of the British Parliament (January 27, 1806) that the remains of the statesman, William Pitt, be interred at the public charge, and a monument be erected to his memory in Westminster Abbey. The motion was opposed, among others by Mr. Windham, who began his speech as follows : " However painful I may feel the situation in which I stand, I feel that there is a duty imposed upon me that I am bound to discharge. Nothing can be more easy and satisfactory than to comply with that advice which has been given to all parties, not to let their political hostilities be carried to the grave, and that on such an occasion as this they should bury all animosities. For my part, the only difficulty I should find in complying with this advice is that I have no political animosities to bury. Although I join sincerely in admiration of the great talents of the Right Honorable gentleman who is now no more, yet I think that those talents cannot be said to have been fortunate in the results ; and I must observe that, by the custom of this country, and, indeed, by the custom of every nation at all times, these extraordinary honors are only conferred where there is a certain union of merit and success." *Success*, then, is claimed by this speaker as a necessary element in life to deserve public gratitude. How different is the standard by which Demosthenes, in his oration on the Crown, bids the Athenians measure the merit of their dead ! " It cannot be," he says—" no, my countrymen, it cannot be true that you have acted wrong in encountering danger bravely for the liberty and safety of all Greece ! No, by those generous souls of ancient times who were exposed at Marathon ; by those who stood arrayed at Platæa ; by those who encountered the Persian fleet at Salamis ; by those who fought at Artemisium ; by all those illustrious sons of Athens whose remains lie deposited in the public monuments !—all of whom received the same honorable interment from their country ; *not those only who prevailed, not those only who were victorious;* and with reason. What was the part of gallant men they all performed ; their success was such as the Supreme Arbiter of the world dispensed to each."   As a stream cannot flow higher than its source, so public virtue will not be more lofty than that of the models proposed for its admiration.   Crown success, and you cast disinterested virtue from its throne.

385. In order to collect arguments in praise of our hero we are to consult the *topics of persons,* explained before (numbers 119, 120).   It is in order to consider here more directly what are **the qualities of men** which chiefly claim the honors of panegyric.   They are all those powers and faculties which are not only productive of blessings for their possessors, but which, moreover, contribute to the happiness of others ; the καλόν of the Greeks as distinguished from the ἀγαθόν.   The whole scope, then, of demonstrative oratory, as Aristotle expresses it (*Rhet.,* i. 9), is the καλόν—*the honorable;* and he devotes a whole chapter to the consideration of what things are honorable. Quintilian classifies these topics and bids us consider :

386. 1. **What preceded the birth of the person** praised : the place of his birth, his parents and ancestors.   "It will be honorable to them either to have equalled the nobility of their forefathers or to have ennobled an humble origin by their achievements."   He adds such occurrences as denoted future eminence (b. iii. c. 1).

387. 2. **The qualities of his mind, body, and external circumstances.**   "All advantages which are external to us are not subjects of praise to a man merely because he possessed them, but only in case he employed them to good purpose.   For wealth and power and influence, as they

offer more opportunities for good or evil, afford the surest test of our morals, since we are sure to be either better for them or worse" (ib.)

Cicero applies the same remark to personal qualities, such as birth, beauty, strength. "These," he says, "carry with them no real praise, for praise is strictly due to virtue alone" (*De Or.*, ii. 84). Still, he directs the panegyrist to treat of all such qualities, inasmuch as they have afforded opportunities for the practice of virtues. He suggests, as more important topics for laudation, wisdom, greatness of soul—which considers all human affairs as mean and inconsiderable—eminent power of mind, and eloquence ; but chiefly the virtues of clemency, justice, benignity, fidelity, and fortitude. Finally, he extols above all others such brave achievements as men undertake with much toil and danger to themselves, while no good results from such actions to the doers, but all the advantages are for their fellow-men or for the commonwealth. To have borne adversity with wisdom and fortitude he justly classes with the more brilliant heroism of generous devotion.

388. **3. Whatever follows the person's death.** Such are the tribute of respect that posterity pays to his memory, the documents of his genius left behind. Children reflect glory on their parents, cities and institutions on their founders, arts on their inventors, sciences on their promoters, etc.

389. There are **three modes of proceeding** in arranging the materials. **1.** The **biographical** panegyric follows the order of time ; it is easy and pleasing, provided dignity be maintained and admiration increase as we proceed.

2. The **ethical or moral** species reduces the good qualities of the person praised to certain groups or leading virtues. Isocrates and Pliny pursued the former, Cicero the latter process.

3. Some French panegyrists **combine the advantages of both** by exhibiting distinguished virtues as displayed in successive periods of a person's life. Such is the beautiful funeral discourse pronounced by Fléchier over the Duchess of Montausier.

390. **In the development** the following **rules** should be observed :

1. The praise bestowed must be *truthful*, really deserved. We may, however, cover with the veil of silence what is no fit matter of praise ; we may extenuate such faults as are abundantly atoned for by transcendent merit—"a proceeding," says Adams (Lect. x.), "perfectly consistent with the pure morality of that religion which teaches that charity covers a multitude of sins."

2. The encomium should be *specific*, not general : only what is uncommonly honorable is worth exalting. The selection of incidents is a crucial test of a speaker's tact and genius.

3. While *climax* is required to keep up admiration, it should be remembered that an attempt at exaggeration may readily become a step from the sublime to the ridiculous.

4. Lofty *moral sentiments* must be inculcated, not in a dry, didactic manner, but, as is usually done in epic and dramatic poetry, by the exhibition of heroic virtue.

5. The *style* must be elegant, or even magnificent, worthy of the subject, of the occasion, of the sentiments aroused.

To the specimens referred to in the course of these precepts we may add, with high commendation, several discourses of Daniel Webster, in particular his two orations at Bunker Hill, his speech on occasion of the extension of the Capitol, and his eulogy of Washington.

391. We insert an extract from his **Second Oration at Bunker Hill**: "The Bunker Hill Monument is finished. Here it stands. Fortunate in the high natural eminence

on which it is placed, higher, infinitely higher, in its object and purpose, it rises over the land and over the sea; and, visible at their homes to three hundred thousand of the people of Massachusetts, it stands a memorial of the last and a monitor to the present and to all succeeding generations. I have spoken of the loftiness of its purpose. If it had been without any other design than the creation of a work of art, the granite of which it is composed would have slept in its native bed. It has a purpose, and that purpose gives it its character. That purpose enrobes it with dignity and moral grandeur. That well-known purpose it is which causes us to look up to it with a feeling of awe. It is itself the orator on this occasion. It is not from my lips, it could not be from any human lips, that that strain of eloquence is this day to flow most competent to move and excite the vast multitudes around me. The powerful speaker stands motionless before us. It is a plain shaft. It bears no inscription fronting to the rising sun, from which the future antiquary shall wipe the dust. Nor does the rising sun cause tones of music to issue from its summit. But at the rising of the sun and at the setting of the sun, in the blaze of noonday and amid the milder effulgence of lunar light, it looks, it speaks, it acts, to the full comprehension of every American mind and the awakening of glowing enthusiasm in every American heart."

ARTICLE III. ACADEMIC LECTURES.

392. Many lectures are of a panegyrical kind, whether their subject be one of the arts and sciences, as music, astronomy; or some city or country, as Rome, Ireland; or some historical personage, as Jefferson, Columbus; or some association or institution, as the Jesuits, the Freemasons; or some moral virtue, as temperance; or some remarkable undertaking, as the Arctic explorations, etc., etc.

Other lectures, it may be on the same subjects, aim more at communicating knowledge than at exciting admiration. Of this class the ancients have not treated ; their method of communicating knowledge was by conversation, as we see in the dialogues of Plato, imitated by Cicero.

With us **academic lectures** form an important variety of demonstrative eloquence. They may be defined as methodical discourses professing to give instruction. We have likened demonstrative orations to poetry ; panegyrics correspond to epic, academic lectures to didactic poems.

393. These lectures may, according to their various kinds of audiences, be assigned to **three classes.** They may be addressed by a scientific or a literary man : 1. To his pupils, as in universities ; 2. To his equals, as in scientific academies or societies ; 3. To the general public. To these distinctions will correspond very perceptible differences in the manner and style of the compositions.

394. **1.** From their professor **pupils** justly expect correct information, methodical arrangement, and clear development expressed in precise language. These qualities are essential in such lectures, but ornament of the more modest kind is not excluded ; it may be used to great advantage to keep up attention and interest by adding beauty to utility. Its amount will vary with the matter treated, with the taste of the audience, and the genius of the speaker. Blair's *Lectures on Rhetoric*, J. Q. Adams' *Boylston Lectures*, Olmsted's *Lectures on Natural Philosophy* are examples in point.

395. **2.** When a lecturer addresses his **equals** he is expected to exhibit something excellent, worthy of the attention of the learned. This excellence may lie chiefly in the matter, as when he can give a deeper insight into a difficult subject. In this case he needs no higher qualities of style than those expected from the professor. When the matter

is more ordinary he must have recourse to all the charms
of a highly-polished but still modest style and delivery, to
satisfy and please a critical audience. For then the attention of the hearers, not being chiefly occupied with the
matter treated, nor diverted by practical reflections on the
business in hand, as happens on other occasions, will be
fixed on the speaker and the manner of his performance.

396. **3.** When the lecturer addresses **the general public**
it is necessary (*a*) that he choose a theme of general interest ; (*b*) that he treat it in a popular form, with clearness
and elegance, and not without some feeling—not, indeed,
with such pathos as shall move the audience to action, but
such as will keep sympathy alive and thus insure attention.
Here, if anywhere, the speaker must observe the golden
rule which bids him *miscere utile dulci*—" to season the useful with the pleasurable." Such lectures, being usually intended as intellectual entertainments, must, like poetry, observe the rule of Horace :

> " Mediocribus esse poetis
> Non homines, non Di, non concessere columnæ."

> " For God and man and lettered post denies
> That poets ever are of middling size."
>
> —*Francis.*

Let no one, then, presume to offer such literary entertainments unless he can produce something uncommonly good,
at least relatively to the audience. On occasions when unusual interest attaches to the matter treated the manner is
of less importance.

397. The **style** suited for the last two varieties of academic lectures should be such as Cicero requires for all
demonstrative oratory (*Or.*, 11, 13) : " A graceful, easy, and
flowing kind of style, with musical sentences and sonorous
words—a style better suited for show than for contest, ap-

propriate in gymnasiums and schools, but excluded from the forum." "This is, as it were, the nurse of that style which we wish to develop. By this a copious supply of words is provided, and their construction and harmony move with greater freedom. Eloquence trained with such care afterwards acquires its own color and strength."

ARTICLE IV. MINOR COMPOSITIONS.

398. Of these we shall treat under the following heads :

1. **Exhibition speeches** should usually have the qualities explained in connection with the third variety of lectures. Their principal object is to impress the audience with a favorable opinion of the scholars' proficiency. The pleasure afforded the auditors is a secondary but still an important object. Hence the compositions should be adapted to the capacity and, as far as taste will permit, to the predilections of the hearers. It is well to study variety both in the subjects and in the forms of such discourses, and to combine in the exhibition as many sources of interest as possible. Still, the literary merit of the compositions and their proper delivery will ever form the chief qualities of exhibition speeches. It is usually desirable to find a link of unity—*i.e.*, some leading thought which will unite all the pieces of an entertainment. Trite subjects should be avoided ; also such as the hearers happen to be just then surfeited with. Classical and academic subjects are often as new to the audience as they are suitable to the scholars.

399. **2. Congratulatory addresses**, at installations, anniversaries, or presentations, etc., should above all express regard and affection for the person addressed. They will usually contain praise. Now, it is one of the most difficult arts to praise delicately ; it requires the choicest thoughts and the most tasteful expressions. Praise which is **too**

direct brings blushes to a modest face and is offensive. Praise ambiguously expressed may suggest a doubt of its sincerity. Great simplicity may appear unbecoming, and extreme elegance may savor of affectation. It is in the middle region between these extremes that we must look for that delicate and original manner which imparts to such compositions their greatest charm. A few more hints may be added: (*a*) Avoid unmeaning expressions, commonplace remarks, platitudes, which render insupportable what has been a thousand times expressed the same way; (*b*) To add novelty, profit by any present or peculiar circumstance, public or private, which may give an air of actuality to what is naturally formal; (*c*) Beware of alluding to anything that may cause any one the slightest feeling of discomfort; for this purpose you must realize the situation of the person addressed and of all concerned.

Cicero's Oration for Marcellus is a conspicuous model. An address of Henry Clay to Lafayette (*Am. Eloq.*, ii. p. 316) is less artistic, but direct and manly.

400. **3. Occasional speeches,** at a social gathering, or in answer to a congratulation, etc., require that the speaker understand well the expectation of the hearers, and do not disappoint it; hence (*a*) He should not speak on a theme totally foreign to the occasion, nor treat his subject so as to cool enthusiasm; (*b*) He should not exceed, in length or in amount of earnestness, what the hearers are prepared for at the time; (*c*) The speaker may either confine himself to remarks strictly pertinent to the occasion, or, if a longer speech appears to be in order, he may direct the thoughts and feelings of his audience into a wider channel; as, at a military banquet, he might eulogize a soldier's career.

As a rule, brevity, wit, and brilliancy, or polite good humor and strong common sense, are the qualities most highly appreciated on such occasions; if there be any defect, let it be in favor of brevity.

The first and second volumes of Webster's *Works* (Boston edition, 1872) contain a great variety of occasional speeches, many of which are models in their kind.

CHAPTER IV.

SACRED ORATORY.

401. We are now to treat of the **highest and most important** species of eloquence. Sacred oratory promotes the reign of peace, justice, and true wisdom upon earth as much as is done by all the other branches of oratory together ; but besides it affects chiefly and primarily the eternal happiness of every individual man. "Of all the works of God," said St. Dionysius the Areopagite, "the most godlike is the salvation of souls." For this purpose the Son of God himself deigned to come down upon the earth ; and he has left his Church to continue his work through her ministers till the end of time. "As the Father has sent me, I also send you" (John xx. 21), said our Blessed Saviour to his apostles ; and he gave them and their successors a special mission to use sacred eloquence as one of their chief instruments when he said : "Go ye therefore and teach all nations. . . . And behold, I am with you all days, even to the consummation of the world" (Matt. xxviii. 19, 20). No man can aspire to a more glorious career than the sacred ministry. It is most honorable in life : "How beautiful are the feet of them that preach the gospel of peace, of them that bring glad tidings of good things !" (Rom. x. 15) ; and it is more exalted still beyond the grave : "For they that instruct many to justice shall shine as stars for all eternity" (Dan. xii. 3). We shall first consider the sources of success in this manner of eloquence.

ARTICLE I. SOURCES OF SUCCESS.

402. As the task of the sacred orator is so sublime and important, he must be disposed for his duties by a special preparation. This preparation is twofold, as it regards both the *Providence of God* and the *co-operation of man.*

403. 1. It is **the part of God's Providence** (*a*) To provide in all generations a sufficient number of men with the proper talents, opportunities, etc., to become fit instruments for the work of the sacred ministry; (*b*) To enlighten them with grace to understand the blessings attached to this divine mission; (*c*) Through those who exercise authority in his Church, to select wisely among them that offer themselves for the task; and (*d*) To impart to them, when properly prepared, the special mission without which no one should presume to enter on this holy career. "How can they preach unless they be sent?" asks St. Paul (Rom. x. 15); and St. Francis of Sales writes: "No one should preach who is not possessed of three things—a good life, a good doctrine, and a lawful mission" (*On Preaching*). This mission, together with the supernatural grace to perform successfully the duties of such office, is conferred on the aspirant through the Sacrament of Holy Order.

404. 2. On **the part of man**, the candidate for this honor must earnestly co-operate with the divine grace, striving to acquire that learning and those virtues which will make him a fit instrument of the Spirit of God for the sanctification of those to be confided to his care. And, first of all, he must select this career for no unworthy motives, but only for those purposes for which it is designed by our Blessed Redeemer—*i.e.*, for the salvation and the sanctification of souls, not for the sake of honor or other temporal advantages. It is especially by this proper dispo-

sition of the heart that a divine *vocation* to the ministry is known to exist. Whoever (*a*) is actuated by such virtuous intention, and (*b*) is not prevented by want of health or talent, nor by the necessity of his parents, from embracing this holy profession, (*c*) provided he be admitted by those in authority, ought to conclude, says St. Liguori, that he has a true vocation (*Duties and Advantages of the Religious State*, p. 185). He truly enters by the right door of which Christ spoke when he said : " He that entereth in by the door is the shepherd of the sheep ; to whom the porter openeth, and the sheep hear his voice ; . . . and the sheep follow him, because they know his voice, etc." (John x. 2–4). But those who choose this state of life for temporal profit the Saviour calls hirelings, of whom no good can be expected : " The hireling flieth, because he is a hireling and has no care for the sheep " (ib. 13). The candidate, once admitted, must apply himself to the acquisition of those qualities which will enable him in due time to exercise worthily his sublime duties; in particular he must acquire *virtuous habits* and *abundant knowledge.*

§ 1. *A Virtuous Life.*

405. His life should be adorned not only with the natural or social virtues, which we have shown to be necessary for every orator (b. i. c. ii.), but besides with those higher virtues which, being of a supernatural kind, dispose him to produce supernatural fruit. He will need in particular :

1. **A lively faith**; for in explaining the division of oratory into its different species we have shown (p. 220) that sacred oratory is distinguished from the other species by this peculiarity : that it addresses hearers who view things in a supernatural light—*i.e.*, in the light of faith as distinguished

from the dimmer light of natural reason. The more an orator is thus divinely illumined the more he is capable of enlightening others on their highest interests.

2. The spirit of prayer; for the effect, being superhuman, needs a copious supply of the divine assistance ; now, this is chiefly obtained by prayer.

3. Humility—*i.e.*, the sacred minister must be sincerely convinced that he is unworthy of so sublime a vocation, and that he is powerless to produce the effects for which he labors, except inasmuch as the Spirit of God shall use him as an instrument : " When you shall have done all the things that are commanded you, say : We are unprofitable servants " (Luke xvii. 10). Humility will also enable the preacher to seek God's glory and not his own in the labors of his ministry.

4. Confidence in God, who is accustomed to effect most important results with weak instruments when those whom he chooses to employ, no matter how insignificant in other respects, yield a faithful co-operation to divine grace.

5. An ardent zeal for the honor of God and the salvation of men. This zeal will make the sacred orator exert himself to the utmost of his power, and thus obtain abundant blessings. For, as St. Ignatius explains, the more liberal a man shall show himself towards God the more liberal he shall find God towards him, and the more fit shall he daily become to receive in greater abundance his graces and spiritual gifts.

§ 2. *Abundant Knowledge.*

406. The knowledge possessed by the priest should, if possible, be very extensive, as becomes his exalted character. Besides the knowledge necessary for all orators (b. i. c. iii.), he will need, for sacred eloquence, in particular:

1. Literary ability. that he may be able to set forth

heavenly doctrine in a style suited to its dignity. "We are the ambassadors of Christ," says St. Paul (ii. Cor. v.) ; now, the ambassadors of a king should strive to inspire respect for their lord and for the mission entrusted to them. Besides, the good effected in the hearts of men by the word of God is so precious that no effort should be spared to attract hearers ; now, beauty of language is a powerful attraction. Still, attention to ornament should never interfere with clearness of instruction and power of persuasion. Here the golden mean is of the highest importance, as St. Augustine beautifully explains in his treatise on *Christian Doctrine*. He condemns, indeed, all affected ornament by which the preacher would seek his own glory rather than the glory of God and the good of souls ; but he praises the cultivation of an attractive style, and he adds : "I should probably never have been converted if I had not been attracted to his instructions by the eloquence of Ambrose." The proper style for sacred oratory is judiciously discussed by Rev. T. J. Potter in his *Sacred Eloquence*, pp. 323, etc. See also Rollin's *Belles-Lettres* (vol. ii. c. iii. 3).

407. The following extract from Cardinal Newman's *Essays on University Subjects* (Ess. ii.) conveys a clear idea of that manly style which we conceive as especially becoming the oratory of the pulpit. Newman applies it to all manner of compositions :

"A great author is not one who merely has a *copia verborum*, whether in prose or verse, and can, as it were, turn on at his will any number of splendid phrases and swelling sentences ; but he is one who has something to say and knows how to say it. I do not claim for him, as such, any great depth of thought, or breadth of view, or philosophy, or sagacity, or knowledge of human nature, or experience of human life, though these additional gifts he may have, and the more he has of them the greater he is ; but I ascribe to him, as his characteristic gift, in a large sense the faculty of expression. He is master of the twofold λόγος, the thought and the word, distinct but inseparable from each other. He may, if so be, elaborate his compositions, or he may pour out his improvisations, but in either case he has but one aim, and is conscientious and single-minded in fulfilling it. That aim is to give forth what he has within him; and from his very earnestness it comes to pass that, whatever be the splendor of his diction or the harmony of his periods, he has with him the charm of an incommunicable simplicity. Whatever be his subject, high or low, he treats it suitably and for its own sake. . . .

"He writes passionately, because he feels keenly; forcibly, because he conceives vividly; he sees too clearly to be vague; he is too serious to be otiose; he can analyze his subject, and therefore he is rich; he embraces it as a whole and in its parts, and therefore he is consistent; he has a firm hold of it, and therefore he is luminous. When his imagination wells up it overflows in ornament; when his heart is touched it thrills along his verse. He always has the right word for the right idea, and never a word too much. If he is brief it is because few words suffice; if he is lavish of them, still each word has its mark, and aids, not embarrasses, the vigorous march of his elocution."

408. The poet Cowper has correctly conceived the proper style of sacred eloquence:

> " I venerate the man whose heart is warm,
>   Whose hands are pure, whose doctrine and whose life
>   Coincident, exhibit lucid proof
>   That he is honest in the sacred cause. . . .
>   I would express him simple, grave, sincere;
>   In doctrine incorrupt, in language plain,
>   And plain in manner; decent, solemn, chaste,
>   And natural in gesture; much impressed
>   Himself, as conscious of his awful charge,

> And anxious mainly that the flock he feeds
> May feel it, too ; affectionate in look,
> And tender in address, as well becomes
> A messenger of grace to guilty men."

>   " In my soul I loathe
> All affectation.   'Tis my perfect scorn
> Object of my implacable disgust.
> What ! will a man play tricks, will he indulge
> A silly fond conceit of his fair form
> And just proportion, fashionable mien
> And pretty face, in presence of his God ?
> Or will he seek to dazzle me with tropes,
> As with the diamond of his lily hand,
> And play his brilliant parts before my eyes,
> When I am hungry for the bread of life ?
> He mocks his Maker, prostitutes and shames
> His noble office, and, instead of truth,
> Displaying his own beauty, starves his flock !
> Therefore avaunt all attitude, and stare,
> And start theatric, practised at the glass !
> I seek divine simplicity in him
> Who handles things divine."

> —*The Task.*

409. **2. A sound knowledge of philosophy.** *Logic* will give him that correctness of thought which should characterize all his teaching ; *metaphysics* will aid him in mastering the more profound questions of theology ; *ethics* will enable him to apply abstract principles judiciously to the circumstances of his hearers.

410. **3. A thorough knowledge of theology, Church history,** and all those matters which directly belong to his office.   Of these we shall speak more fully when treating of the Topics of Sacred Oratory (Art. iii.)

On the subject of **varied learning** we may remark that, while it is important, it is not essential for the sacred orator ; a saintly priest of moderate talents and of no great

learning may often accomplish wonders in the pulpit. St.
Francis de Sales quotes some examples of this success, and
he adds : " The preacher is learned enough when he does
not aim at appearing more learned than he is. If we cannot speak well on the mystery of the Trinity, let us leave
it alone; there is no want of more useful subjects " (*On
Preaching*).

ARTICLE II. THE SUBJECTS OF SACRED ORATORY.

411. As the end of sacred oratory is chiefly supernatural, the principal means employed must also be supernatural. Hence the **subjects** treated should, as a rule, belong to
the **supernatural** order—*i.e.*, they should direct men to work
for the happiness of heaven. That happiness is not obtained, nor are the means to attain it known, by natural reason alone; they are, therefore, called supernatural. They
have been made known to mankind by divine revelation, especially through the Son of God himself. These teachings
are proposed to us by the Catholic Church, and we are enabled by the light of faith to accept them in their fulness.
It is the task of sacred oratory to explain these teachings,
to apply them to the conduct of the hearers, and to urge
compliance with the obligations they impose.

412. Hence it is clear what subjects are appropriate in
the pulpit. The most proper are those most emphatically
taught by Christ through the Church. No idle discussions, then, on abstruse speculations, much less uncertain tenets or theories, belong to sacred eloquence. The
priest speaks as one having authority. " These things
speak, and exhort, and rebuke with all authority " (Tit. ii.
15). But he has *authority* to teach, as doctrine, only that
which the Church teaches concerning faith and morals.
He is not commissioned to teach in the pulpit systems of
philosophy and the physical sciences. With St. Paul let

him teach Christ and Him crucified, the Wisdom of God, the Redeemer of man ; His commandments, especially love of God and of the neighbor ; His be·ititudes ; His sacraments ; His examples, especially of meekness and humility ; the hope of heaven and the fear of hell ; obedience to all lawful authority and fidelity to the faith ; the practice of all virtues and the avoidance of all vices.

The sacred orator must prudently apply these and the other doctrines to the special circumstances of his hearers ; he must point out dangers to his flock, occasions of sins and errors, refute false teachings, especially those prevalent at the time. This task is usually most successfully accomplished by a full and clear exposition of true doctrine rather than by direct controversy, which is rarely desirable.

413. **Philosophical subjects** are not altogether excluded from the pulpit ; but they should be treated in the light of revelation as well as reason. They serve to strengthen in the faith those who are brought into frequent contact with unbelievers ; and where faith is dim or extinguished altogether human reason may lead men back to God and to his holy Church.

414 To make a **judicious selection** of appropriate subjects the sacred orator will consider the special circumstances of—

1. **His audience**: their age, mental capacity, disposition of heart, their special wants, their surroundings, etc., adapting himself mainly to the needs of the majority, without neglecting to suggest some wholesome thoughts for the consideration of the others. He can provide for all minds by explaining a doctrine of the Church so lucidly that all present cannot help understanding it. Let him ever beware of talking over the heads of his audience with the view of reaching the more educated few.

2. His own person: his age, capacity, time allowed for preparation, proper length of intended sermon, etc.   Minute applications of doctrines to the morals of his audience are less becoming in a young speaker; nor can every orator do justice to very difficult subjects.   It would be unwise for a priest to attempt a matter which requires much preparation, at times when he is overburdened with other necessary work.   Lastly, there are subjects which can scarcely be properly treated within the few minutes to which prudence or charity often compels the orator to restrict his discourse.

3. The ecclesiastical seasons.   It is very desirable that the faithful be made to enter into the spirit of the principal feasts and special seasons of the Christian year.   These are intended to keep the most important truths of religion before the minds of the faithful.   To promote this same purpose still further the Church assigns certain *Gospels and Epistles* to be read on the various Sundays.   These portions of the Holy Scriptures are so selected that, if properly explained, they will remind the faithful of all the great truths of religion at least once a year.   From these a text is usually chosen to be developed in the Sunday sermon.

Still, there are often special reasons to depart from this order of explanations for the greater good of the greater number.   Where the same priest addresses the same congregation every week it may often be useful to follow for a time a **regular course of instructions;** *e.g.,* on the Creed, the Commandments, the Sacraments, etc.   A clear and practical explanation of such matters is often as interesting to the audience as it is instructive.

To be interesting is certainly important in all sacred discourses; but interest depends far less on the novelty of the subject than on the lucid and sensible way in which it is treated: *Non nova, sed nove*—" Not new things, but in a new way "—is an old proverb most applicable in this matter. When the sermon is not an explanation of the Epistle or Gospel of the day it is better to say so openly, assigning a reason for this departure from ancient custom, than to attempt a forced and unnatural union of subjects.

ARTICLE III. THE SPECIAL TOPICS OF SACRED ORATORY.

415. After considering what subjects the sacred orator is expected to treat we must next examine the sources from which he draws his arguments. He treats undoubtedly most noble and most important themes, and still he often finds it more difficult to arouse a lively attention in his audience than any other professional speaker. The indifference of the hearers usually results from their familiarity with all the arguments proposed. Now, a powerful help to treat an old subject in a new way is a thorough study of the genuine topics of sacred eloquence, an exploring for one's self of the fountain-heads of Catholic thought. He who takes an argument at second-hand will not treat it with half the freshness of another speaker of equal talent who has drawn the argument from an original source. The first class of sources consists of the **Intrinsic Topics**. These are not peculiar to any species of oratory : they are applicable, and even indispensable, to all the species, and the sacred orator should apply to his subject the precepts we have laid down in our Second Book (chapter iii.) The **Extrinsic Topics**, on the contrary, are more or less peculiar in each species ; we shall here briefly explain those of sacred oratory.

§ 1. *The Holy Scriptures.*

416. The **Holy Scriptures** hold the first rank among the treasures of sacred eloquence. They are the written word of God, and the priest is the ambassador of God ; they are

therefore his credentials and his letters of instruction. In them he will find not only the chief truths he is to proclaim, but also the most conclusive proofs, the clearest illustrations, and the most impressive means of persuasion. What an abundance and variety the sacred books contain of facts, maxims, figures, and parables, and especially of the very words spoken by the Redeemer! All texts of Holy Writ possess a peculiar unction which belongs to no other writings. But it is better to explain clearly a few well-chosen texts than rapidly to accumulate a large number of them. For this purpose the priest must carefully study the true meaning of each passage quoted.

417. The texts of Holy Writ may be taken in **three different meanings**—the *literal*, the *mystical*, and the *accommodated*.

1. The **literal**, or historical, meaning is that sense which the words directly convey when read in connection with the context and the traditional interpretation which has been ever given of them in the Church. The Council of Trent forbids any one to interpret the Scriptures in a sense opposed to the unanimous teachings of the holy Fathers. In matters of faith and morals we cannot expect to make new discoveries.

2. The **mystical**, or spiritual, sense is the meaning conveyed, not directly by the words, but by the facts narrated. Thus that the blood of a lamb saved the Israelites from the sword of the destroying angel is the historical fact related in the twelfth chapter of Exodus ; but that the *Lamb of God* was by his blood to save all mankind from sin and hell is the spiritual, or mystical, sense of the same chapter. The lamb foreshadowed Christ ; that which foreshadows another is called the *type*, and the thing foreshadowed is the *antitype*.

3. The **accommodated** sense is a meaning which the texts

of Holy Scripture do not bear in the context, either directly or indirectly, but which is assigned to them by the pious ingenuity of men. This accommodation of texts rests on the same principle that recommends the use of tropes in literature. Thus what is said in the Scriptures of patient Job may be applied to any good man who displays great fortitude ; and as St. Paul was called by the Lord *a vessel of election to carry his name before the gentiles*, this title may well be applied to such an apostle as St. Francis Xavier. Such applications of texts are extensively used by many of the holy Fathers, in particular by St. Bernard, who almost speaks in Scripture language. St. Jerome deals more in the literal sense, and is imitated by Bourdaloue ; while Massillon rather imitates St. Augustine and St. Gregory in the frequent use of the accommodated sense.

It is evident that the accommodated meaning has no force in argumentation, except so far as it makes known the teaching of the holy Fathers ; it has the weight of human, not of divine, authority. It is not reverential to apply sacred texts to entirely profane matters ; nor is it wise, even on religious subjects, to accommodate a text to meanings that have no relation to its obvious signification.

418. Rhetoricians point out **various ways in which a text can be properly developed.** These are the principal :

1. Quote the interpretations that the holy Fathers have given of the text. These are found collected and discussed in the invaluable commentaries on the Holy Scriptures of Cornelius à Lapide, Maldonat, etc.

2. Develop every word of the text.

3. Confirm the text by comparison with others of similar import.

4. Explain it by contrast with other sayings of Holy Writ.

5. Apply the topic of circumstances.

6. Examine the cause or reason of the assertion made.

7. Apply the words to various classes of men or things.

8. Adduce examples in confirmation of the truth proposed.

§ 2. *The Holy Fathers.*

419. Divine Providence has bestowed upon the Church, from the earliest ages of its existence, a number of men remarkable alike for their learning and for their saintly lives, who in copious writings, especially in commentaries on the Holy Scriptures, have explained the faith for all succeeding ages. Even when viewed with the eyes of reason alone it is evident that their interpretations concerning matters of faith and morals must possess great authority, as they were men of very superior minds, who lived in lands and times contiguous to those in which the apostles had preached—men familiar with ancient manners and languages, and with the usages and the traditions of the Church in early times. To this natural weight of their testimony must be added the more important fact that the Church of God has honored many of them as **Doctors** especially enlightened by the divine Spirit to explain the faith. Not that she considers any of them as infallible, but their united testimony she receives as decisive in all matters of faith and morals on which they profess to state the doctrine of the apostles. Among the Fathers, St. Jerome is the most illustrious interpreter of the literal sense of Scripture, St. Augustine, St. Ambrose, and St. Gregory of the mystic. St. Chrysostom's eloquent orations exhibit most happily the manner in which sacred texts are to be developed and applied.

420. **Quotations** from such authorities are certainly most suitable to impress upon the faithful the truth and the importance of the doctrines explained in a discourse. But,

unfortunately, in these days of secular knowledge many Christians are too ignorant of Church history to appreciate such matters as they ought; hence it is often necessary to add to the quotations such explanations as will make those revered names more fully known to the people. They were giant minds, and their hearts were the abodes of the Spirit of Wisdom. Rollin goes so far as to say (*Belles-Lettres*, vol. ii. p. 358) that a preacher is censurable for preferring his own poor thoughts to those of such great men, who, by a special privilege, were destined to be the lights of the world. Still, every preacher must adapt his arguments to the minds of his own particular audience. Besides, not every thought in the writings of the Fathers would be pertinent at present, as many of their illustrations are taken from the imperfect scientific notions of their day; they would be the first to discard such passages if they lived at present.

The Second Plenary Council of Baltimore speaks thus (n. 136): "We earnestly exhort (the priest) to study night and day—*diurna et nocturna manu verset*—the venerable Fathers of the Church, Ambrose, Chrysostom, Augustine, Leo, Gregory, and Bernard, and especially the Holy Scriptures; for the nearer he shall approach the fountain the more pure and fresh will be the waters which he can draw."

421. Some of the holy Fathers afford us not only arguments but also the noblest models of sacred oratory. St. Gregory Nazianzen is remarkable for the regularity and the dignity of his orations; St. John Chrysostom offers the most perfect forms of discourses of every kind, from the magnificent panegyric to the most familiar instruction. Their orations are better models of composition for the pulpit than the writings of the apostles themselves. For although the latter contain, as do all the Holy Scriptures, lofty and tender thoughts, brilliant and charming figures,

deepest pathos and most sublime conceptions, still the sacred writers had no need to employ what St. Paul calls *the persuasive words of human wisdom* (1 Cor. ii. 4), for they had miracles to arrest the attention of the world "*in showing of the spirit of power*" (ib.) *Nec ipsos decet alia* (*eloquentia*), *nec alios ipsa*, says St. Augustine (*De Doct. Christ.*, iv. 6)—"No other eloquence became them, and theirs would become no one else." Let the speaker who works miracles like them imitate their style of rhetoric, if he can; but ordinary human agents must have recourse to human skill in their exertions for the good of souls.

§ 3. *Theological Writings.*

422. Theological writings comprise the decrees of Councils and of Supreme Pontiffs and the works of the illustrious theologians. These are the fountain-heads from which exact knowledge of religion ought to be drawn. These, therefore, a priest ought to consult upon such matters of difficulty as he may have to explain. He may read sermons to study the best way of developing his thoughts; but the thoughts themselves, the doctrines to be proposed, and the chief arguments to be urged in support of them he ought not to look for in sermon-books but in theological treatises.

A definition pronounced by a general council or by the Sovereign Pontiff speaking *ex cathedra*—*i.e.*, teaching as the head of the entire Church—puts the matter thus defined beyond all doubt or questioning. As for the unanimous teaching of theologians on any matter, it would be, to say the least, highly rash to impugn it. Such points as are disputed by theologians are not to be treated in ordinary sermons. The **Catechism of the Council of Trent** contains an authentic collection of all the doctrines usually to be explained to the people and of the proofs chiefly to be urged in their support. This work is most highly recommended by the Sovereign Pontiffs Clement XIII., Pius VI., and Pius IX., and by the Fathers of the Second Plenary Council of Baltimore (n. 133).

§ 4. *The History of the Church and Ascetic Writings.*

423. By the **History of the Church** we mean not only the public events connected with the conversion and the sanctification of the nations, the dangers, the sufferings, and the successes of the ecclesiastical rulers, but also the more hidden virtues of the great servants of God, especially of those proposed for public veneration. The **lives of the saints** exhibit all the Christian doctrine in examples; and examples are more powerful than words. We have mentioned before that all popular orators use the topic of *example* copiously and most effectively; there are special reasons why the sacred orator should do the same. He has in the saints of the Church a host of far more brilliant models of every virtue than a profane speaker can find among the heroes of the world. But we shall speak of this matter more fully when treating of the sacred panegyric.

424. By **ascetical works** we mean such writings as teach the faithful how to sanctify their lives by the practice of constant virtue, so as to approach more and more nearly to a state of Christian perfection. Some of the most distinguished theologians have written on this matter, in particular St. Thomas Aquinas, St. Bonaventure, Bellarmin, Lessius, and St. Alphonsus of Liguori. Among those authors who have confined themselves to asceticism Thomas à Kempis holds the first place; Rodriguez, De Ponte, Segneri and Pinamonti, Croiset, Judde, and St. Jure are conspicuous; Father Faber, of the London Oratory, is highly esteemed.

The sacred orator who would neglect to study ascetic works and the lives of the saints would be apt to omit in his discourses an important portion of Christian teaching and to disappoint the more devout portion of his flock. This defect would be considerable, as souls striving after perfection are far dearer to God and render him far more glory than a much larger number of ordinary Christians.

Of the lives of the saints the Oratorian series and the collection of Rev. F. X. Weninger, S.J., are replete with unction and edification ; but many prefer the learned volumes of Alban Butler, as being written in a more critical style and better adapted to the taste of the British and American public.

425. St. Francis of Sales ranks the **study of nature** and of the natural sciences among the topics from which the sacred orator should draw copious illustrations. Both the Scriptures and the Fathers have given the example of this practice. *Go to the ant, you sluggard*, says Holy Writ (Prov. vi. 6), and it reminds us that *the heavens proclaim the glory of God* (Ps. xviii. 1), and that *the invisible things of God are clearly seen by the things that are made* (Rom. i. 20). But when the priest deals with science it should be certain science, no uncertain theories. Illustrations taken from nature are far preferable to those taken from *profane literature ;* the latter are rarely noble enough to be used in connection with sacred subjects. Of *pagan fables* St. Francis of Sales remarks that they are scarcely ever appropriate in the pulpit, " for the idol Dagon is not to be placed with the ark of the covenant " (*On Preaching*).

426. To enable him to draw freely on all these sources the orator should accustom himself **to take notes** of any useful facts, sayings, or thoughts that he may meet with in his reading or in his own meditations. This practice is in common use among the learned. St. Francis Xavier says : " Be assured that what we commit to paper is imprinted more deeply upon the mind : the very trouble of writing .

it and the time spent in doing so engrave the matter on the memory. Even those thoughts which move us considerably will leave no lasting fruit behind them, unless we note them down while our impressions are still fresh." To this practice Cardinal Wiseman owed that wonderful facility with which he could lecture learnedly on almost any subject at short notice. Various methods of thus collecting notes are in use ; one of the most practical is to have always at hand a blank-book the pages of which are marked alphabetically, so that any item may at once be entered on the proper page. Brief notes, not long extracts, are recommended (*Sacr. Eloq.*, ib.)

427. When thoughts have been collected they must be **arranged and developed** according to the rules laid down in our Third and Fourth Books. Whatever in these matters is peculiar to sacred oratory we shall treat in the remaining three articles, in which we shall consider three classes of sacred discourses : 1. *Didactic ;* 2. *Exhortatory ;* and 3. *Festive.*

ARTICLE IV. DIDACTIC SPEECHES.

428. Religion ought to be taught in such a manner that *veritas pateat, veritas placeat, veritas moveat*—"that truth shall be made luminous, pleasing, and persuasive." Now one and then another of these three qualities is chiefly desired. **Didactic** speeches aim directly at making the truth *luminous.* Since to teach religion is emphatically the mission of the sacred orator—*Go teach all nations*—didactic speeches are the most important portion of his eloquence. If these be well managed the other kinds may, strictly speaking, be dispensed with. A pastor who teaches his flock excellently leaves little or nothing to be desired ; while one who moves and pleases, but neglects to impart proper instruction, fails in one of his chief duties. *Docere necessitatis est*—" To teach is a matter of necessity "—says St.

Augustine (*De Doctr. Christ.*, iv. 12) ; and we may add that it is as fruitful as it is imperative. Bossuet is said to have worked more conversions by his *Exposition of Christian Doctrine* than by all his other writings and his grand orations. In this country, in particular, explanations of religion are productive of the richest fruits ; for a thorough knowledge of its dogmas and of the grounds of faith is indispensable for those who live in a non-Catholic community, and at the same time the acquisition of it is beset with more difficulty, where so many are educated in secular schools. Even those who are learned in other respects are often very ignorant in religious matters. But the people here are of an inquiring mind and willing to be instructed.

Didactic oratory may assume various forms and pass under various names, such as *lectures, conferences, dogmatic sermons, familiar instructions, catechisms*, etc. Let that form and that name be preferred which appear, under the circumstances, the best suited to do good to souls. All the various forms may be reduced to two classes : *dogmatic discourses* and *familiar instructions*.

§ 1. *Familiar Instructions.*

429. We begin with **familiar instructions,** as being more indispensable and of more frequent use. In these the sacred orator has the highest models before him. For of this kind were the teachings of our Blessed Saviour himself, such were the instructions of the apostles and of apostolic men of all ages. St. Cyril of Jerusalem, St. Gregory of Nyssa, and St. Augustine not only were devoted to this practice, but they have also written special works on this subject. Familiar instructions constituted the principal mode of evangelizing with such missionaries as St. Vincent Ferrer, St. Dominic, St. Francis Xavier, St. Francis Regis, and St. Liguori.

430. The most necessary instructions are those called **catechetical.** This word comes from the Greek κατὰ ἦχος, *by sound,* and properly means *oral* instructions ; but the term is now usually applied to instructions *by questions and answers.* They are of four principal kinds : those for little children, those in preparation for the first Holy Communion, the catechisms of perseverance, and catechetical instructions for adults.

The subject is too extensive for full development in this work ; these **directions** may be briefly given :

1. The catechist of children should gain the esteem, the confidence, and the affection of every child. For this purpose a firm tone and manner are found most expedient when addressing boys collectively, mild and gentle ways when singly ; with girls the opposite course is more advisable.

2. He should excite emulation by all proper means.

3. He should talk little : the less said the more learned, provided every word be clear and exact.

4. Every catechist should adapt himself to the capacity of his hearers, taking up, even with adults, only one idea at a time, and making that as clear as possible to every one present ; using familiar but not vulgar words ; introducing well-chosen illustrations after the example of our Divine Saviour himself.

5. When one idea has been well explained he should elicit answers by appropriate questions, easy but never trifling. With adults, however, this practice may be omitted, as care should be taken not to cause them any public confusion.

6. He should show the practical bearing of every truth explained, often adding cases of conscience suited to the intelligence of his hearers, and teaching them how to lead fervent Christian lives.

7. He should add such proofs of doctrine as can readily be understood and appreciated ; he will thus indirectly refute the errors of the day, and arm his hearers against the objections of heretics and infidels.

8. He will show forth the beauty of religion and the exceeding goodness of God ; but he must also inspire the fear of the Lord, which is the beginning of wisdom.

9. He will frequently exhibit models of virtue in the lives of the saints, and strive to inspire all with a lively devotion towards the Blessed Virgin Mary.

Some popular specimens of catechetical instructions are found in Furniss' *Tracts*, in St. Liguori's *Commandments and Sacraments*, and in Perry's *Instructions*. See also St. Augustine, *De Doctrina Christiana ;* Rev. F. Hamon's *Treatise on Catechism ;* Potter's *Pastor and People* (c. vi.), etc.

431. II. **More connected instructions** require a somewhat different mode of treatment. Like all regular discourses, they should have unity of subject. The matter treated, being thus limited, admits of more thorough development. These instructions may be connected into a regular course with very great advantage to the hearers. " There is no art or science," says Fénelon, " that is not taught in consecutive order and methodically ; and it is only religion that, by abuse, is taught otherwise." Copious **exposition** is the manner of development best suited for such explanations ; we must, therefore, refer the student of oratory to the precepts given on that subject in the fourth chapter of our Fourth Book.

432. As regards the **order** to be observed in these discourses, the precepts of our Third Book will be a great help. We shall here give **one example** of their application. Suppose an instruction is to be prepared on one of the virtues or vices. It may contain : **1.** A correct *definition* of the subject, followed by a clear explanation ; hence may be derived the marks by which it is known.

2. *Motives* for embracing the virtue or avoiding the vice, drawn from the consideration of its nature, its causes, its effects, and the other intrinsic sources—authorities and examples taken from the Holy Scriptures, the Fathers, the lives of the saints, etc.

3. *Means* to acquire the virtue or to avoid the vice ; particular applications to present circumstances, etc.

Human motives may be usefully proposed ; but the main thoughts of the instruction should be Christian. Each virtue may be *contrasted* with its opposite vice ; but faults against purity should be treated of but briefly and very discreetly ; the chastisements inflicted on such sins may be proclaimed with earnestness. The discourse of Bourdaloue on this vice, and that of Massillon on the Prodigal, are commendable models.

§ 2. *Dogmatic Lectures.*

433. **Dogmatic lectures** differ from familiar instructions —**1.** In their general *tone*, which is more elevated, more dignified.

2. In their *style*, which is more elaborate, more oratorical.

3. In the *matter* treated, which is more confined to the doctrine itself, and contains less application to the hearers.

4. In the *manner* of development, which is more philosophical, more argumentative.

434. To dogmatic lectures apply the precepts which we have laid down in our Fourth Book (c. iv. §§ 2, 3) *On Reasoning* and *Refutation.* Such discourses usually begin with a solemn *enunciation* of doctrine, which is next *explained* in a clear and impressive manner, exhibiting not only its true meaning, but also its importance, its beauty, its advantages. Then they proceed to prove or establish the truth of the doctrine. Starting from undoubted prin-

ciples, the *reasoning* should be logical and cogent. It should not be proposed in the dry manner of scholastic disputation, but in a popular way, with appropriate illustrations. *Refutation* may often be necessary. But, as objections can be strikingly proposed in a few words, while answers to them may require patient reasoning, great care should be taken lest the objections make a stronger impression on the hearers than the refutations.

The *Points of Controversy* of Father Smarius, S. J., referred to above, contain some **models** of considerable merit. Cardinal Wiseman's *Lectures on the Doctrines of the Church* are learned and elaborate.

435. **Controversial lectures** are such as attack error directly. They may sometimes be useful, or even necessary ; but there is one objection against them which is not inconsiderable—viz., that they may hurt the feelings of those in error, and thus provoke rather than allay opposition. If used, they require careful attention to the *oratorical precautions* explained above (b. iv. c. iv. art. ii § 3). Dogmatic lectures do not give offence, and can be so managed as to attain almost all the advantages of controversy.

436. In this age of spreading infidelity it is more than ever necessary to make the faithful familiar not only with the doctrines but also with the solid proofs of their religion, that they may repel the sophistical objections urged against the faith. It has become necessary to defend the very first principles of revelation. But, whatever the errors of the day may be, the one central truth must ever be held before the eyes of all that there is a living voice on earth ever teaching the nations, that the Church is divine and imperishable, and that she speaks through the lips of her infallible pontiff. If an audience appears too destitute of faith to profit by direct dogmatic teaching, there are effective examples in Fathers Lacordaire, Ravignan, and Felix

to show how a zealous priest can adapt himself to difficult circumstances. For instance, Father Felix, addressing his worldly-minded audience, treats successively of—1. The necessity of *moral progress*, as regards science, art, society ; 2. The impediments of progress—cupidity, avarice, etc.; 3. The sources of progress—sanctity, humility, etc. From all this he argues the divine perfection of the Christian religion : *Crescamus in illo per omnia qui est caput, Christus*—" That we may in all things grow in him who is the head, Christ " (Eph. iv. 15). Thus some application to practice, some pathetic appeal to the heart, or at least some gentle persuasion should accompany the teaching of dogmatic truth.

ARTICLE V. EXHORTATORY DISCOURSES.

437. **Exhortatory** discourses aim directly at moving the will of the hearers. But before the will can be efficaciously moved the mind must be convinced. Thus combining conviction with persuasion, and using the arts of pleasing as means to obtain the main object, exhortatory discourses afford ample room for all the resources of eloquence. They may assume the form of the *set moral sermon* or of the *homily.*

§ 1. *The Set Moral Sermon.*

438. While almost every precept laid down for oratory in general is applicable to the **set moral sermon,** we shall briefly notice a few points of special importance :

1. A marked **unity** should prevail in the discourse. The reason is that the point urged in such speeches is supposed to be important, and men are so constituted that they will not take any important resolution unless all their attention be concentrated on one point. Still, the one point urged should not be so limited as to apply to a portion only

of the audience. On the contrary, to every class of the hearers some way should be suggested in which it applies to themselves. The right idea of **unity in moral sermons** is thus expressed by Cardinal Newman : " Summing up, then, what I have been saying, I observe that, if I have understood the doctrine of St. Charles, St. Francis, and other saints aright, *definiteness of object* is in various ways the one virtue of the preacher ; and this means that he should set out with the intention of conveying to others some spiritual benefit ; that with a view to this, and as the only ordinary way to it, he should select some distinct fact or scene, some passage in history, some truth, simple or profound, some doctrine, some principle, or some senti-ment, and should study it well and thoroughly, and first make it his own, or should have already dwelt on it and mastered it, so as to be able to use it for the occasion, from an habitual understanding of it ; and that then he should employ himself, as the one business of his discourse, to bring home to others and to leave deep within them what he has, before he began to speak to them, brought home to himself. What he feels himself, and feels deeply, he has to make others feel deeply ; and in proportion as he compre-hends this he will rise above the temptation of introducing collateral matter, and will have no taste, no heart for going aside after flowers of oratory, fine figures, tuneful periods, which are worth nothing unless they come to him spon-taneously and are spoken ' out of the abundance of the heart.' "

439. **2.** Let no attempt be made to move the will before **conviction** is secured. Still, on many occasions conviction may well be presumed in the faithful, especially in those who are well instructed and whose minds are not darkened by the false maxims of the world. But in most cases it will be found useful to lay down some solid proofs of the

doctrine before applying it to practical conclusions. For conviction must ever be the guide of conduct, and in producing conviction natural reason is intended by Divine Providence to be the handmaid of revelation. *Rationabile obsequium vestrum*—" Your reasonable service "—is demanded (Rom. xii. 1).

440. Some rhetoricians call this combination of dogma with exhortation a mixed kind of oratory; it matters little by what name it is called, but it is certainly a most useful kind, especially in this rationalistic age.

To give **an example.** Suppose the discourse is on eternal punishment. The text may be : " Depart from me, ye cursed, into everlasting fire, which was prepared for the devil and his angels" (Matt. xxv. 41). A purely dogmatic sermon might prove : 1. That there is a hell ; 2. That it is eternal. A purely exhortatory sermon might —1. Inculcate a holy fear of God's justice, without any explicit reasoning ; 2. Exhort to avoid sin. The following plan would combine the advantages of both kinds : 1. There is an eternal hell, solidly proved ; 2. It awaits all those who refuse obedience to God—applying this to various classes of sinners.

441. **Mission sermons** need not be separately treated of : they are moral or exhortatory discourses on the most important practical doctrines of the holy faith. The Italian missionaries Segneri and Sinescalchi are remarkable for their powerful orations in this species of sacred eloquence. Still, in imitating them it must be remembered that they addressed a people very different in many respects from the English-speaking public, and that every speaker must adapt his treatment of his subject to his own special audience.

442. Of exhortatory speeches generally, besides the sermons of the holy Fathers referred to before, we have in the

Church a considerable number of illustrious **models.** The principal are the great preachers of the golden age of literature in France. Massillon, Bourdaloue, Brydaine, though they preached frequently before corrupt courts accustomed to flattery, ever bore aloft the pure standard of Christian dogma and morality, and urged the practice of virtue with all the liberty that becomes the minister of God and all the ability that could be expected of such representative men.

§ 2. *The Homily.*

443. The term **Homily** is derived from the Greek ὁμιλία, *familiar intercourse*, and was used by the holy Fathers to designate their familiar instructions. As these speeches were usually, though not always, commentaries on the Holy Scriptures, the word homily came to be used to denote explanations of Holy Writ; this is its ordinary meaning at present. When chiefly didactic it should be classed with familiar instructions; but it is often moral or exhortatory, owing to the copious practical applications to which it readily lends itself.

The homily has the great advantage of directly presenting the word of God; it is, therefore, full of divine unction. It may be *simple, oratorical*, or *mixed.*

444. I. The **simple homily** lays down no one proposition, aims not at unity of purpose; but it explains familiarly some verses of Holy Scripture, adding illustrations and practical applications to the hearers. It contains three parts—an exordium, an explanation, and a conclusion. The *exordium* arouses attention by commending the importance of the doctrine, the applicability of the passage to present circumstances, its connection with what precedes, etc. The *explanation* develops the meaning of the words, removes misunderstandings, suggests practical applications. These last should be obvious, not far-fetched or unnatural

Some speakers are fond of introducing long digressions ; but this practice is as injurious to the peculiar unction of the homily as it is offensive to literary taste, which requires some kind of unity in all compositions. The *conclusion* is an earnest exhortation to some practical resolution. (See *Pastor and People*, p. 141, etc.)

The holy Fathers were accustomed to explain whole books of the Scriptures in connected homilies ; the practice appears to have many advantages, and is recommended by the Council of Trent ; it exists in Italy. In most other countries the simple homily is usually applied to the Epistles and Gospels of the Sundays and feast-days, as is done by Goffine ; it is a convenient practice for hard-worked priests who can devote little time to preparation. Fénelon, in his *Dialogues on Eloquence*, advocates it ; but St. Francis of Sales finds great fault with its want of unity.

445. II. **The oratorical homily** is not subject to this defect, and it strives to combine in one speech all the advantages of the simple homily with those of the set moral sermon or dogmatic lecture. In fact, it is nothing else than a regular oration which draws all its leading arguments from one short passage of the Holy Scriptures, and directs them all to establish one great truth or inculcate one practical lesson. No manner of sacred oratory is more powerful or more impressive than this. It requires a certain grasp of intellect and some earnest meditation to compose it, but it demands no extraordinary talents, and still it produces most beneficial results. Would it were more frequently employed !

Those **passages of the Bible are best suited** for this purpose which fully develop one chief idea ; many such occur.

1. In the *discourses* of Christ and in the *Epistles* of the Apostles : *e.g.*, the sixth chapter of St. John's Gospel (v. 26 –71), on the Holy Eucharist ; the twenty-fifth of St. Mat-

thew (v. 31–46), on the Last Judgment ; the sixth of St. Matthew (v. 19–34), against solicitude for earthly possessions ; the fifteenth chapter of the first Epistle to the Colossians, on the Resurrection, etc.

2. Many *narrations* of facts ; *e.g.*, Dives and Lazarus, the Marriage Feast of Cana, the Deluge, Jonas at Ninive, the Cure of the Paralytic by Saints Peter and John, any miracle of the Saviour, etc.

3. *Parables*, as of the Prodigal, the Good Samaritan, the Good Shepherd, the Nuptial Garment, the Wise and the Foolish Virgins, etc.

4. *Facts used as allegories.* Thus St. Augustine exhibits the restoration of a soul to grace in the raising of the youth of Naim to life and health. Massillon's homily on the raising of Lazarus is a masterpiece of this kind (see it analyzed in *Pastor and People*, p. 149, etc.)

446. III. **The mixed homily** consists of two parts. In the first a clear and interesting exposition is given of the Gospel or Epistle of the day ; the second part makes the moral applications. This method is usually followed by St. John Chrysostom. It is more regular than the simple homily, and, if forcibly applied to inculcate one moral point, it may be made very impressive. The parables of our Divine Saviour usually inculcate one great lesson, and may easily be treated in this regular form. The first part, for instance, might describe the wanderings and the return of the Prodigal, exhibiting the exceeding mercy of the father; while the second part would display the charity of our heavenly Father towards repenting sinners (*Pastor and People*, p. 144).

An example is found in Canon Oakeley's lectures entitled *The Priest on the Missions*. In his appendix he shows how the parable of the Wise and the Foolish Virgins may be thus very impressively developed (pp. 229 to 234).

ARTICLE VI. FESTIVE ORATIONS.

447. The work of glorifying God and of teaching and sanctifying the nations is performed by the Church in no slight measure through her solemn festivals. These speak a language of their own well suited to raise the heart of man from the vain pursuits of earth to the praise of God and the desire of heaven. On days when the churches are decorated to the best advantage, when the altars are adorned with choicest flowers and numerous burning tapers, when the sacred ministers wear the most precious vestments, and when music and incense raise every heart to heaven, it is certainly unbecoming that the sermon should be made up of common thoughts expressed in homely phrases. Festive oratory is necessary on festive occasions, and no speech can be too beautiful for solemn feasts. Not vanity but duty requires that the priest shall exert himself to the utmost to make his hearers enter into the spirit of the Church. Such has ever been the practice of the saints—of St. Chrysostom, St. Basil, St. Ambrose, St. Augustine, St. Leo, St. Bernard, etc. *Omnia tempus habent* —" All things have their season "—says Ecclesiastes (iii. 1), and this is emphatically the case with the festivals of religion.

Festive orations, provided their style be adapted to the intelligence of the hearers, are usually full of instruction and exhortation to every one present. They may expound the meaning of the mystery celebrated, or extol the wisdom or the goodness of God revealed in the dogma ; they may exalt the Lord in the servants whom he wishes to honor, and thus propose lofty models for imitation. Hence it may be said with truth that demonstrative orations are even more appropriate in sacred than in profane · eloquence. Festive orations may be of three classes : discourses *on the mysteries, panegyrics of saints,* and speeches on *various occasions.*

§ 1. *Discourses on the Mysteries of Religion.*

448. The **mysteries of religion** most solemnly honored by the Church are those which have immediate reference to the Redemption. Such are the solemnities of the Birth of Christ, of his Manifestation to the Gentiles, of his sacred Death, his glorious Resurrection and Ascension into heaven, of the Descent of the Holy Ghost at Pentecost, and of the Holy Eucharist. Such also are the wonders of grace accomplished in his Blessed Mother, her Immaculate Conception, the Annunciation of the Angel, her Nativity, and her Assumption.

These festivals afford the sacred orator excellent opportunities to proclaim the principal truths of religion in a manner at once most honorable to God and most useful to the hearers. He may treat them in various ways :

449. 1. **Dogmatically,** thus answering all the purposes of the dogmatic lecture, and that under circumstances peculiarly favorable to render the truth clear, interesting, and impressive.

2. **Morally,** exhorting the faithful to enter into the spirit of the solemnity for the glory of God and their own sanctification.

But, whether treated dogmatically or morally, festive orations should exhibit a lofty conception of the mystery, set forth with appropriate beauty of style.

450. **Bourdaloue,** in his sermon on the **Resurrection of our Lord,** combines all these sources of success in a masterly manner. Taking for his text the words of the angel, *He is risen, he is not here ; behold the place where they laid him,* he contrasts these with the inscriptions on other tombs, *Here lies,* and displays in his *introduction* the glory of the sepul-

chre of Christ. He next lays down his *dogmatic proposition :* " The Resurrection of Christ is—(*a*) The foundation of our faith, as it is the principal proof of his divinity ; (*b*) The foundation of our hope, being the pledge of our resurrection." Then follows a triple *moral application :* (*a*) To the incredulous, who refuse to believe ; (*b*) To sinners, who believe, but live as if they did not believe ; (*c*) To good Christians, who look forward to their own resurrection.

451. **Cardinal Wiseman's** volume of *Sermons on our Lord and the Blessed Virgin Mary* contains some noble specimens of festive oratory. He concludes his oration on the triumph of the **Cross** as follows :

" O blessed Jesus ! may the image of these sacred wounds, as expressed by the Cross, never depart from my thoughts. As it is a badge and privilege of the exalted office to which, most unworthy, I have been raised, to wear ever upon my breast the figure of that Cross, and in it, as in a holy shrine, a fragment of that blessed tree whereon thou didst hang on Golgotha, so much more let the lively image of thee crucified dwell within my bosom, and be the source from which shall proceed every thought and word and action of my ministry ! Let me preach thee, and thee crucified, not the plausible doctrines of worldly virtue and human philosophy. In prayer and meditation let me ever have before me thy likeness, as thou stretchest forth thine arms to invite us to seek mercy and to draw us into thine embrace. Let my Thabor be on Calvary ; there it is best for me to dwell. There thou hast prepared three tabernacles : one for such as, like Magdalen, have offended much, but love to weep at thy blessed feet ; one for those who, like John, have wavered in steadfastness for a moment, but long again to rest their head upon thy bosom ; and one whereinto only she may enter whose love burns without a reproach, whose heart, always one with thine, finds its home in the centre of thine, fibre intertwined with fibre, till both are melted into one, in that furnace of sympathetic love. With these favorites of the Cross let me ever, blessed Saviour, remain in meditation and prayer and loving affection for thy holy Rood. I will venerate its very substance, whenever presented to me, with deep and solemn reverence. I will honor its image, wherever offered to me, with lowly and respectful homage. But still more I will hallow and love its spirit and inward form, impressed on the heart and shown forth in the holiness of life. And, O divine Redeemer ! from thy Cross, thy true mercy-seat, look down in compassion upon this thy people. Pour forth thence abundantly the streams of blessing which flow from thy sacred wounds. Accomplish within them, during this week of forgiveness, the work which holy men have so well begun, that all may worthily partake of thy Paschal Feast. Plant thy Cross in every heart ; may every one embrace it in life, may it embrace him in death ; and may it be a beacon of salvation to his departing soul, a crown of glory to his immortal spirit ! Amen."

§ 2. *Panegyrics.*

452. Panegyrics rank among the most magnificent specimens of oratory. These are even more appropriate in sacred than in profane eloquence, as the praise of sanctity is more exalted than that of civil virtue, and heroism is nowhere so conspicuous as in the saints. Besides, the saints are not only models but also intercessors with God.

We have treated the composition of panegyrics in considerable detail under the head of Demonstrative Oratory. A few points are peculiar to the pulpit. The sacred orator must give his chief attention to the praise of Christian virtues, exhibiting his hero as habitually inspired by motives of supernatural faith, hope, and charity, as referring all to God and loving his neighbor for the sake of God. Gifts of grace are to be referred to as evidences of the favor of Heaven. Miracles must certainly not be omitted, for, as the angel said to Tobias (ii. 7), *it is honorable to reveal and confess the works of God.* Besides, nothing is so striking to man as the supernatural manifestations of divine power in behalf of the Church and her saints. But great care should be taken to designate nothing as miraculous which is not proved to be so; and the Second Council of Baltimore (139) very justly observes that learned men smile and non-Catholics are offended at the narration of pious stories which are not well authenticated, and it adds that Gospel truth does not need the support of idle legends.

453. For **models** of religious panegyrics we may refer to the eloquent oration of St. John Chrysostom on St. Ignatius, and to his less lofty but not less charming encomium of Saints Maximin and Juventin.

I. He divides the crown of **St. Ignatius** into the wreath of his episcopacy and the wreath of his martyrdom.

1. Taking apart the *wreath of his episcopacy*, he finds in it : (*a*) The dignity of the office itself ; (*b*) The character of those who consecrated him ; (*c*) The uncommon fortitude needed by a bishop in his time ; (*d*) The importance of the city of Antioch confided to him ; (*e*) The dignity of St. Peter's former chair.

2. He unfolds the *wreath of his martyrdom* in a reasoned narrative of his imprisonment, his travels to Rome, his sufferings there ; and he describes in brilliant colors the triumphant return of his remains to Antioch.

In the peroration he summons various classes of supplicants to receive favors at the saint's tomb.

454. II. The panegyric of **Saints Maximin and Juventin** follows the historical order.

Introduction : Various and ever beautiful are the saints of God, the rich treasures of the Church.

Exposition of Julian the Apostate's persecution.

Narration—1. The confession of the two soldiers : (*a*) Their zealous language ; (*b*) Their arrest ; (*c*) Their life in prison ; (*d*) Snares laid to entrap them.

2. Their martyrdom : (*a*) Their glorious death ; (*b*) Collection of relics.

Peroration extols the saints and invites to confidence in their intercession.

§ 3. *Speeches on Special Occasions.*

455. The sacred orator may often be called upon to discourse on **special occasions** which require special thoughts and peculiar treatment. Some of these occasions are *entirely sacred*, such as a ceremony of ordination, of religious profession, a first Mass, a first Communion, the consecration of a church, etc. Others are *partly profane*, such as the inauguration of a dignitary, the opening of a school, the blessing of a military standard or of a public building, the celebration of solemn obsequies, etc.

On all occasions two great objects must be kept in view : 1. To understand the expectation of the hearers, so as not to disappoint them : and 2. To raise their thoughts to a level suitable to the dignity of the speaker's priestly character.

456. 1. In order **to realize the expectation of the audience** he should avoid introducing subjects or arguments alien to the occasion, or treat the matter in a way which may damp their enthusiasm. On the contrary, he must sympathize with those present and make himself the interpreter of their sentiments. These sentiments he will direct into a proper channel, then widen and deepen it as much as his genius and his discretion will allow. For instance,

at the blessing of a military standard he may exalt the love of country as a virtue sanctioned by religion, and then make a soldier's devotion to his flag appear in all its heroism. He will illustrate it by examples of Christian warriors, thus arousing military and religious enthusiasm.

457. **2. To elevate the subject**: (*a*) When the occasion is entirely sacred, the holy thoughts which it inspires are to be developed and displayed in all their richness ; (*b*) If partly profane, some great principle is to be introduced which will bring the theme within the province of religious eloquence. In either case it will generally be most appropriate to explain the ceremony or the occasion, and thus derive the thoughts from the very nature of the subject, its effects, circumstances, etc. Father McCarthy's discourse on religious vows, and Father T. N. Burke's at the opening of the month of May, are examples in point.

458. Discourses at solemn obsequies are more frequent than any other occasional speeches. They are specifically called **Funeral Orations** when they praise the dead for the edification of the living. Not every speech at a funeral attempts this task, nor should it do so. The Second Council of Baltimore (143), while approving the practice of preaching at funerals, cautions the priest against the bestowal of unmerited praise, and it suggests that on many occasions it may be most appropriate to preach on the duty of praying for the departed or on the wholesome remembrance of death.

In this matter of funeral orations the great pulpit orators of France stand unrivalled. Bossuet, above all, appears to have reached an ideal excellence before which criticism is lost in admiration.

459. One great difficulty in this kind of speeches is that the matter of praise is in great part profane, and often blended with objectionable items or with sucn as may give

offence.   The management of such matters requires a delicate tact.   Every point treated must be, as it were, purified and sanctified, and that without any misrepresentation or exaggerated praise.   No pain must be caused to sorrowing friends ; silence and charity may cover many a fault, or a moral wound may be uncovered to show how it has been healed.   (See n. 400.)   Thus Fléchier beautifully exhibits the momentary defection of Turenne as eclipsed by the remainder of his career, and Bossuet the longer defection of Condé as atoned for by his repentance.   At the funeral of Henrietta Anne of England, Duchess of Orleans, Bossuet diverts attention from her example, which was not edifying, to the lesson which her death teaches the world.   We shall finish these precepts with a quotation from that eloquent oration.   It begins thus : " I was, then, still destined to render this funeral duty to the most high and most puissant princess, Henrietta Anne of England, Duchess of Orleans.   She, whom I had seen so attentive while I rendered the same duty to the queen, her mother, was to be so soon after the subject of a similar discourse, and my sad voice was reserved for this sorrowful ministry. O vanity !   O nothingness !   O mortals ignorant of their destiny !   Would she have believed it six months since ? And you, sirs, would you have thought, while she shed so many tears in this place, that she was so soon to reassemble you here to weep over herself ?   Princess, worthy object of the admiration of two great kingdoms, was it not enough that England mourned your absence without being yet reduced to mourn your death ?   And France, who saw you again with so much joy, environed with a new renown— had she now no other pomps, no other triumphs for you, on your return from that famous voyage whence you had brought back so much glory and hopes so fair ?   ' Vanity of vanities, and all is vanity ! '   It is the only word which remains to me ; it is the only reflection which, in so strange an occurrence, a. grief so just and so sensible permits me to use. Neither have I searched the sacred volumes to find in them a text which I could apply to this princess. I have taken, without study and without choice, the first words which Ecclesiastes presents to me, in which, although vanity has been so often named, it still appears to me not sufficiently so for the design which I propose to myself. I wish, in a single misfortune, to deplore all the calamities of the human race ; and, in a single death, to show the death and the nothingness of all human grandeur. This text, which suits all the conditions and all the events of our life, by a particular reason becomes suitable to my unhappy subject ; for never have the vanities of the earth been so clearly exposed nor so loftily confounded. No ; after what we have just seen, health is but a name, life is but a dream, glory is but a phantom, accomplishments and pleasures are but dangerous amusements : all is vain in us except the sincere avowal which we make of our vanities before God, and the settled judgment which makes us despise ourselves."

THE END.